Published by
Big Enough Productions
www.bigenough.co.uk/books

15 THINGS SCHOOL DOESN'T TEACH YOU

WHAT WE ARE TAUGHT IS NOT WHAT WE REALLY NEED TO KNOW

MARCO CABRIOLU

Copyright © 2025 by Marco Cabriolu

Copyright Notice

All rights reserved. No part of this book may be reproduced, copied, distributed, transmitted, or stored in any form, digital, audio, or print, without the publisher's or copyright holder's prior written permission. Unauthorized distribution of this publication is strictly prohibited.

Limitation of Liability

The accuracy and completeness of the information contained in this book have been carefully reviewed. However, neither the author nor the publisher assumes any responsibility for possible errors, omissions, or misinterpretations. The use of the information provided is entirely at the reader's discretion and responsibility. Under no circumstances shall the author or publisher be held liable for any damages, losses, or consequences resulting directly or indirectly from using the content in this book.

Legal Notice

This book is protected by copyright and is intended for personal use only. It is prohibited to modify, distribute, sell, quote, or paraphrase any part of the content without the author's or copyright holder's written consent. Any violation will be prosecuted in accordance with applicable laws.

Disclaimer

The content of this book is provided solely for informational, educational, and entertainment purposes. While every effort has been made to ensure the accuracy of the information, no express or implied guarantees are provided. The opinions expressed by the author do not replace legal, financial, or professional advice. Readers are encouraged to consult qualified professionals before making any decisions based on the information contained in this book.

For rights and permissions, please contact:

Big Enough Productions Ltd.

71-75 Shelton Street, Covent Garden

London - UK WC2H 9JQ

publishing@bigenough.co.uk

"The money that we possess is the instrument of liberty; that which we lack and strive to obtain is the instrument of slavery."

JEAN-JACQUES ROUSSEAU

CONTENTS

Note To Readers	9
Introduction	11
Doubts, Mistakes, Successes and Life Lessons	17
1. How to Think	23
2. The importance of Traveling	35
3. The basics of Success	53
4. How to build a Career	81
5. How to create a Business	99
6. How to be a Good Partner	123
7. How to communicate Well	143
8. How to create an Impact	167
9. How to Manage Time	199
10. How to Negotiate	219
11. How to Sell	239
12. How to Manage Money	257
13. How to Invest Money	271
14. How to obtain Economic Freedom	295
15. How to deal with Failure	313
Conclusion	339

NOTE TO READERS

This book does not offer a magic formula for getting rich, nor does it claim to provide miraculous advice on how to invest your money and guarantee success. What you will find here is a different way of looking at things that challenge what you were taught during your school years. It offers a new perspective that may open your eyes and help you see beyond conventional beliefs.

As you read this book, you may notice that certain concepts appear repeatedly across different chapters. This is intentional: repetition helps solidify the key ideas in your mind, making them easier to remember and apply.

Each chapter stands on its own and can be read independently. I've structured the book this way to allow you to explore the topics in whatever order you prefer. You're free to jump from one section to another, go back or move forward, choosing the reading path that suits you best.

This book does not provide financial advice or an investment recommendation. The shared information is intended solely for informational and educational purposes, based on my experience and observations over the years.

Financial and investment decisions always involve risks. They should be made mindfully, supported by thorough research, and, if necessary, assisted by qualified professionals.

This book aims to help you develop an entrepreneurial and strategic mindset, offering reflections on how to approach money, investments, and the creation of income streams. However, every financial decision is personal and must be assessed according to your needs, goals, and skill set.

INTRODUCTION

From my earliest school years, I always wondered whether what I was learning would actually be useful in real life. I remember sitting at my desk while the teacher explained trigonometry or Latin syntax, and my mind would wander elsewhere: *Will any of this really help me build a future?*

I believe most people have had the same doubts. At school, we're taught how to solve complex equations, memorize dates from historical events, and recite poetry, but we're never shown how to earn or manage money, start a business, build wealth, or navigate the real world.

I've always approached things a little differently. I learned to read at four, and a year later, I was already writing short essays, thanks to my mother, a primary school teacher, who recognized my creative streak early on. She never forced me to follow a rigid path but encouraged me to explore. She would give me a blank sheet and a challenge: create a story from scratch, maybe starting with a place and two characters. That's how my love for creative writing began.

But it wasn't just writing that excited me. At six years old, whenever relatives or friends visited, I'd walk around with my little notebook, jotting down all my project ideas. I still remember the day I showed one of my favorite uncles, a surveyor by profession, my design for a pedal-powered biplane. I had imagined and drawn that aircraft in great detail, and he didn't laugh at me. Instead, he encouraged me and gave me advice about proportions and measurements. Shortly afterward, with my grandfather's help, that biplane was built with wooden planks and parts from an old bicycle.

Not all my projects were as I imagined, but every mistake taught me something. I learned that creativity without action is just an illusion. You must try, fail, and adjust your course to build something real.

As I grew older, I realized something: the world doesn't reward dreamers, at least not those who keep their dreams confined to their heads.

During my childhood, like many kids, I lived in a world built by my imagination, where anything was possible, and fantasy fueled every idea. But as we grow up, we see too many people stop dreaming, trapped by society's expectations and predefined paths. Today, I observe young people and notice how their curiosity seems to fade. They no longer ask questions out of a desire to understand but accept everything passively, as if what they're taught were unquestionable truths with no alternatives.

I often felt like an idiot for asking so many questions in class, sometimes out of genuine interest. Other times, I was naturally inclined to doubt everything and take nothing for granted. Only later did I realize that asking questions helped me remember lessons better. I only needed to read the assigned pages once or twice, which was enough. It wasn't that I had a phenomenal memory. It was because I asked questions and tried to connect everything to something concrete.

But I kept wondering: *Do I really need to know how to work with radicals or translate from Latin? Will Kant's philosophy help me pay the bills? Will trigonometry help me earn a living? Or studying art history, memorizing Leopardi's "A Silvia" or Foscolo's "I Sepolcri," translating Dante's Divine Comedy into prose... and so on?*

What we learn at school may not seem helpful at the time, but eventually, it becomes relevant. I found the answers to those questions only later when I entered the world of work.

Latin, art history, philosophy, and all the other subjects shaped my thinking, giving me a foundation for understanding the world and appreciating what surrounds me. This background has become a constant source of inspiration, especially for me, as I work in a creative field like cinema, poetry, and the arts in general.

But of all the things we learn at school, very little is practical. When we leave that environment, we're left to figure things out on our own. Only then do we realize that school didn't prepare us for the real challenges of life.

No one ever taught us how to earn money independently, manage our finances to avoid hardship, start a business and make it thrive, or invest wisely so our money works for us. No one taught us the importance of effectively dealing with people, negotiating, selling, or communicating. Yet these essential skills are needed to survive in the real world, and school barely touches on them.

When we finish compulsory education, most of us feel lost and confused. We're pressured to make a decision about choosing a university at an age when we're not ready for such a significant choice. We're told that this decision will shape our future. But how many people actually graduate from university? How many end up working in the field they studied for?

We've always been told: *Get a degree, and you'll land a great job!* But are we sure about that? Because the facts and statistics say otherwise.

Thousands of graduates cannot find jobs in their fields, and many are forced to accept underpaid work despite holding degrees. The system trains employees but doesn't teach them to be independent.

Having a degree doesn't necessarily mean you're smarter.

People often confuse education with intelligence. Intelligence lies in the ability to reason and connect causes and effects based on what you know or what you need to learn. Education, on the other hand, is often just a collection of knowledge, which, in many cases, relies simply on good memory.

If we examine the business world, we'll notice that many of the most successful entrepreneurs never earned a degree. Steve Jobs, co-founder of Apple, dropped out after a few months. Richard Branson, founder of the Virgin Group, never finished high school. Mark Zuckerberg left Harvard to concentrate on Facebook. Amancio

INTRODUCTION

Ortega, the visionary behind Zara, left school at 14. The list continues on.

There are even entrepreneurs who only completed elementary school and still managed to build business empires, proving that success doesn't depend on a piece of paper but on the ability to think innovatively and act with effective determination

Don't get me wrong; I'm not saying studying is useless. I'm saying it's just not enough.

School trains us to be cogs in a machine, but it doesn't teach us how to build our own machine. That's the real problem.

The school doesn't offer any alternatives. You can't make a living solely by quoting Dante Alighieri or reciting a sonnet by William Shakespeare.

There was a time when supermarkets, grocery stores, and malls didn't exist. If you wanted to eat, you had to learn how to hunt. If you sought shelter, you had to build it yourself. There were no hunting or fishing stores and no hardware shops to buy ready-made tools. You had to create them from the raw materials that nature provided. The knowledge needed for survival wasn't learned in classrooms but was passed down from elders. Young people learned by observing, gaining direct experience, making mistakes, and correcting them until they became skilled enough to be self-reliant.

Today, our minds are filled with theoretical knowledge, but do we really know how to navigate life independently? Independence isn't gained through a diploma but through the ability to earn and manage money, understand the tax system to avoid exploitation, invest wisely, build a career, and make informed decisions.

None of these skills are taught in school, so we enter the workforce with a diploma, facing a sea of uncertainty

This book was born from reflections on the paradox of what we're taught versus what we actually need to know. In the end, surviving isn't only about finding food; it's about learning how to live in a world that, if you don't learn to master it, will ultimately end up mastering you.

I want to share 15 fundamental lessons that school never taught us, which I believe are essential for navigating life and the world of work.

INTRODUCTION

These are practical and motivating insights for anyone who wants to launch a project, build wealth independently, and is ready to shift their perspective and start thinking like an entrepreneur.

My goal is to inspire readers to achieve financial independence and establish a strong foundation for the long term. It's not just about earning money; it's about learning how to make money work for you.

If you prefer to believe that school has all the answers, then this book isn't for you. However, if you're ready to view things from a different perspective and create success in life and work, then let's embark on this journey together.

DOUBTS, MISTAKES, SUCCESSES AND LIFE LESSONS

I like to think of myself as a creative entrepreneur, but in truth, I'm just someone who has turned his passions into a path to walk every day. I grew up in a typical Italian family, with a mother who was a schoolteacher and a father who was a chemical analyst. Two wonderful people who, however, had no entrepreneurial experience to share with me. I had no role models to follow and no manuals to study. All I had was curiosity and an unstoppable drive to create something of my own.

I've always had a strong interest in business. When I was seven years old, I would set up little street markets at the corner of my street. I would collect comic books, old magazines, party favors, toys, and other unused yet good-quality items from our home and my grandparents' place, price them, and try to sell them to anyone who walked by.

I wasn't just doing it for fun, even though it felt like a game to me; I was motivated by the idea of making money. My maternal grandmother gave me my first piggy bank, and I was determined to fill it. With those few coins, I could buy spare parts for my bike, visit the small grocery store on the main street for ice cream and strawberry bubble gum, or grab soccer sticker packs to complete my collection album.

I was a budding salesman, and without even realizing it, I had grasped a fundamental business principle: selling in bundles was more profitable and quicker. So, when I found a customer—someone kind enough to entertain my little entrepreneurial game—I would pitch them a package deal, explaining how much more convenient it was to buy multiple items at once. However, my best idea was the surprise bags. I was fascinated by the concept of leveraging other kids' curiosity, and I quickly understood that the unknown sold better than the known. So, I'd create mystery bags filled with a mix of stickers, figurines, small toys, or quirky items. The element of mystery made the purchase more exciting, and soon, surprise bags became my best-selling product. I sold them faster than anything else and made a significantly higher profit margin.

That little game started producing real results. Without knowing it, I was already learning marketing, sales strategies, and pricing concepts that would be useful years later. Thinking back now, it makes me smile.

Later, when I started playing drums, my city and the nearby towns were full of bands and, of course, drummers. I quickly realized I had to become self-sufficient, replacing drumheads, fixing hardware, repairing cracked cymbals…, and even repainting drums to give them a new life.

Over time, more and more drummer friends asked me to repair their gear, and almost without realizing it, I discovered another way to make some extra money. Between gigs (which at the time paid very little or nothing at all), I had an idea: why not buy used drum kits, refurbish them, and resell them?

With my drummer friend Williams, who was skilled with paint and finishes, my garage periodically transformed into a mini restoration workshop. I bought used drum sets and, after making repairs and repainting, sold them as refurbished. And it actually worked!

Whenever I spotted an opportunity to earn more money, it felt like a game. It wasn't just about earning money; it was about experimenting, understanding how things worked, and trying new paths. Above all, it was about never leaving an idea unexplored.

When I graduated from high school, almost all my classmates

already knew exactly which university to attend. They had a clear plan: medicine, law, engineering. I didn't. None of those paths felt right for me. I only knew one thing: I was passionate about music. I started playing drums at eleven, and over time, my dream became clear: I wanted to be a musician, travel the world, and turn my passion into a profession.

For my parents, this idea was unacceptable. They believed the right path led to a "real" job and a stable career. But deep down, I knew that wasn't my direction. So, I left my homeland, Sardinia, and moved to New York. I had no concrete plan, but I was sure that learning English would open new opportunities for me.

In New York, I enrolled in a private English language school with a business focus while continuing my drum studies at a music school. During the English course, we had to choose a field for hands-on experience. One option was an internship at a casting agency for film and television. I accepted without much thought. That decision changed the course of my life.

After that adventure, I returned to Italy with a fresh vision for the future. I wanted to create something of my own. I hadn't attended film school, screenwriting courses, or directing classes. I learned everything on the job by observing, experimenting, making mistakes, and starting over. Lacking experience and capital, and with an idea still taking shape, I decided, at just twenty years old, to launch my first business, offering services in film and advertising right there in my beloved Sardinia, where I was born and raised.

Many told me I was crazy; cinema wasn't a business on that island. But to me, it felt like a blank canvas waiting to be painted. I saw untapped land, a market to build from scratch, an opportunity.

I got started with a computer, a small video camera, a digital camera, and an internet connection from my family's garage. I created a database of over 1,000 locations and a casting archive of around 2,000 extras and artists. I began contacting companies, and against all odds, the first jobs started rolling in. My business was up and running. But, as often happens, early success brought new challenges.

This type of business worked only during the warmer months, while in the off-season, income dried up. So, I decided to diversify and accepted a proposal to co-found a sports facility management company with two partners. It was a disaster. I was the only one truly committed, while the other two were barely involved. The business didn't take off, and I lost both time and money. But I learned a vital lesson: never go into business with people who don't share your vision.

I ended up in the red, and my debts started piling up. I felt like I was trapped in a tunnel with no way out. Then, one day, while looking at photos I had taken in New York, I paused at one of Times Square. Those huge digital billboards ignited a spark in me: Why not bring that idea to my city?

I began researching and discovered a company in Puglia that manufactured remote-controlled LED video screens. I reached out to them for pricing and specifications. The cost was exorbitant, nearly as much as a small apartment in the suburbs. Instead of thinking, "I can't afford it," I shifted my mindset to, "How can I afford it?" I started pre-selling advertising space to local business owners, and in less than a month, I raised enough money to make the down payment and launch the project. In no time, I had developed a new source of income.

That experience taught me that success largely depends on how we think and respond to challenges. From that moment on, I began to see business opportunities everywhere. Over the years, I've developed a variety of entrepreneurial projects, from creating an interactive shopping card, to founding the first clothing outlet in Sardinia to launching an online film festival that I eventually sold to an American client. I've written, directed, and helped produce ads for more than 50 international brands, and I've collaborated with talents from around the world.

I've lived in various countries, and working on international productions has allowed me to collaborate with renowned creatives. To date, I've written over 40 original stories and screenplays, 3 international TV formats, and the plots of 5 television series. I work as a producer and director, building a network that spans cinema, advertising, and television.

But more than anything, I've learned this: wealth isn't just about money; it's about mindset.

Over the years, I've learned to turn every mistake into an opportunity and capitalize on the things I've always loved doing. Writing has become one of my most valuable assets, and I've begun investing in intellectual property as a long-term strategy resource.

My life is a constant blend of music, film, advertising, books, and entrepreneurial ideas. Every passion and interest I've pursued has almost naturally evolved into a tangible project. In recent years, I've even delved into writing books, eager to explore another way of expressing myself, communicating, and sharing.

Today, I've chosen to focus exclusively on what I truly enjoy, dedicating my time to doing what I love and sharing the insights I've gained throughout this intense and fascinating journey.

And if I told you how many business ideas cross my mind every day, well, I'd probably need ten lifetimes to pursue them.

So here I am, eager to share some of my experiences with you, hoping it might inspire you to pursue what truly makes you happy.

This book was born from a desire to share what I've learned along the way.

It doesn't matter where you start or how many obstacles you face; what matters is how you think, react, and turn difficulties into challenges and growth.

If there's one thing I can tell you for sure, it's this: success isn't about luck. It's about mindset and action.

There are those who make things happen and those who merely watch them unfold. It's up to you to choose which side you're on. Be the protagonist of your own life; take control!

1 HOW TO THINK

Everything we are stems from the way we think. Our thoughts are not just fleeting mental impulses but powerful forces shaping our reality. Every experience we have and every goal we achieve originates in our minds. This means the quality of our lives is directly influenced by the quality of our thoughts.

Many people believe that life is shaped by luck or external circumstances, but the truth is that our perception of the world results directly from our inner dialogue. If we think we are destined to fail, we will subconsciously act in ways that confirm that belief. Conversely, if we believe we can succeed, we'll start making decisions and taking actions that lead us in that direction.

A classic example is two people facing the same challenge: one sees it as a chance for growth, while the other views it as an insurmountable obstacle. Their experiences will be radically different, not because of the situation itself, but because of their mindset.

Positive thoughts provide us with energy, confidence, and determination. They fuel our motivation and help us overcome difficulties. When we believe in our abilities and cultivate an optimistic mindset, we create a mental state that supports success.

On the other hand, negative thoughts generate fear, insecurity, and mental blocks. They make us doubt ourselves and blind us to opportunities. If we constantly repeat phrases like "I'm not good enough" or "I'll never make it," we are programming our minds for failure.

HOW TO CULTIVATE A WINNING MINDSET

1. **Become aware of your thoughts** – The first step to changing your mindset is recognizing negative thoughts. Pay attention to how you speak to yourself and replace each limiting thought with an empowering affirmation.
2. **Visualize success** – Picture yourself achieving your goals. Visualization creates a mental model that makes concrete action easier.
3. **Surround yourself with positivity** – The people you spend the most time with influence your mindset. Choose to be around those who inspire and motivate you.
4. **Replace fear with confidence** – Every time doubt arises, remember that you have the ability to face any challenge. Courage isn't the absence of fear; it's the decision to act despite it.
5. **Practice gratitude**. Being thankful for what you have shifts your focus from what's missing to what's already present, increasing your sense of abundance and well-being.

HOW TO THINK ABOUT MONEY DIFFERENTLY

Since childhood, many of us have heard phrases like "We can't afford that" or "Money doesn't grow on trees," planting seeds of scarcity and limitation. These ideas take root in our thinking and shape our relationship with money, making us believe there are unbreakable limits to our financial potential. But if we truly want to achieve financial success, we need to learn to think differently.

Throughout my entrepreneurial journey, I've realized that the key is not to focus on what's missing but on how to bridge the gap. A great read on this topic is ***"Rich Dad, Poor Dad"*** by Robert Kiyosaki. It emphasizes the importance of asking the right question: Instead of saying, *"I can't afford it,"* we should ask, *"How can I afford it?"* A simple shift in perspective can open up a world of opportunities.

SCARCITY MINDSET VS. ABUNDANCE MINDSET

This difference in language changes everything. Saying *"I can't afford it"* shuts down our minds. It's a dead end, a block that prevents us from seeking solutions. The brain stops working and stops thinking creatively.

In contrast, when we ask ourselves, *"How can I afford it?"* We activate our brains differently. The question is no longer a wall stopping us; it's a door opening to endless possibilities. That's how we begin to find new paths, new ideas, and new solutions.

Let me give you a real example. When I returned to Sardinia after living in New York, I wanted to start a business in film and advertising production. I had big ideas but zero capital. If I had thought, *"I can't afford it,"* I probably would have given up. Instead, I asked, *"How can I start this business without money?"*

I began seeking alternative solutions: I made use of the equipment I had, transformed our family garage into an office with my parents' help, and created a photo archive featuring thousands of locations to attract clients. Before long, the first jobs started coming in. It wasn't about resources; it was about mindset.

THE POWER OF THE RIGHT QUESTIONS

If you want to transform your relationship with money and opportunity, you have to start asking the right questions.

If you focus on what you lack, you'll only find more limitations. But if you start focusing on solutions, your brain will uncover new paths.

Here are a few questions that can make a real difference:

- Instead of saying, *"I don't have enough money to start a business,"* ask: *"How can I find the resources to launch my project?"*

- Instead of saying, *"I can't buy that house,"* ask: *"How can I create a financial plan to afford it?"*
- Instead of saying, *"I'll never earn enough,"* ask: *"What skills can I develop to increase my income?"*

Every great success begins with the right question asked at the right time. The answer is always within us; we just need to seek it out with the right approach.

APPLYING THIS MINDSET IN DAILY LIFE

Changing how you think about money and opportunity doesn't happen overnight; it takes small, daily steps.

Here are a few practical tips that worked for me:

1. **Change your language** – Every time you're about to say *"I can't afford it,"* pause and reframe it as *"How can I afford it?"*
2. **Write down your solutions** – Keep a journal of the ideas that arise when you ask constructive questions. The best insights often come from simple reflection.
3. **Build financial skills** – Learn to manage money strategically. Study investments, business, and resource management.
4. **Surround yourself with a winning mindset** – Avoid people who see only obstacles, and spend time with those who spot opportunities. The energy of those around you will shape your mindset.
5. **Make financial creativity a habit** – Don't wait until you're "rich" to think like a successful person. Start now, and look for solutions regardless of your current situation.

THE MOST IMPORTANT LESSON

When I decided to install the first LED advertising screen in my city, I didn't have the money to do it. But instead of thinking, *"I can't afford it,"* I asked, *"How can I afford it?"* The answer was simple: find customers before even having the product.

So I went around the city, spoke to dozens of business owners, and offered them advertising space on a screen that didn't exist yet. Within a month, I had raised enough money to pay the deposit and start the installation.

If I had said, *"I can't afford it,"* that screen would never have existed. Yet, in under two months, I had a new business and built a network of clients who would later entrust me with other advertising work.

Financial success doesn't just depend on how much you earn but on how you think about money.

Every time you hear yourself say, *"I can't afford it,"* stop. Reframe. Ask yourself, *"How can I afford it?"* It's in that simple shift of perspective where life-changing solutions lie.

Remember: Money is never the limit. The real limit is only how you choose to think.

THE POWER OF MINDSET

Have you ever noticed that when you focus on something—a problem, a desire, a goal—everything around you seems to reflect it? It's not magic; it's simply how our minds work. This phenomenon is often referred to as the **Law of Attraction**, a principle suggesting that our thoughts and emotions shape our experiences.

Personally, I've always believed that mindset is one of the most powerful tools we have. I didn't discover this from a book but through my own experience. However, when I read *"The Law of Attraction – Ask and It Is Given"* by Esther and Jerry Hicks, I found confirmation of something I had already observed in my life.

HOW THE LAW OF ATTRACTION WORKS

The Law of Attraction is based on three core principles:

1. **Thoughts generate energy** – Every thought impacts our reality. Positive thoughts attract positive experiences, while

negative thoughts lower our frequency and lead to difficult situations.
2. **Focus amplifies reality**. The more we focus on something, the more it manifests in our lives. If we obsess over a lack of money, we'll continue to experience scarcity. But if we focus on abundance, we'll start noticing opportunities for financial growth.
3. **Emotions drive attraction** – Thinking positively isn't enough; we must also *feel* positive. Our feelings are the true engine of our destiny.

FROM THEORY TO PRACTICE: APPLYING THE LAW OF ATTRACTION

Being aware of these principles is not enough; you must practice them. Here are some key steps I've applied in my own life.

1. Clearly define what you want

If you don't have a clear vision of what you want, how can you expect to achieve it? When I started my first business, I had a vague idea: I wanted to work in film and advertising. However, opportunities began appearing when I set specific goals, built a location archive, attracted international productions, and created a client network.

Practical Exercise: Write your goals in detail. Instead of saying, "I want more money," try: "I want to earn €5,000 per month by the end of the year doing work I love."

2. Visualize your success every day

Each morning, before starting the day, I imagine I've already achieved my goals. When I wanted to install my first LED advertising screen, I pictured it already turned on, with ads rotating and people watching. That gave me incredible energy to take action.

Practical Exercise: Spend 5–10 minutes a day visualizing your success. Picture the details: how you feel, what you see, who's with you. The more you do it, the more your brain starts working in that direction.

3. Use positive affirmations
What you say to yourself has a huge impact on your reality. I learned to replace phrases like "I'll never make it" with "I will find a solution."

Here are a few affirmations you can try:

- "I'm capable of achieving any goal."
- "I attract abundance and opportunity into my life."
- "I'm surrounded by positive and successful people."

Practical Exercise: Practice these each morning and evening with feeling and conviction.

4. Replace negative thoughts with positive ones
Our brains tend to dwell on worries. During a tough period, I kept thinking, "What if everything fails?" That thought was paralyzing. I had to retrain my mind and replace it with, "What can I do today to improve my situation?"

Practical Exercise: When you notice a negative thought, stop and reframe it positively. For example, instead of "I'll never make it," try "Every day, I grow stronger and more capable."

5. Practice gratitude
One of the most powerful tools for attracting positivity is gratitude. When I focus on what I already have rather than what I lack, my perspective shifts.

Practical Exercise: Write down at least three things you're grateful for every day. This will shift your mental focus from lack to abundance.

6. Take action aligned with your desires

Thinking and hoping isn't enough; you must act. When I wanted to expand my business, I didn't just visualize it. I contacted potential clients, studied marketing strategies, and took calculated risks.

Practical Exercise: If you're looking for a new job, start sending resumes, improving your skills, and networking with people in your industry. The universe responds to those who are ready to receive.

OVERCOMING DOUBTS AND MENTAL BLOCKS

Many people question the Law of Attraction because they don't see immediate results. But the secret is consistency. If you've spent years cultivating a scarcity mindset, you can't expect to change it overnight. It takes time to reprogram your subconscious and align with the vibration of success.

When facing obstacles, ask yourself:

- *Do I truly believe in what I want?*
- *Am I acting in alignment with my goals?*
- *Am I letting fear or doubt sabotage my growth?*

When I began investing in the advertising sector, I had no experience. Instead of focusing on the risks, I chose to concentrate on the opportunities. I studied, consulted with experts, and took small steps. Eventually, the results came. It wasn't luck; it was a combination of the right mindset and action.

The Law of Attraction isn't magic; it's a principle based on how we think and act. If we nurture thoughts of success, act with confidence, and sustain a positive attitude, we will draw what we desire into our lives.

Remember: Our greatest power is our mind. Let's use it wisely to create the life we want.

THINK AND ACT LIKE A MILLIONAIRE: THE GOAL IS TO BE WEALTHY, NOT JUST APPEAR RICH

Many people dream of becoming rich, but how many truly focus on *building* wealth rather than just *appearing* wealthy? The difference between those who accumulate solid assets and those who live for appearances lies in mindset and daily actions.

True millionaires don't just flaunt luxury; they build their fortunes through smart financial strategies, targeted investments, and a growth-oriented mindset. The secret isn't merely earning massive amounts but also adopting habits and making decisions leading to genuine financial freedom.

At the beginning of my entrepreneurial journey, I experienced a difficult period. The obstacles seemed endless, and I questioned whether I had made the right choice. I felt out of control, and frustration grew.

That's when my dear friend Davide gave me a book that deeply impacted me: *"The Instant Millionaire"* by Mark Fisher. More than just a finance manual, it's a story that teaches how successful people think. The biggest lesson I took from it was that wealth isn't just about money; it's about mindset, attitude, and action. If you want to be rich, you must first think and act like someone who is.

The first step to becoming wealthy is eliminating limiting beliefs. Many people grow up thinking that making money is hard or that it's only for the privileged few. This scarcity mindset blocks them and keeps them from seeing opportunities.

Millionaires, on the other hand, think completely differently:

- They believe that wealth is abundant and available to anyone willing to work for it.
- They focus on opportunities rather than difficulties.
- They see problems as challenges to overcome, not insurmountable obstacles.
- They continually invest in their education and personal growth.

Practical Exercise: Observe your thoughts about money. Do you often say, "I can't afford it" or "Getting rich is impossible"? Try changing your inner dialogue with positive affirmations like:

- "How can I increase my income?"
- "Money is abundant, and I can attract it into my life."

HABITS THAT LEAD TO WEALTH

Thinking big is the first step, but without action, it remains a dream. Millionaires don't wait for the perfect moment; they act, experiment, and learn from their mistakes.

Here are some of the key habits:

1. Take Responsibility for Your Finances

A millionaire doesn't let fate or circumstances decide for them. They take control of their money, manage it carefully, and plan strategies to grow it.

- Learn to save and invest wisely.
- Avoid unnecessary debt and frivolous spending.
- Set clear financial goals and track your progress.

2. Invest in Yourself and Your Education

Wealth doesn't come by chance; it results from effectively applying skills and knowledge. Millionaires dedicate time and resources to their personal growth.

- They read books on finance, business, and personal development.
- They attend courses and seminars to enhance their skills.
- They seek mentors and role models to learn from.

Practical Exercise: Dedicate at least 30 minutes a day to reading books on financial management and investing. Even one book can give you life-changing ideas!

3. Create Multiple Streams of Income

Relying on a single paycheck is risky. Millionaires diversify their incomes to increase their financial security and accelerate their wealth accumulation.

- They start businesses and side hustles.
- They invest in real estate, stocks, or other opportunities.
- They create products or services that generate passive income.

4. Take Calculated Risks

Financial success requires courage and vision. Millionaires don't fear the risk; they manage it intelligently.

- They thoroughly analyze decisions before taking action.
- They are willing to fail and learn from their mistakes.
- They see risk as a growth opportunity, not a threat.

Practical Exercise: Identify one area in your life where you've avoided taking a risk because you feared failure. Take one small step in that direction, assess the risk carefully, and don't let fear hold you back.

5. Surround Yourself with Successful People

The environment around us greatly influences how we think and act. Millionaires choose their company wisely.

- They spend time with motivated, ambitious, success-driven individuals.
- They avoid negative people who only see problems and limitations.
- They build a network of contacts that inspires and supports their growth.

Practical Exercise: Create a list of the five people you spend the most time with. Do they contribute to your growth or confine you to your comfort zone?

THE MISTAKE TO AVOID

Many people go into debt to purchase luxury cars, designer clothes, and costly accessories, thinking that appearances equal success. However, true millionaires prioritize wealth-building before they spend on personal purchases luxury.
The difference between looking rich and being rich:

- **Buying things to impress others** vs. Investing to grow wealth
- **Living beyond your means** vs. Living below your means while building assets
- **Spending money on liabilities** (cars, fashion, luxury vacations) vs. Spending money on assets (investments, education, business)

Golden Rule: Build wealth first, then enjoy it. Don't do it the other way around!

Remember: The goal isn't to appear wealthy; it's to actually be wealthy. And that's achievable for anyone willing to cultivate the right habits and persist over time.

IN SUMMARY

Becoming wealthy is not just a matter of luck; it's about mindset and action.

Thinking like a millionaire involves believing in yourself and adopting an abundant mindset. Acting like a millionaire requires making smart decisions, investing in yourself, creating multiple income streams, and practicing financial discipline.

2 THE IMPORTANCE OF TRAVELING

Travel is one of the richest and most transformative experiences we can have. It opens doors to new worlds, allows us to experience different cultures firsthand, and gives us the chance to discover parts of ourselves we didn't know existed.

Let's explore how important travel is for inspiration, living, experimenting, observing, documenting, reflecting, sharing, and getting ready to embark on a journey that may change your life.

Travel is not just a leisure activity; it's a powerful tool to broaden your mind, expand your perspective, and spark new ideas. Every place we visit, every person we meet, and every culture we explore offers us stimuli, insights, and opportunities we would never encounter by remaining in our comfort zone.

From my earliest trips abroad, I discovered that the world is filled with business models, work approaches, and mindsets that can be adapted into successful ventures. Some of the best insights I've ever gained came from simply observing what was happening beyond my usual environment.

TRAVEL AS A SOURCE OF CREATIVITY AND INNOVATION

Changing your environment is a catalyst for creativity.
Why does travel inspire new ideas?

- It exposes you to various cultures and perspectives.
- It removes you from your daily routine, allowing you to view things with fresh eyes.
- It introduces you to business models, strategies, and trends that can be adapted to your own situation.
- It forces you to confront unexpected situations, enhancing your problem-solving skills and resilience.

Practical Example: *Richard Branson got the idea for Virgin Airlines after having a negative experience with an airline while traveling in the Caribbean. Rather than complaining, he recognized an opportunity: he chartered a plane, sold tickets to other stranded passengers, and transformed a problem into a business.*

Howard Schultz, the founder of Starbucks, was inspired to create a unique coffeehouse experience after visiting Italian cafés, where coffee was not merely a drink but a cultural and social ritual. He turned a simple café into a global brand by adapting Italian coffee culture to the American market.

Practical Exercise: Reflect on a travel experience that changed your perspective. How could you use that to foster your business or personal growth?

OBSERVE AND ADAPT: BRINGING WINNING IDEAS BACK HOME

You don't need to reinvent the wheel; many successful ideas are born by adapting existing models.
How to spot business ideas abroad and adapt them to your market:

- **Observe what works in other countries:** What are the emerging trends in innovative cities like New York, London, Tokyo, or Berlin?
- **Analyze how people live and consume products:** Do you notice significant differences compared to your country?
- **Focus on unmet needs:** Is there a service or product abroad that could succeed in your local market?
- **Study the idea's adaptability:** Is the concept replicable? Is it culturally acceptable? Can it be improved to better suit your audience?

Practical Examples: *The Escape Room concept, which began in Asia as an interactive puzzle-based experience, was adapted in Europe and the U.S. with innovative formats, becoming one of the most popular entertainment trends in recent years.*

Glovo and Deliveroo introduced the on-demand food delivery concept, already established in the U.S., to Europe, customizing it to meet local needs and consumer habits.

Practical Exercise: Think about a business idea you saw abroad that could thrive in your country. How could you adjust it to be successful in your local market?

TRAVEL AS AN OPPORTUNITY FOR NETWORKING AND PROFESSIONAL GROWTH

Travel isn't just about observation; it's also about connecting with the right people.

Where to find networking opportunities while traveling:

- **International conferences and trade shows:** Industry events are ideal for connecting with investors, partners, and innovators.
- **Global coworking spaces:** Shared workspaces where

professionals and entrepreneurs can collaborate, exchange ideas, and ignite opportunities.
- **Local events and networking groups:** Meetups, workshops, and gatherings provide unique insights into local markets.
- **Universities and startup accelerators:** Ideal places to discover new ideas and talent.

Practical Example: *Numerous entrepreneurs have built strategic partnerships by attending events like Web Summit, CES in Las Vegas, or the American Film Market, where global connections frequently evolve into business opportunities.*

Practical Exercise: Organize a trip aimed at attending a networking event or exploring an innovative entrepreneurial ecosystem.

EXPLORE WITHOUT BIAS: LEARNING FROM DIFFERENT CULTURES

Sometimes, the greatest lessons come not from a business model but from adopting a different mindset.

What can you learn from other cultures?

- **Asian community spirit:** Japanese and Chinese companies prioritize teamwork and collective growth.
- **American innovation:** A bold and experimental approach to business.
- **Scandinavian work-life balance:** Emphasizing well-being to boost productivity.
- **Mediterranean hospitality:** Focusing on human connection and customer service.

Practical Example: *In Denmark, the concept of 'hygge' (comfort and well-being) has emerged as a global trend, influencing design, tourism, and lifestyle sectors.*

Practical Exercise: Reflect on a cultural value you observed in another country and think about how it might be applied to your business or lifestyle.

PUTTING TRAVEL LESSONS INTO ACTION

Travel inspires, but inspiration must be translated into action.
How to turn a travel experience into something concrete:

- Keep a travel journal for business insights or personal reflections.
- Create a contact list and stay in touch with the people you've met.
- Identify a new habit or strategy to integrate into your work or life.
- If you notice a promising business idea, begin testing it on a small scale in your market.

Practical Example: *After a trip to Asia, many entrepreneurs brought the bubble tea concept to Europe, turning it into a growing trend.*

Practical Exercise: Write down three things you've learned from your travels and how you can apply them to enhance your career or business.

TRAVEL IS MUCH MORE THAN VISITING NEW PLACES

- Observe what works abroad and assess how to adapt it to your country.
- Use your trip to network and create meaningful connections.
- Study cultural differences and learn new business and lifestyle strategies.
- Turn inspiration into action: jot down ideas, experiment, and test new opportunities.

Remember: The world is full of ideas, innovations, and growth opportunities. You just have to know how to spot them.

TRAVEL TO GROW, INNOVATE, AND CREATE OPPORTUNITIES

As we've mentioned, travel is more than just moving from one place to another; it's an experience that can transform your worldview, enhance your creativity, and provide new personal and professional perspectives. Every journey is an opportunity to learn, experiment, connect, and draw inspiration from new cultures and ways of life. Often, the most innovative ideas in both business and personal growth are born while traveling.

Let's explore how mindful travel can help you develop new skills, step outside your comfort zone, and even discover business opportunities that you can adapt and bring back to your own country.

TRAVELING WITH AN OPEN MIND: DON'T JUST BE A TOURIST: LIVE THE JOURNEY

The most meaningful journey isn't taken with a camera in hand but experienced with an open mind.

How to turn travel into a growth experience:

- **Immerse yourself in the local culture:** Participate in traditions, discover daily habits, and live the country as the locals do.
- **Try local food:** Cuisine is a fundamental cultural expression, taste traditional dishes and learn their history.
- **Engage with local people:** Learn about their perspectives, life experiences, and dreams.
- **Learn something new:** Languages, traditional arts, local sports, every culture has something unique to teach you.

Practical Example: *Anthony Bourdain didn't just eat at famous restaurants; he sat down with everyday people to hear their stories and understand culture through food.*

Practical Exercise: What's one local habit you discovered while traveling that you could integrate into your daily life?

TRAVEL AS A TOOL TO STEP OUT OF YOUR COMFORT ZONE

Nothing changes you more than a challenge in an unfamiliar context.
Strategies to push beyond your limits:

- **Travel alone at least once:** It will make you more independent and confident in your abilities.
- **Try a different lifestyle:** Spend a few weeks or months living in a city with habits vastly different from your own.
- **Treat unexpected events as opportunities:** Every travel mishap can become a lesson.

Practical Example: *Elizabeth Gilbert, in her book Eat, Pray, Love, used travel to discover new ways of living and to find inner balance.*

Practical Exercise: What's one out-of-your-comfort-zone experience you could try on your next trip?

LEARNING NEW SKILLS THROUGH TRAVEL

Every culture has something unique to teach you.
Examples of skills you can learn while traveling:

- Cooking traditional dishes
- Practicing martial arts or local sports
- Learning meditation or wellness techniques
- Exploring new technologies or business models

Practical Example: *Many digital entrepreneurs discovered the concept of remote work while traveling in countries like Thailand, where digital nomad culture is well established.*

Practical Exercise: Choose a destination and find a local activity you can learn to enrich your travel experience.

TRAVELING TO CREATE IMPACT AND LEAVE A LEGACY

Travel is not just about receiving experiences but also about giving value.

How to make travel meaningful:

- Join volunteer or social impact projects
- Share your knowledge with local communities
- Support sustainable tourism and local economies

Practical Example: *Many travelers have found purpose through experiential tourism, such as volunteering in Africa or supporting educational projects in South America.*

Practical Exercise: What's one way you could give back to a place you visit?

Travel is much more than seeing new places; it's about living, learning, connecting, and being inspired.

- Live every journey with curiosity and an open mind
- Step outside your comfort zone and try new things
- Observe business trends and ideas to adapt to your country
- Network and build global connections
- Learn new skills and apply the lessons to your life

Remember: Travel can change your perspective, your business, and your life.

LEARNING TO OBSERVE: LOOKING IS NOT ENOUGH; YOU MUST TRULY SEE

Observation is one of the most underrated skills and one of the most powerful tools for understanding the world, improving your learning ability, and uncovering new opportunities.

It's not enough to simply look; observing involves noticing details, understanding dynamics, and reading between the lines of what's happening around you.

Learning to observe can transform how you interpret the world and make decisions, whether you're traveling, doing business, or improving your personal relationships.

There's a big difference between looking at something and truly observing it.

How to sharpen your observation skills:

- **Take time to slow down:** Rushing is the enemy of observation. Pause and analyze your surroundings.
- **Cultivate a curious mindset:** Ask why something is done a certain way and try to understand the context.
- **Use all your senses:** Don't rely solely on sight. Pay attention to sounds, smells, and textures.
- **Notice habits and behaviors:** How do people interact? What patterns repeat?
- **Train yourself to spot hidden details:** What changes in an environment from one day to the next? What elements reveal a place's culture?

Practical Example: *Many writers draw inspiration from closely observing people in public spaces, capturing gestures, expressions, and details that make their stories more authentic.*

Practical Exercise: On your next outing, choose a crowded place and observe people for 10 minutes. What details do you notice that you would normally overlook?

OBSERVATION AS A TOOL FOR PERSONAL GROWTH

Observing others helps us better understand ourselves.
How observation can improve your life:

- **It helps you make better decisions:** Noticing details and behaviors enables you to assess situations and people more accurately.
- **It boosts your emotional intelligence:** By observing facial expressions and body language, you learn to interpret others' emotions more effectively.
- **It makes you more empathetic:** Understanding different habits and cultures enhances your ability to connect with others.
- **It allows you to anticipate problems and find solutions:** Identifying early signs before they escalate into issues is a key skill in any setting area.

Practical Example: *Many successful entrepreneurs closely observe their customers, in stores or on social media, to understand exactly what they need and how to improve their products.*

Practical Exercise: Try listening to a conversation (without interrupting) and focusing not only on the words but also on the tone of voice and body language.

OBSERVING THE WORLD TO DISCOVER NEW OPPORTUNITIES

Many great ideas are born simply by observing what's missing or what could be improved.
How to find inspiration through observation:

- **Watch what's happening in foreign markets:** Is there a product or service that could succeed in your country?

- **Observe everyday problems:** The best inventions solve common, small issues. What inefficiencies do you notice in your routine or in others'?
- **Analyze trends:** What's changing in people's behavior? What new needs are emerging?
- **Listen to people's feedback:** Often, customers express problems and desires that can be turned into business ideas.

Practical Example: *Sara Blakely noticed that many women struggled to find comfortable shapewear and created Spanx. Thanks to her insight, she became a billionaire.*

Practical Exercise: Identify at least one common problem in your daily life that could be solved with an innovative product or service.

IMPROVING BUSINESS AND COMMUNICATION THROUGH OBSERVATION

Being observant is essential in both business and interpersonal relationships.
How to use observation professionally:

- **Study your competitors:** What are they doing differently or better than you?
- **Analyze customer reactions to your products or services:** Observe how they use them, listen to their feedback, and note their challenges.
- **Pay attention to non-verbal signals in conversations:** Body language often conveys more than words.
- **Sharpen your storytelling:** People are drawn to authentic stories and vivid details. Observing and understanding your audience helps you to tell more powerful stories.

Practical Example: *The most attentive professionals know that real success doesn't lie only in selling, but in understanding people's behavior and needs to offer tailored solutions and improve the overall customer experience.*

Practical Exercise: If you run a business, spend a day observing your clients or users and note at least three things you could improve.

TRAINING THE MIND TO NOTICE EVEN SMALL CHANGES

People who observe carefully are able to catch details that others miss. *Exercises to develop a more detail-oriented mind:*

- **Keep a daily journal:** Writing down your observations strengthens your attention to detail.
- **Change perspective:** Observe a familiar place as if seeing it for the first time.
- **Practice visual memory**: After visiting a new place, try to recall as many details as possible.
- **Ask open-ended questions:** Actively listening to others helps you understand their needs and perspectives.

Practical Example: *An experienced detective notices small details that others ignore, like a change in the environment or an inconsistency in someone's behavior. This skill allows them to solve intricate cases.*

Practical Exercise: Next time you enter a new space, try to memorize as many details as you can, then check how much you actually remembered.

Learning to observe is a fundamental skill that can improve your life, career, and relationships.

- Observe consciously and use all your senses.
- Use observation to better understand yourself and others.
- Leverage it as a tool to discover business ideas and opportunities.
- Sharpen your ability to notice details to improve communication and decision-making.

Remember: The world is full of valuable information. You just need to learn to see it differently.

DOCUMENT, REFLECT, AND SHARE: GIVING VALUE TO YOUR EXPERIENCES

Traveling, exploring, and observing the world are incredibly enriching experiences, but what makes them even more valuable is the ability to document, reflect on, and share them with others.

Writing, recording, and sharing your experiences bring meaning to the moments you've lived, help you remember details you might otherwise forget, and inspire and inform others.

Let's explore how to document our experiences effectively, reflect on what we've lived, and share our message with the world while maintaining the authenticity of those experiences.

DOCUMENTING: WHY WRITING OR RECORDING YOUR EXPERIENCES MATTERS

We don't travel just to see but also to remember and learn.

Benefits of documenting your experiences:

- **Long-term memory:** Emotions and details fade over time. Writing helps keep memories alive.
- **Mental clarity:** Putting your experiences into words helps you reflect and make sense of events.
- **Creative inspiration:** A travel journal can become a source of ideas for future projects.
- **Sharing with others:** Your stories can inspire and help others live similar experiences.

Practical Example: *Explorers of the past, like Marco Polo, carefully documented every detail of their travels, describing not just the places they visited, but also the cultures, customs, and emotions they experienced. Thanks to their notes, future generations could learn about distant worlds and find inspiration for new discoveries.*

Practical Exercise: Consider starting a travel journal if you've never tried it. You don't need to write daily; just note the meaningful details or emotions you experience.

REFLECT: TURNING EXPERIENCES INTO LEARNING

It's not enough to live an experience; you need to understand its value and the lessons it brings.

How to reflect on your experiences:

- **Ask meaningful questions:** What did I learn from this trip? What struck me the most? What emotions did it stir in me?
- **Analyze personal changes:** How have I changed after this experience? What beliefs did I begin to question?
- **Recognize moments of growth:** What challenges did I face, and how did I overcome them?

Practical Example: *After a trip to India, Steve Jobs reflected on simplicity and essentialism, concepts that would later influence Apple's minimalist product design.*

After spending time in a place with a completely different culture, many people realize just how relative their perspectives and habits are. This awareness helps them become more open, flexible, and adaptable to new situations.

Practical Exercise: After a meaningful experience, write down three things you learned and how they could influence your future.

SHARE: TELLING YOUR STORIES WITHOUT LOSING AUTHENTICITY

Sharing is powerful, but it must be done with intention.

How to share effectively:

- **Be authentic:** Don't try to impress others; tell your story as you truly lived it.
- **Use engaging language:** Describe not just the events but also the emotions and sensations.
- **Find your personal style:** Whether it's a journal, blog, podcast, or social media, choose the method that best suits how you express yourself.
- **Give value to others:** Share tips, lessons learned, and reflections that might help your audience.

Practical Example: *Ernest Hemingway used his travels and life experiences as inspiration for his novels, transforming reality into narrative without ever losing its authenticity.*

Practical Exercise*:* Write a short post or article about an experience that left a mark on you. Aim to capture its essence in a sincere and meaningful way.

THE ROLE OF TECHNOLOGY: SOCIAL MEDIA AND CONSCIOUS SHARING

Social media offers a platform for sharing, but it should be used wisely.

Strategies for balanced sharing:

- **Live the moment first; then share it:** Enjoy the experience without feeling pressured to document it for social media immediately.
- **Don't chase perfection:** The most authentic and spontaneous content often has more impact than perfectly curated posts.
- **Be selective:** Not everything needs to be shared. Choose the moments that truly mean something to you and your audience.
- **Engage with your audience:** Sharing also means listening.

Reply to comments, start conversations, and exchange stories with others.

Practical Example: *Many digital storytellers have built communities by sharing real experiences, showing the behind-the-scenes of their adventures, and offering practical advice instead of flawless images.*

Practical Exercise: Spend a day without posting anything on social media; just live the moment for yourself. Then, write about how it felt and whether it changed your perception of the experience.

STORYTELLING TO INSPIRE: THE POWER OF STORIES

Stories are the most powerful way to convey a message.
How to tell a story that leaves a mark:

- **Create a clear narrative:** Start by providing context, describing the key moment, and concluding with a reflection.
- **Use sensory details:** Describe colors, sounds, scents, and emotions to make the reader feel immersed in the story.
- **Include a message:** Every story should leave something meaningful with the listener or reader.

Practical Example: *Brandon Stanton created* Humans of New York *by collecting authentic stories from people, proving how storytelling can forge deep connections.*

Practical Exercise: Tell a life-changing experience in less than 300 words. Try to make it engaging and meaningful.

Documenting, reflecting, and sharing isn't just about telling an experience: it's about giving it meaning and passing it on

- Write or record your experiences to preserve memories and give them value over time.

- Reflect on your experiences to draw lessons and new perspectives.
- Share authentically, with the aim of inspiring and building connections.
- Use technology mindfully; don't let it distract you from living in the moment.

Remember: Experiences become more powerful when they're understood and shared.

IN SUMMARY

Travel is an experience that enriches and transforms us deeply. It allows us to discover parts of ourselves we didn't know existed and pushes us to see life through new eyes. Traveling to be inspired, live, experiment, observe, document, reflect, and share is the key to success in life.

Through travel, we can find inspiration, fuel our creativity, and uncover our passion. Fully embracing each moment of our journeys helps us explore, learn, step outside our comfort zone, and face life's challenges head-on.

Careful observation of our surroundings helps us capture the details, stories, and nuances we might otherwise miss. This enhances self-awareness and deepens our understanding of the world.

Documenting our experiences, whether in a travel journal or a blog, helps us reflect on our lives, remember the most meaningful moments, and share our stories with others.

Sharing our travel experiences inspires others to begin their own journeys and live their best lives. While we can share photos, thoughts, and emotions through social media, it's also essential to be present and enjoy the moment. Travel is meant to be lived fully without being overly distracted by screens.

When we travel, we discover not only the beauty of the world but also the beauty within ourselves. Every journey is an opportunity to grow, learn, and transform. It allows us to step away from the daily routine, explore new horizons, and open our minds to fresh ideas and perspectives.

Travel teaches us the value of flexibility and adaptability. It shows us how to embrace change and seize life's opportunities. It also reminds us to be grateful for what we have and for the experiences we live.

Travel is an endless source of inspiration, knowledge, and transformation. Traveling to be inspired, to live, to experiment, to observe, to document, to reflect, and to share helps us succeed in life. It opens doors to new worlds, enriches us, and encourages us to live our lives to the fullest.

Don't miss the opportunity to begin your journey and discover what's waiting for you.

3 THE BASICS OF SUCCESS

Let's dive deeper into the essential foundations for achieving success in life through passion, stepping out of your comfort zone, consistency, action, reflection, innovation, and problem-solving. Get ready to discover these qualities' transformative power in your life.

Passion is the fuel that drives our ambitions. Work no longer feels like a sacrifice when we're genuinely engaged in something. It becomes an opportunity to grow, learn, and improve. It's no coincidence that successful people share one common trait: they love what they do. But how do you discover your passion? And more importantly, how can you turn it into something concrete that enhances your life and maybe even generates income?

HOW TO DISCOVER YOUR PASSION?

Some are born with a clear calling, while others need to explore, try things, and experiment until they find that spark. Personally, I've always been drawn to creativity and entrepreneurship, but it took me time to figure out how to channel that energy into something tangible.

Here are some questions to help you uncover your passion:

- What would you do even if you weren't getting paid?
- What activities make you feel alive and energized?
- What topics do you speak about with enthusiasm?
- What makes you lose track of time?

Practical Example: *I realized that my excitement grew every time I talked about business ideas. I understood that it wasn't just an interest. It was a real passion.*

Practical Exercise: Make a list of activities that excite you; things you'd do even without getting paid.

TURNING PASSION INTO A LIFE PROJECT

Having a passion is great, but it remains a hobby without a plan.
If you really want to turn it into something bigger, you need to find a way to make it productive.
How to do that?

- **Study the field you're passionate about:** read books, take courses, learn from the best.
- **Find a way to apply it in the real world:** it could become a job, a business, or a profitable hobby.
- **Experiment without fear of failure:** the first step is simply to try.

Practical Example: *If I'm passionate about fitness, I could start sharing my journey on social media, obtain certification, and perhaps even launch my own business in the field.*

Practical Exercise: Identify one way you could integrate your passion into your daily life in a productive way.

OVERCOMING CHALLENGES AND STAYING FOCUSED

Even when you're following your passion, obstacles are inevitable.
The difference between those who succeed and those who give up lies in the ability to stay focused despite difficulties.
Strategies to stay motivated:

- **Remember why you started**—keep your vision in mind.
- **Surround yourself with encouraging people**—avoid those who bring you down.
- **Embrace failure as part of the journey**—every mistake is a growth opportunity.

Practical Example: *If I'm passionate about music but struggling to get noticed, I can remind myself that every great artist began from the bottom and had to face criticism and setbacks.*

Practical Exercise: Write a motivational phrase you can read every time you hit a roadblock.

PASSION AS A TOOL FOR DIFFERENTIATION

Those who are passionate about what they do naturally stand out.
Enthusiasm and dedication are visible in every project and make you professionally and personally more attractive.
How to use passion to stand out:

- **Be authentic:** passion can't be faked. Be yourself.
- **Add value with your uniqueness:** do things your own way, in your own style.
- **Become a reference point:** share your knowledge and inspire others.

Practical Example: *If I love cooking and create a blog with unique recipes, my passion will shine through the content and attract a loyal audience.*

Practical Exercise: Identify one way your passion can make you unique in your field.

THE CONNECTION BETWEEN PASSION AND SUCCESS

The most successful people in the world share a common trait: they are passionate about what they do.

Passion fuels the energy to improve, innovate, and confront challenges head-on.

What Do Successful People Have in Common?

- They don't work just for money but to create something meaningful.
- They face obstacles with determination because they love what they do.
- They radiate energy and inspire others.

Practical Example: *Steve Jobs was committed to perfection in his products due to his passion for technology and design. That's what made him a pioneer.*

Practical Exercise: Write the name of a person you admire for their passion, and analyze what led them to success.

Find your passion, nurture it every day, and use it as a lever to build the future you want.

Remember: Passion is the force that can turn an ordinary life into an extraordinary one. It's not merely an emotion; it's a powerful engine that, when nurtured, can lead you to unimaginable results.

LEAVING YOUR COMFORT ZONE: THE FIRST STEP TOWARD SUCCESS

The comfort zone is a mental space where we feel safe. There are no risks, no surprises, and everything is under control. It is a perfect refuge... or so it seems.

The problem? Staying there too long stifles personal and professional growth.

There were moments when I found myself trapped in a routine that felt safe but also stagnant. I was afraid to try new things, afraid to fail, and afraid of feeling out of place. Then, I realized that every great opportunity lies outside that comfort zone. And that's where real transformation begins.

WHY STEPPING OUT OF YOUR COMFORT ZONE IS ESSENTIAL

Staying in a predictable environment comes at a high cost. We might not notice it immediately, but over time, it deprives us of growth and opportunity.

How the comfort zone can hold you back:

- **It blocks personal growth** – Without new challenges, we don't develop new skills.
- **It traps you in routine** – Too much predictability leads to boredom and stagnation.
- **It limits opportunities** – Often, the best opportunities arise from unexpected and unfamiliar situations.

Benefits of Leaving Your Comfort Zone:

- **Increased self-confidence** – Every obstacle overcome boosts your self-esteem.
- **Expanded opportunities** – New experiences and connections can open unexpected doors.

- **Greater adaptability** – The world changes fast; those who adapt quickly have the upper hand.

Practical Example: *I was afraid of public speaking and avoided every opportunity to engage in it. Then one day, I agreed to give a presentation. I was nervous and made mistakes, but I ended up receiving compliments. That's when I realized that the only way to overcome fear is to face it.*

Practical Exercise: Think of something you've always wanted to do but have avoided because of fear or insecurity. What is the first small step you can take to face it?

HOW TO RECOGNIZE WHEN YOU'RE STUCK IN THE COMFORT ZONE

Often, we don't even realize we're trapped in routine.
Here are some signs:

- You repeat the same activities without variation.
- You avoid challenges out of fear of failure.
- You feel bored or dissatisfied but keep postponing change.

Practical Example: *For years, I said I wanted to learn a new language, but I never took the first step. It wasn't a lack of time; it was the fear of feeling inadequate. Then I started with just ten minutes a day and discovered that even a little effort led to real progress.*

Practical Exercise: Create a list of things you've always wanted to do but have delayed. What is the reason for each delay?

PRACTICAL STRATEGIES FOR LEAVING YOUR COMFORT ZONE

You don't have to completely change your life overnight. The secret is to take small, consistent steps.
Ways to expand your comfort zone:

- **Try something new every week** – A new hobby, a different route to work, or a new social interaction.
- **Surround yourself with people who challenge you** – Those who encourage your growth are your best allies.
- **Accept failure as part of the process** – Every mistake is a step forward, not a setback.

Practical Example: *I used to avoid conversations with strangers. Then I started with small steps: chatting with the barista and asking a question to someone at the gym. Now I feel more confident and natural when interacting with others.*

Practical Exercise: Write down three activities that fall outside your usual routine and commit to doing at least one of them this week.

THE ROLE OF MINDSET IN STEPPING OUT OF THE COMFORT ZONE

The way we perceive change determines our level of success.

If we see success as a threat, we'll stay stuck. If we view it as an opportunity, we'll grow.

Mindsets to develop:

- **Growth mindset** – Every challenge is a chance to learn.
- **Resilience** – Initial discomfort is normal. Accept it and keep going.
- **Openness to risk** – Failure isn't the end; it's part of the journey.

Practical Example: *I used to believe I wasn't suited for business until I decided to give it a try. I encountered failures multiple times, but each experience taught me something valuable.*

Practical Exercise: Whenever you experience mental resistance to change, write down a positive alternative thought.

SUCCESS AS A RESULT OF ACTION OUTSIDE THE COMFORT ZONE

Successful people have embraced risk and uncertainty.
Here's what they have in common:

- They started before they felt 100% ready.
- They learned to handle criticism and failure.
- They stepped up and discovered new opportunities.

Practical Example: *J.K. Rowling wrote Harry Potter while dealing with financial difficulties and facing numerous rejections from publishers. If she had allowed her fear of failure to stop her, we wouldn't have one of the most iconic books in history today.*

Practical Exercise: Note the name of someone you admire and examine how they stepped out of their comfort zone to achieve success.

Stepping out of your comfort zone doesn't mean jumping without a parachute. It means accepting new challenges and facing them with determination.

Each time we push past our limits, we expand our potential and open the door to new possibilities.

Remember: Growth begins where your comfort zone ends. Change is scary, but fear is just a sign that you're on the right path.

CONSISTENCY: THE REAL SECRET TO SUCCESS

Success is never the result of luck or a sudden breakthrough. It's the result of consistent effort, small, daily steps taken even when no one is watching.

I learned this over time after observing many talented people waste their potential because they expected instant results. I also witnessed seemingly "average" or even "mediocre" individuals achieve incredible things simply because they never stopped.

Many believe success depends on talent or luck. In reality, talent without discipline won't get you very far, while consistency, even in the absence of extraordinary gifts, can lead to amazing outcomes.

Why consistency is the key to success:

- **It outlasts temporary motivation** – Initial excitement fades, but discipline keeps progress alive.
- **It creates continuous improvement** – Even small daily efforts produce extraordinary results over time.
- **It builds reliability and credibility** – Being consistent makes you someone others can count on.

Practical Example: *When I started writing my first book, I was full of energy. However, after a month, my motivation began to fade. I was tempted to quit, but I pushed myself to write at least 500 words each day. One year later, the book was finished. It wasn't talent that completed it; it was" consistency.*

Practical Exercise: Write down a skill or goal you want to improve and take small daily actions to achieve it.

HOW TO BUILD THE HABIT OF CONSISTENCY

Consistency isn't a natural talent; it's a habit you build. Like all habits, it develops over time through repetition.

Steps to build consistency:

- **Start small** – It's better to do a little every day than a lot once a month.
- **Create a routine** – Tie the activity to a specific time of day.
- **Avoid distractions** – Find an environment that supports focus.
- **Track your progress** – Seeing improvement helps maintain motivation.

Practical Example: *I used to tell myself that I didn't have time to read books. Then I decided to dedicate just thirty minutes each day to reading, without waiting for the 'perfect moment.' After six months, I had finished several books and felt enriched. All it took was consistency.*

Practical Exercise: Choose a habit you want to build and select a specific time of day to practice it without interruptions.

HOW TO OVERCOME DIFFICULT MOMENTS

Even with the best discipline, there will be days when you feel like giving up.

The difference between those who succeed and those who quit is the ability to keep going, despite the challenges setbacks.

Strategies to stay consistent in tough times:

- **Remember why you started** – Reconnect with your original vision to find motivation.
- **Adapt your approach** – If a method doesn't work, change strategy instead of giving up.
- **Find support** – Surround yourself with people who encourage you and keep you accountable.
- **Accept "off" days** – Even if you can't give 100%, doing something is better than nothing.

Practical Example: *When I launched my first business, there were moments when it felt like everything was going wrong. I could have given up, but instead, I focused on making small daily progress. Ultimately, that steady effort resulted in success.*

Practical Exercise: Create a strategy for managing challenges associated with a goal you are pursuing.

SUCCESS IS THE SUM OF SMALL ACTIONS REPEATED

Many people give up on their dreams because they seek instant results. However, true success is built over time.

Examples of success through consistency:

- Top athletes train daily, even when they lack motivation.
- Successful entrepreneurs continuously improve their products and strategies.
- Individuals who attain financial freedom achieve it through steady, consistent investing rather than relying on luck.

Practical Example: *Warren Buffett didn't become a billionaire through a single lucky investment. He accumulated his wealth through discipline and consistent investing over time.*

Practical Exercise: Write down a long-term goal and outline the daily or weekly steps required to achieve it.

CONSISTENCY AS A COMPETITIVE ADVANTAGE

We live in a world where many people start things with enthusiasm but abandon them quickly.

Being consistent automatically sets you apart and gives you a competitive edge.

How to use consistency as an advantage:

- **Keep going when others quit** – Persistence will move you forward.
- **Become someone others can rely on** – This builds your reputation.
- **Demonstrate reliability and discipline** – Opportunities come to those who show steady commitment.

Practical Example: *Many people start a blog or a YouTube channel but* *quit after a few months. Those who stick with it for years build a real audience and achieve long-term success.*

Practical Exercise: Identify one area of your life where you can stand out simply by being more consistent than others.

The secret to success isn't about starting with enthusiasm; it's about continuing after that enthusiasm fades.
Consistency allows you to achieve your goals, develop new skills, and outpace the competition.

Remember: It's not the fastest runner who wins the race, but the one who keeps running until the end.

ACTION: THE KEY THAT TURNS DREAMS INTO REALITY

Ideas alone aren't enough. I've met people with brilliant insights and ideas that could revolutionize an entire industry, yet they never accomplished anything. Why? Because they never took action.

They spent their time planning, thinking, perfecting the details, and waiting for the perfect moment to start. The problem is that the perfect moment doesn't exist.

Success doesn't happen all at once; it results from consistent action. Even the most brilliant project remains merely an idea if it's never put into practice.

Let's explore how to overcome inertia, develop the habit of action, and confront the fear of making mistakes.

ACTION MATTERS MORE THAN PERFECTION

Many people hesitate to take action because they want everything to be perfect before getting started. I've learned the hard way that taking action is the true improvement engine.

Why you should take action now:

- **Action brings experience** – You can't learn to swim by reading a book; you must jump in the water.
- **Perfection is an illusion** – Waiting until you're 100% ready often results in never starting.
- **Doing is better than overthinking** – Success comes to those who experiment, adjust, and improve along the way.

Practical Example: When I decided to start my first business, I didn't have all the answers. However, I knew that if I didn't take action, I'd remain stuck. So, I launched the project, learned from my mistakes, adjusted, and improved. If I had waited for the perfect plan, I'd still be planning today.

Practical Exercise: Choose a goal you've been postponing for too long, and take the first step today, even if it's a small one. Just do it.

OVERCOMING THE FEAR OF FAILURE

The biggest mistake you can make is doing nothing out of fear of failure. Failure is not the end; it's a valuable lesson that brings you closer to success.

How to face the fear of taking action:

- **Accept that mistakes are part of the journey** – Every success is built on overcoming failures.
- **Start with small actions** – You don't need a giant leap. Begin with something manageable.
- **Change how you view failure** – It's not defeat; it's a necessary step toward growth.

Practical Example: When I decided to direct my first film, I had a thousand doubts. What if it wasn't good enough? What if nobody liked it? I waited too long for the perfect budget, the best equipment, and the ideal cast. Eventually, I told myself: 'It's better to shoot something imperfect than not shoot at all.' That first step was crucial in turning an idea into reality.

Practical Exercise: Write down a past mistake and describe what you learned from it.

FROM INTENTION TO ACTION: HOW TO CREATE AN EXECUTION PLAN

Having a goal is essential, but without a clear plan, you risk becoming stagnant. Effective action stems from a solid foundation strategy.

Tips to turn an idea into action:

- **Define your goal clearly** – The more specific it is, the easier it will be to achieve.
- **Break the goal into small steps** – A big goal may seem overwhelming, but small steps make it manageable.
- **Set deadlines** – Without a deadline, you'll keep postponing.
- **Take immediate action on a simple task** – Start with something easy to build momentum.

Practical Example: *I wanted to start an online business, but I kept putting it off. Then I decided to break the process down: On the first day, I bought the domain; on the second day, I created the logo; on the third day, I drafted the website. After a month, I was up and running.*

Practical Exercise: Identify an important goal for yourself and divide it into five manageable steps you can begin immediately.

BUILDING THE HABIT OF ACTION

Action should become a habit, not an exception. The more you act, the more natural it becomes to take action without hesitation.

Strategies to develop the habit of action:

- **Do something every day, even something small** – It doesn't matter how much; what matters is to keep going.
- **Eliminate excuses** – Always find a reason to act, not to delay.

- **Develop a solution-oriented mindset** – Instead of focusing on problems, concentrate on how to overcome them.

Practical Example: *When I wanted to improve my fitness, I kept making excuses. Then I decided to start with just 20 minutes of exercise each day. It didn't seem like much, but that small habit transformed everything.*

Practical Exercise: Choose an activity you wish to make a habit and establish a small daily action to start with.

ACTION: THE DIFFERENCE BETWEEN THOSE WHO SUCCEED AND THOSE WHO DON'T

Many people have big dreams, but few take the steps to make them happen.

The difference between those who succeed and those who fall behind is simply this: one takes action, while the other does not.

It's good to remember the traits of successful people:

- They act before they feel ready.
- They know that improvement happens along the way.
- They turn every mistake into a growth opportunity.

Practical Example: *Many people wanted to start a YouTube channel but waited too long. Others began with poor-quality videos and progressively improved over time. Today, they are among the world's top content creators, earning substantial amounts of money.*

Practical Exercise: List three actions you can take today to get closer to your goals.

Success doesn't come to those with the best ideas, but to those who act consistently and with determination.

Taking action means overcoming fear, embracing failure, and continually improving.

Remember: Action is the key that transforms dreams into reality. Stop waiting for the perfect moment; start now.

REFLECTION: THE SECRET TO GROWTH AND IMPROVEMENT

In today's fast-paced world, we're often pressured to rush from one goal to another without taking the time to reflect. However, without reflection, there is no genuine growth; we risk repeating the same mistakes and losing our direction.

Reflection turns experience into wisdom. It's not just an exercise in memory but a strategic habit that allows us to analyze our journey, evaluate successes and failures, and make continuous improvements.

WHY IS REFLECTION ESSENTIAL FOR SUCCESS?

Many people work hard but never pause to evaluate if they're on the right track direction.

Benefits of reflection:

- **Enhances decision-making** – Understanding what worked in the past helps make better choices for the future.
- **Boosts self-awareness** – Reflecting on emotions, reactions, and behaviors allows you to gain a deeper understanding of yourself.
- **Averts repeated mistakes** – Without reflection, we risk repeating the same errors continuously.
- **Keeps you focused on your goals** – Analyzing your progress helps maintain the correct direction.

Practical Example: *After completing my first screenplay, I realized how essential it was to review every aspect of the process. I examined what worked well in the story and what could be improved, from the narrative structure to the rhythm of the dialogue. That reflection enabled me to approach future projects with greater awareness and confidence.*

Practical Exercise: Spend five minutes at the end of the day reflecting on one thing you did well and one area where you could improve.

HOW TO PRACTICE REFLECTION EFFECTIVELY

It's not enough to merely think about the past; reflection needs to be structured to yield genuine insights results.

Techniques for reflective thinking:

- **Keep a reflection journal** – Writing down successes, challenges, and lessons learned helps to organize your thoughts.
- **Ask targeted questions** – Ask yourself: What did I learn today? What could I have done better?
- **Use the three-step rule** – 1) Analyze an event, 2) Identify the lesson, 3) Decide how to apply it in the future.
- **Create quiet moments** – Dedicate time to reflect without distractions to encourage mental clarity.

Practical Exercise: Each week, write down three things you've learned and how to apply them.

REFLECTION AS A TOOL FOR PERSONAL GROWTH

Reflection isn't just about improving your work; it also enhances your mindset and well-being.

How to use reflection for personal development:

- **Analyze your emotions** – Understanding your reactions helps improve stress management and relationships.
- **Identify recurring patterns** – If a problem keeps resurfacing, reflection can help you discover better solutions.
- **Make more intentional decisions** – The more we reflect on our experiences, the greater our ability to choose grows wisely.

Practical Example: *When I realize that I tend to be overly perfectionistic and micromanage every time I manage a team, I can reflect on how to give my team more autonomy to achieve better results.*

Practical Exercise: Each evening, write down one moment from your day when you experienced a strong emotion and explore what caused it.

AVOIDING PARALYSIS BY OVERANALYSIS

Reflection is only useful if it leads to concrete actions. Otherwise, it can become a trap, and overthinking can block progress.
How to avoid overthinking:

- **Set a time limit for reflection** – Obsessing over a mistake without taking action doesn't help.
- **Focus on solutions, not just problems** – Reflection should result in practical improvements.
- **Accept that not everything has an immediate answer** – Some lessons require time to understand.

Practical Example: *After making a mistake on set, instead of dwelling on it for days, I asked myself: 'What can I do now to avoid this next time?' That mindset helped me turn errors into tools for growth.*

Practical Exercise: If you catch yourself overthinking a problem, write down three practical actions you can take to deal with it.

CREATING A CONSISTENT REFLECTION HABIT

To fully benefit from reflection, it should become a regular practice.
How to integrate reflection into daily life:

- Use a journal or digital notes to capture your thoughts and track your progress.

- Reflect at the end of each week on your successes and the challenges you encountered.
- Share your reflections with someone you trust to gain new insights perspectives.

Practical Example: *Every Sunday evening, I take 10 minutes to write about what I've learned throughout the week and what I want to improve on next. This simple habit has contributed to my growth both personally and professionally.*

Practical Exercise: Set a daily reminder to take a few minutes for personal reflection.

Reflection is a powerful growth tool that turns experiences and mistakes into opportunities for improvement. Those who reflect strategically gain an advantage over those who proceed without analyzing their situation.

Remember: True change occurs when we gain insights from our experiences. Reflect, learn, and continue to improve.

INNOVATION: THE SECRET TO STANDING OUT AND GROWING

In a constantly evolving world, innovation is what separates those who adapt and grow from those who fall behind. It's not enough to follow the rules of the game; you have to rewrite them.

Innovation doesn't just mean inventing something entirely new; it's about discovering better, more efficient, and more creative ways to do things. Innovators don't merely follow others; they forge new paths, create new solutions, and open up new opportunities.

The world is always changing. If you don't innovate, you risk being left behind.

Why is innovation essential?

- **It sets you apart from the competition** – If you do what everyone else does, you'll get the same results.
- **It helps you solve problems more effectively** – Innovation finds new solutions to old problems.
- **It allows you to seize opportunities before others** – The best opportunities go to those ready to change.

Practical Example: *When I wrote my first screenplay, I realized my idea didn't align with the industry's traditional standards. Instead of feeling discouraged, I opted for an innovative approach, focusing on a more visual and less conventional narrative. I organized a reading with friends and colleagues to evaluate its effectiveness, gathering valuable feedback to refine the story. The result? A screenplay that stood out for its unique style and caught the attention of potential producers, opening new doors for me in the industry.*

Practical Exercise: Identify a part of your life or work where you can adopt a more innovative approach.

HOW TO DEVELOP AN INNOVATIVE MINDSET

Innovation isn't just for entrepreneurs or scientists; anyone can develop a creative mindset and a willingness to embrace change.

Traits of an innovative person:

- **Endless curiosity** – Always ask, "Why do we do it this way?" and "How could we do it better?"
- **Openness to change** – Those who resist new ideas get stuck in the past.
- **Constant experimentation** – Don't hesitate to try new things.
- **Ability to connect different ideas** – The best innovations often come from blending concepts from different fields.

Practical Example: *When I worked on my first film, I had a very limited budget, but I discovered creative ways to shoot spectacular scenes using* *minimal resources. I experimented with new filming techniques, utilized natural lighting, and explored unusual locations that gave the film a distinctive flair.*

Practical Exercise: Every day, challenge yourself to find a better or more efficient way to accomplish something in your routine.

PRACTICAL INNOVATION: HOW TO APPLY IT IN LIFE AND BUSINESS

Innovation isn't just theory; it must be applied to deliver results.
Where can you apply innovation?

- **At work** – Automate repetitive tasks, use new digital tools, find more efficient ways to manage time.
- **In business** – Analyze what your competitors are doing and think of ways to improve or change your approach.
- **In your personal life** – Change habits, discover new methods to be more productive, explore fresh ideas.

Practical Example: *When I created an ad for a major client looking to stand out, I broke away from traditional formats. Instead of a conventional ad, I printed it upside down on a full page of one of the magazines I produced. It sparked curiosity among readers, who physically turned the magazine to check if it was a mistake. The result? The ad garnered much more attention than traditional ones, proving that a touch of innovation can make a significant difference.*

Practical Exercise: Identify an aspect of your life or work that you want to improve and write down three ways you could innovate in that area.

OVERCOMING THE FEAR OF CHANGE

Many people resist innovation because they fear change or failure.
How to overcome the fear of innovating:

- **Recognize that failure is a part of the process** – Every innovation stems from trial and error.
- **Don't wait for perfection to act** – Innovation demands ongoing experimentation.
- **Surround yourself with those who embrace change** – Positive influences foster creativity.

Practical Exercise: Identify a situation where you have avoided change due to fear and write down one action you can take to face it.

CREATING A COMPETITIVE ADVANTAGE THROUGH INNOVATION

The most successful people and companies are those that continuously innovate.

- Amazon revolutionized e-commerce with cutting-edge logistics.
- Tesla transformed the automotive industry by investing in electric vehicles before anyone else.
- Steve Jobs reshaped consumer technology by converting the phone into a digital device ecosystem.

How can you use innovation to stand out?

- Monitor the market and pinpoint areas for improvement.
- Examine the strategies of successful companies and tailor their approaches to fit your context.
- Continuously seek new opportunities; don't hesitate to experiment.

Practical Exercise: Write down one innovative idea that you could apply to your job or a personal project.

Innovation is not a luxury; it is necessary for those who want to stand out and succeed.

You don't have to be a genius to innovate; just be curious, open to change, and willing to experiment.

Remember: Don't merely adhere to the rules of the game. Forge new rules and transform your ideas into reality.

PROBLEM SOLVING: THE KEY TO OVERCOMING CHALLENGES

Life and work present numerous challenges. Success doesn't rely on the absence of problems but on the ability to confront them effectively. Problem-solving is a crucial skill that distinguishes successful individuals from those who remain stuck when facing difficulties.

Creating a strategic approach to problem-solving allows you to turn challenges into opportunities, enhance your decision-making, and tackle difficult situations with confidence and clarity.

PROBLEM SOLVING AS A SUCCESS MINDSET

Many people see problems as insurmountable obstacles. Successful individuals, instead, treat them as challenges to be solved with creativity and logic.

How to change the way you see problems:

- **View the problem as a growth opportunity** – Every difficulty teaches something new.
- **Develop a solution-oriented mindset** – Focus on what you can do, not on what you can't control.
- **Avoid being overwhelmed by emotions** – Approach problems with logic and calmness, not letting yourself be consumed by them.

Practical Example: *Often, when I write a screenplay, I face a problem that appears simple but is actually quite complex: how to create an original, engaging story without a large budget. Rather than becoming discouraged, I view these limitations as an opportunity. I set the story in fewer locations and* *concentrate on intense dialogue and building tension. Ultimately, this approach strengthens the script and makes it more impactful.*

Practical Exercise: Consider a recent problem and note what you can learn from it for the future.

SOLVING A PROBLEM

Problem-solving isn't just improvisation; following a clear method helps you find effective solutions.
5 Steps to Solve Any Problem:

1. **Define the problem** – What's the real root cause?
2. **Analyze your options** – What possible solutions exist?
3. **Evaluate risks and benefits** – What's the most effective and sustainable solution?
4. **Act quickly** – A perfect solution tomorrow is worth less than a good one today.
5. **Assess the results** – Did the solution work? What can I improve next time?

Practical Example: *If my business is losing customers, I can analyze the feedback, identify the problem (pricing, quality, service), and test strategies to win them back. For instance, I could offer a personalized service or enhance client communication.*

Practical Exercise: Use these five steps to address a current problem you're facing.

CRITICAL THINKING VS. CREATIVE THINKING IN PROBLEM SOLVING

There are two primary approaches to problem-solving: critical thinking and creative thinking.

Critical Thinking:

- Analyzes data and facts logically.
- Weighs pros and cons rationally.
- Eliminates unrealistic options and focuses on practical solutions.

Creative Thinking:

- Discovers unconventional solutions.
- Tests innovative approaches.
- Employs intuition and brainstorming to generate new ideas.

Practical Example: *If a restaurant has few customers, critical thinking can be used to evaluate service quality and pricing. Conversely, creative thinking might inspire the introduction of a themed menu or special events to attract more patrons.*

Practical Exercise: Select a problem and apply both critical and creative approaches to develop varied solutions.

HOW TO OVERCOME CHALLENGES IN PROBLEM SOLVING

Sometimes, even with the best methods, problems seem unsolvable. Here's how to tackle the most common obstacles.

Strategies to overcome roadblocks:

- **Break the problem into smaller parts** – Solving one piece at a time makes it feel less overwhelming.
- **Change your perspective** – Ask yourself: "How would a successful person handle this situation?"
- **Seek help or external feedback** – Sometimes, a different viewpoint can reveal the solution.
- **Avoid procrastination** – Delaying off will not make the problem disappear; it will only make it harder to confront.

Practical Example: *While working on an ad production, I encountered* *last-minute issues with the shooting location. Instead of panicking, I promptly reached out to alternatives, reassessed the production plan, and quickly found a solution. The result? A successful commercial despite the obstacles.*

Practical Exercise: Identify a complex problem and divide it into 3–5 smaller, more manageable micro-problems.

PROBLEM SOLVING AS A COMPETITIVE ADVANTAGE

In the world of work and entrepreneurship, the most sought-after people are those who can solve problems.

Why being a problem solver makes you more competitive:

- Companies seek individuals who provide solutions rather than those who complain.
- Problem solvers adapt more effectively to market changes.
- Problem-solving is the cornerstone of innovation and leadership.

Practical Example: *Steve Jobs addressed the issue of complicated user interfaces in computers. At a time when PCs were hard to use, he introduced the Macintosh, featuring an intuitive graphical interface and a mouse, revolutionizing the tech industry and making computers accessible to everyone.*

Practical Exercise: Identify an issue within your business or industry and write down a potential innovative solution.

Problem-solving is one of the most powerful skills you can develop. Those who seek solutions instead of complaining always have an edge.

Remember: There are no problems without solutions, only problems that haven't been approached correctly yet.

IN SUMMARY

We've explored the essential foundations for achieving success in life. Passion, stepping out of your comfort zone, consistency, action, reflection, innovation, and problem-solving are powerful tools that can help turn your dreams into reality.

Remember that success requires commitment, determination, and an open mindset. Be prepared to leave your comfort zone, face challenges with courage, and constantly innovate.

With these tools at your disposal, you'll be equipped to overcome any obstacle and achieve the success you deserve in life.

4 HOW TO BUILD A CAREER

Let's explore how to overcome the fear of asking, the importance of public relations, and how to turn opportunities into profit. By mastering these essential skills, you'll be able to make the most of every opportunity that comes your way.

Many people give up on their dreams not because they lack talent or ability but because they don't dare to ask. We're often held back by the fear of rejection, humiliation, or judgment. Yet, asking is the first step toward receiving.

Successful people don't wait for opportunities to fall from the sky; they actively seek them out by asking questions, requesting help, negotiating terms, and building connections.

WHY ASKING IS ESSENTIAL FOR SUCCESS

If you don't ask, you don't get it.
  Why is learning to ask so important?

- **It opens new opportunities** – Many possibilities only exist for those brave enough to ask.

- It provides support and resources – No one achieves success entirely alone.
- **It helps you negotiate better conditions** – Asking can earn you benefits that you would otherwise miss.
- **It shows self-confidence** – People respect those who have the courage to express their needs.

Practical Example: *When I decided to start my first service company, I had a solid idea but lacked the funds. Instead of letting that stop me, I asked for help. My parents were the first to support me, and I soon gained backing from industry colleagues, both in Italy and abroad, from Rome to New York. I also had the opportunity to borrow essential equipment to get started. If I hadn't dared to ask, my business would have never taken off.*

Practical Exercise: *Write down three goals you want to achieve and identify someone or a situation where you could ask for them.*

HOW TO OVERCOME THE FEAR OF REJECTION

The fear of asking often comes from the fear of rejection. However, rejection is not failure; it's simply a response.

- **Accept that rejection is part of the process** – Every "no" brings you closer to a "yes."
- **Don't take it personally** – A "no" doesn't define your worth.
- **View rejection as a learning opportunity** – Reflect on what you can improve for next time.
- **Practice with small requests** – Start with simple asks to build confidence.

Practical Example: *When I started working in film production, I often had to reach out to companies and sponsors to request funding. At first, every 'no' felt like a hard blow. But then I realized that each rejection taught me something: I improved my pitch, refined my requests, and learned how to present myself more convincingly. In the end, those early 'no's made me stronger and more determined.*

Practical Exercise: Reflect on a moment when you hesitated to ask due to a fear of rejection, and consider how you might have approached it differently.

THE ART OF ASKING EFFECTIVELY

Asking isn't just about saying, "I want this." You need to understand how to do it correctly to increase your chances of success.
How to make effective requests:

- **Be clear and specific** – People can't read your mind, so explain exactly what you need.
- **Show value** – Clarify why your request benefits the other person as well.
- **Ask with confidence** – Your approach impacts the response: be assertive and direct.
- **Be prepared for a 'no' and know how to pivot** – If you get turned down, inquire if there are alternatives.

Practical Example: *During a film's production, the director needed to shoot at an exclusive location. Instead of simply submitting a standard request, I prepared a proposal detailing how our production would provide visibility for the venue and offered a promotional return for their brand. The result? I secured the location for free in exchange for including some clips in their marketing campaigns.*

Practical Exercise: Draft a request you wish to make, and try to rephrase it more clearly and effectively.

WHERE AND WHEN TO ASK TO MAXIMIZE YOUR CHANCES OF SUCCESS

The timing and context of your request can greatly influence its outcome.

- **Choose the right moment** – A poorly timed request may be ignored or rejected.
- **Identify the right person** – Ask someone who has the authority to help, not someone who cannot.
- **Use the appropriate tone and** language – Adapt your approach to fit the situation and the person you're addressing to.

Practical Example: *Once, I wanted to pitch an idea to a well-known producer, but I was aware that he received dozens of proposals every day. I researched the best time to reach out to him and decided to write after a networking event when he would be more relaxed and open to ideas. As a result of this strategy, I got his attention and secured a follow-up.*

Practical Exercise: Think about a request you made in the past and assess whether the timing and the person were appropriate.

ASKING AS A HABIT: THE 100 REJECTIONS METHOD

Many successful entrepreneurs apply the "100 rejections" method, a technique that teaches you to stop fearing the act of asking.
How does it work?

- **Make 100 requests** in different areas of life (work, relationships, opportunities).
- **Track every "no" and analyze the responses** to refine your approach.
- **Over time, you'll realize that receiving a "no" isn't so bad**, and you'll start getting plenty of opportunities.

Practical Example: *When I launched my publishing company, I faced a significant challenge: attracting advertisers for my magazines without an established portfolio. Instead of feeling discouraged, I chose to reach out to various companies and directly ask for 'help' by offering innovative advertising services, sometimes including discounts or small trial projects to demonstrate my value. Many declined, but some accepted, which helped me* *build credibility and gain experience. If I had stopped asking after the first rejections, my magazines would have never come to life.*

Practical Exercise: Start your own 100 rejections challenge today: make one request each day and monitor the responses.

Asking is a life-changing skill.

- Don't hesitate to express your desires.
- Accept rejection as a natural part of the process.
- Asking with confidence brings you closer to success.

Remember: If you don't ask, the answer will always be "no." Learn to ask with determination, and you'll be amazed by the opportunities that arise.

THE POWER OF PUBLIC RELATIONS: BUILDING CONNECTIONS FOR SUCCESS

We live in a world where success isn't just about skills and knowledge; it's also about the quality of our relationships.

Public relations aren't merely a business marketing strategy; they're an essential skill for creating opportunities and opening doors that might otherwise remain closed.

Knowing how to build and maintain a network of genuine and strategic relationships can make the difference between a stagnant career and one filled with opportunities.

Successful people don't achieve everything on their own; they understand how to connect with the right people at the right time.

WHY IS PUBLIC RELATIONS SO IMPORTANT?

The right relationships can open more doors than skills alone.
That's why building a strong network is essential:

- **They provide access to job and business opportunities** – Many deals arise from referrals and word of mouth.
- **They offer valuable information and resources** – With a solid network, you can discover solutions and fresh ideas more quickly.
- **They help establish a strong reputation** – People tend to trust those who are known and well-connected.
- **They enhance support and personal** growth – The right contacts can help you through tough times with advice and guidance.

Practical Example *When Jeff Bezos launched Amazon, he didn't possess massive capital, but he understood how to cultivate strategic relationships to secure funding and logistical support. He solicited trust from investors, collaborators, and business partners, demonstrating that a revolutionary idea requires a network of believers to thrive. If he hadn't dared to ask, Amazon might never have grown into the giant it is today.*

Practical Exercise: Create a list of five individuals you admire in your field and consider how you might connect with them in a genuine way.

HOW TO BUILD AUTHENTIC AND VALUABLE RELATIONSHIPS

Networking isn't just about knowing more people; it's about building genuine, lasting connections.

- **Give before you ask** – Offer value, support, or advice before expecting something in return.
- **Be genuine and sincere** – People can sense authenticity. Focus on building real relationships, not just opportunistic ones.
- **Stay in touch** – A network needs nurturing. Sending a quick message, sharing a helpful article, or congratulating someone on a success strengthens your bond.

- **Show up at the right events** – Conferences, seminars, and professional groups are ideal opportunities to grow your network.

Practical Example: *I met one of my most important collaborators almost by chance at an event, where we started a conversation without any expectations. I didn't ask him for anything; I simply listened to his perspective and shared mine. Years later, that connection evolved into a strategic partnership that brought great results.*

Practical Exercise: Write down the names of three people you'd like to reconnect with and plan one action for strengthening your relationship with each.

EFFECTIVE NETWORKING STRATEGIES

Effective networking is not merely about exchanging business cards; it involves creating meaningful and mutually beneficial relationships.

- **Ask questions and listen actively** – Showing genuine interest in others fosters stronger connections.
- **Attend networking events with a clear goal** – Understanding what you want enables you to connect with the right people.
- **Use social media strategically** – Platforms like LinkedIn and professional groups can be powerful tools for expanding your network.
- **Follow the 24/7/30 rule** – After meeting someone, send a message within 24 hours, follow up within 7 days, and maintain the relationship over the next 30 days.

Practical Example: *Whenever I attend a film festival or market, rather than simply collecting contacts, I reach out with a personalized message to each person I meet. This helps me build genuine relationships that, over time, can evolve into significant collaborations.*

Practical Exercise: Prepare a 30-second personal introduction to use when meeting new people (your elevator pitch).

AVOIDING COMMON PUBLIC RELATIONS MISTAKES

Building a network takes time and strategy. Avoid these common mistakes:

- **Only focusing on what you can get** – Relationships should be mutual, not one-sided.
- **Failing to follow up after the first meeting** – Relationships need to be nurtured over time.
- **Not adapting your message to the context** – Talking only about yourself without considering the other person's interests will not create real connections.
- **Underestimating the power of kindness and respect** – People remember those who treat them with attention and respect.

Practical Example: *Richard Branson, the founder of Virgin, built his empire not only on innovative ideas but also by nurturing strategic relationships. He made it a habit to personally follow up with those he met, maintaining the dialogue and creating opportunities for collaboration. His ability to connect with partners, investors, and employees was key in transforming Virgin into a global brand.*

Practical Exercise: Write down the name of someone you've recently met and message them to strengthen the connection.

TURNING YOUR NETWORK INTO CONCRETE OPPORTUNITIES

A strong network isn't just a contact list; it's a web of people eager to collaborate.

- Identify key individuals who can help you grow.

- Create value for your network by sharing useful information and connecting people.
- Use every connection as an opportunity to learn something new.
- Don't wait until you need something to build your network relationships.

Practical Example: *Genuine connections can change the trajectory of a career. One day, a colleague introduced me to a producer seeking someone with my exact background. That meeting, stemming from a simple exchange of ideas, evolved into a game-changing collaboration for my professional journey. If I hadn't nurtured sincere relationships and valued each encounter, that opportunity might never have come my way.*

Practical Exercise: Think of an opportunity you want to pursue and ask yourself: which contact could help you in making it happen?

In short:

- Your network serves as your social capital.
- The more authentic connections you foster, the more opportunities will arise.
- Investing in relationships yields long-term benefits across all areas of life.

Remember: Success is never a solitary journey. The right people alongside you can make all the difference.

CREATING YOUR OWN OPPORTUNITIES

Many people spend their lives waiting for the right time, the perfect chance, or for luck to knock on their door. But those who achieve success don't wait; they create their own opportunities.

Initiative, creativity, and the ability to spot hidden potential in every situation are the keys to turning ordinary moments into extraordinary opportunities. The world belongs to those who see opportunities, whereas others see only obstacles.

Success rarely results from chance; opportunities come to those who actively seek them.

- Successful people didn't wait for the perfect moment; they created it.
- Every challenge hides an opportunity for those ready to seize it.
- The first step to creating an opportunity is taking action without waiting for ideal circumstances.

Practical Example: *Sara Blakely, the founder of Spanx, turned a simple idea into a multibillion-dollar empire. With only $5,000 and no prior experience in the textile industry, she created an innovative product and persisted until she secured a meeting with Neiman Marcus executives, persuading them to carry her garments. Thanks to her determination and her ability to create her own opportunities, she became the world's youngest self-made billionaire, according to Forbes.*

Practical Exercise: Write down three situations in your life where you hesitated to take action and consider how you might have transformed those moments into opportunities.

DEVELOPING A PROACTIVE MINDSET

Opportunities don't appear magically. You need the right mindset to spot and seize them.

- Shift your perspective. Instead of thinking, "I can't," ask yourself, "How can I?"
- Always stay curious and open to new possibilities.
- Turn problems into opportunities for growth and innovation.

Practical Example: *Ingvar Kamprad, founder of IKEA, transformed the furniture industry by identifying a market opportunity: offering stylish furniture at affordable prices. He revolutionized the industry by introducing the* *concept of flat-pack furniture, making stylish design accessible to a wider audience.*

Practical Exercise: Whenever you face an obstacle, write down three potential ways to turn it into an opportunity.

HOW TO IDENTIFY HIDDEN OPPORTUNITIES

Opportunities don't always reveal themselves clearly; often, they appear disguised as challenges or complex situations.

- Observe unmet needs in your industry or community.
- Keep your eyes on emerging trends and market shifts.
- Pay attention to people: their needs and frustrations often uncover business or innovation opportunities.

Practical Example: *Airbnb originated from the idea of two young men who couldn't afford their rent and decided to rent out an air mattress in their living room. They turned a personal struggle into an opportunity that revolutionized the travel industry.*

Practical Exercise: Identify three problems you encounter in your daily life and brainstorm innovative solutions for each.

CREATING OPPORTUNITIES THROUGH NETWORKING AND CONNECTIONS

Often, the best opportunities don't come from working alone, but from the people you know.

- Attend industry events, seminars, and professional gatherings.
- Build authentic relationships with people who share your interests.
- Don't be afraid to ask; having the right connections can open new doors.

Practical Example: *Steven Spielberg began his career by sneaking into Universal Pictures' studios and building relationships with producers. That daring move helped him land his first significant opportunities in film industry.*

Practical Exercise: Identify five people who could assist you on your journey and plan one method to reach out to each of them.

TAKE ACTION NOW: THE RIGHT TIME IS NOW

The biggest mistake you can make is to postpone. Every day without action is a lost opportunity.

- Don't wait for the 'perfect moment"; it doesn't exist.
- Take small steps every day to get closer to your goals.
- Experiment, fail, learn, and try again: action is key to progress.

Practical Example: *Jeff Bezos left a stable job to start Amazon in his garage. If he had waited for the perfect moment, the e-commerce giant might never have existed.*

Practical Exercise: Consider one immediate action you can take today to advance toward one of your opportunities.

Opportunities don't come on their own: you have to create them.

- Develop a proactive mindset.
- Learn to identify hidden opportunities.
- Surround yourself with individuals who can help you grow.
- Don't hesitate: take action now.

Remember: The future belongs to those who do not wait but create. Seize the opportunities surrounding you.

TURNING OPPORTUNITIES INTO PROFIT: FROM IDEA TO ACTION

Spotting an opportunity is a crucial step, but simply recognizing the potential of an idea or a connection is not enough. You must know how to turn it into a tangible, profitable outcome.

Too many people identify opportunities for growth or income but lack the knowledge to fully leverage them. True success comes from transforming our network, ideas, and resources into real profit.

FROM OPPORTUNITY TO PROFIT: THE 4-STEP PROCESS

Not every opportunity automatically leads to success. You need a method to turn it into tangible value.

1. **Identify the opportunity's value** – What makes it unique? What problem does it solve?
2. **Define an action plan** – What steps must you take to maximize it?
3. **Monetize your idea or connection** – What's the business model or revenue strategy?
4. **Measure and optimize** – Monitor results and improve the process over time.

Practical Example: *A photographer meets an influencer at a networking event. Instead of just exchanging contact details, he proposes a complimentary photo shoot to demonstrate his skills. The influencer, impressed by his work, begins recommending him to others, turning a simple connection into a steady stream of clients.*

Practical Exercise: Choose a recent opportunity you identified and outline the four steps to turn it into a profit.

KNOWING MANY PEOPLE ISN'T ENOUGH

You should understand how to turn contacts into business opportunities, avoid opportunism, and avoid confusing professional networking with personal friendships.

- **Build strategic relationships** – Focus on connections that offer mutual and professional value.
- **Create a clear, valuable offer** – Explain how you can help your contacts in a specific, professional way without a hidden agenda.
- **Be proactive in proposing collaborations** – Don't wait for others to ask; genuinely offer your value.
- **Follow up over time** – Many business opportunities take shape after multiple meetings and interactions.

Practical Example: An entrepreneur meets a potential client at an event. Rather than engaging in a casual chat, he follows up the next day with an email that presents a concrete idea and offers a free consultation to start. This proactive approach increases the chances of closing a deal without appearing pushy.

Practical Exercise: Think of three professional contacts you've made recently and identify one specific action you can take to turn each into a genuine, mutually beneficial business relationship.

FINDING THE RIGHT MONETIZATION MODEL

Having an idea or a connection isn't enough; you must know how to make it economically viable.

- **Direct sales** – Provide paid products or services based on the identified opportunity.
- **Strategic partnerships** – Seek partners to co-develop and monetize an idea.

- **Long-term value creation** – Establish a recurring revenue system (subscriptions, royalties, affiliate programs).
- **Profit automation** – Develop scalable business models that operate without constant direct involvement.

Practical Example: *A fitness expert creates an online course rather than just working with individual clients. This allows him to scale his business and earn passive income, turning his expertise into a sustainable revenue source.*

Practical Exercise: Choose one opportunity you've identified and select a monetization model to maximize its potential.

RESILIENCE: THE KEY TO OVERCOMING CHALLENGES

Not every opportunity leads to immediate profit. That's where resilience and adaptability come into play.

- **Embrace failure as part of the journey** – Every mistake offers a chance to learn.
- **Adjust your strategy** – If an idea doesn't work, change your approach instead of giving up.
- **Keep your focus on results** – Maintain discipline and consistency throughout time.

Practical Example: *Jeff Bezos started by selling only books on Amazon. When he realized the model worked, he expanded the offerings. If he had remained limited to just books, Amazon wouldn't have become the giant it is today.*

Practical Exercise: Reflect on a moment when you missed the chance to turn an opportunity into profit and consider what you might do differently next time.

CREATING A SYSTEM TO CONTINUOUSLY TURN OPPORTUNITIES INTO PROFIT

Success does not depend on a single opportunity; it results from the ability to consistently repeat the process over time.

- **Create a steady flow of opportunities** – Expand your network and actively seek out new prospects.
- **Establish a system to monetize opportunities** – Automate processes and build scalable strategies.
- **Continuously improve your method** – Analyze results and optimize your approach over time.

Practical Example: *Elon Musk didn't stop at PayPal; he used the capital he earned to launch Tesla and SpaceX, applying the same entrepreneurial mindset to create new profit-generating opportunities.*

Practical Exercise: Create a checklist of actions to ensure every opportunity is fully leveraged and can be replicated in the future.

Identifying an opportunity is only the first step. Genuine success comes from understanding how to turn it into actual profit.

- Develop a clear method to turn opportunities into action.
- Monetize ideas through sustainable business models.
- Don't fear failure, use each experience to improve the process.
- Create a repeatable system to maximize opportunities over time.

Remember: The world is full of opportunities, but only those who can harness them truly succeed.

IN SUMMARY

We've explored ways to overcome the fear of asking, the power of public relations, the creation of opportunities, and strategies for turning those opportunities into profit.

Remember, success doesn't happen by chance; it results from consistent effort, an open mindset, and intentional actions. Don't be afraid to ask; through communication and interaction, you can discover new possibilities.

Public relations are essential for building a support network and forming connections that can unlock unexpected doors.

Don't wait passively for opportunities; be proactive in seeking, creating, and recognizing them when they arise.

Real success lies in the ability to transform and monetize opportunities with determination, discipline, and consistent action.

Always remember that everyone has the potential to achieve success, but it requires ongoing commitment and the courage to face challenges along the way. Don't let fear or insecurity hold you back. Be bold, confident, and willing to leave your comfort zone.

Work hard, keep your mind open, and learn from every obstacle you encounter on your journey.

5 HOW TO CREATE A BUSINESS

As we know, every great success begins with an idea. However, not every idea is destined to work.

Many times, I've gotten excited about a brilliant idea only to realize shortly after that there was no market for it or that I didn't have the right skills to bring it to life. This is frustrating, but it's a necessary step. Choosing the right idea isn't just a matter of intuition; it requires passion, experience, and a concrete market analysis.

Let's look at evaluating and selecting the right idea, reducing the risk of failure, and maximizing the chances of success.

THE IMPORTANCE OF STARTING FROM YOUR PASSIONS

Pursuing something you love is not only more rewarding, but it also boosts your resilience in facing challenges.

Questions to identify your passion:

- What activities excite you and make you lose track of time?
- What topics do you read, study, and research effortlessly?
- If you had unlimited time and money, what would you do?

Why passion matters:

- It keeps you motivated during difficult times.
- It helps you stand out from the competition by conveying enthusiasm and authenticity.
- It makes you more willing to invest time and energy in learning and self-improvement.

Practical Example: *Steve Jobs didn't just create computers; he was passionate about design, technology, and user experience, combining these passions to revolutionize the industry.*

Practical Exercise: Write down your top three passions and consider how they might transform into a business venture.

EVALUATING YOUR SKILLS AND STRENGTHS

Having a passion is not enough: you also need the skills to turn it into a sustainable project.

How to assess your skills:

- What are your strengths, and what do people frequently seek your advice on?
- What professional or personal experiences have provided you with valuable skills?
- What skills could you easily acquire through study and practice?

Key skills to develop:

- **Technical skills**: Specific abilities required in your chosen field.
- **Soft skills**: Leadership, time management, communication, and problem-solving.
- **Digital skills**: Today, nearly every business requires a strong online presence.

Practical Example: *A great chef might have a passion for cooking, but to run a successful restaurant, they also need to develop business management and marketing skills.*

Practical Exercise: Make a list of your main skills and pinpoint the ones that could be useful for your business idea.

ANALYZING THE MARKET AND REAL DEMAND

A viable idea must meet a market need. It cannot become a business if no one is willing to pay for your product or service.

Steps to analyze the market:

- **Study trends**: Which sectors are growing? Are there new technologies or emerging habits?
- **Identify unmet needs**: Are there problems that still lack effective solutions?
- **Analyze the competition**: Which companies are already operating in this field? How can you differentiate yourself?
- **Test public interest**: You can conduct surveys, test a Minimum Viable Product (MVP), or use tools to measure demand.

Practical Example: *Netflix recognized that audiences desired on-demand content, moving beyond the traditional video rental model and reshaping the entertainment industry.*

Practical Exercise: Choose a sector that interests you and identify three common issues you can address with an innovative product or service.

TESTING THE IDEA BEFORE INVESTING SIGNIFICANT RESOURCES

Many entrepreneurial failures arise from premature investments in untested ideas.

Ways to test an idea without significant investments:

- **Develop a prototype or MVP:** A streamlined version of your product to assess interest.
- **Launch a landing page:** A webpage featuring a clear value proposition along with a pre-order or sign-up option.
- **Utilize social media:** Share content to observe how the audience responds to your idea.
- **Consider pre-sales or crowdfunding:** An effective method to validate demand and generate initial funds.

Practical Example: *Dropbox tested its product using a straightforward demo video prior to developing the software, which helped gather thousands of sign-ups and validate the market.*

Practical Exercise: Consider a method to evaluate your idea on a minimal budget before committing to larger investments.

FINDING THE BALANCE BETWEEN PASSION, SKILLS, AND MARKET DEMAND

The ideal concept lies at the intersection of passion, skills, and market opportunity.

The Three-Circle Model:

1. **Passion:** It excites and motivates you over the long term.
2. **Skills:** You are (or can become) good at it.
3. **Market:** There is a real demand for your product or service.

Practical Example: *If you are passionate about photography, possess experience in visual content creation, and see a demand for high-quality images in digital advertising, you could launch a photography business for brands and companies.*

Practical Exercise: Draw three circles representing passions, skills, and market opportunities, and find the ideal overlapping area for your business idea.

Choosing the right idea is the first step toward building a successful business.

- Identify your passions to remain motivated.
- Assess your skills and develop the necessary abilities for success.
- Study the market to ensure there's genuine demand for your idea.
- Test the idea before making significant investments to avoid expensive mistakes.
- Find the ideal balance between passion, skills, and market opportunities.

Remember: An idea alone is not enough; it requires a clear strategy and a strong vision.

THE PURPLE COW

We live in a world filled with products, services, and advertising messages. To succeed, being good is not enough; you must be remarkable.

From my earliest projects, I realized that the market does not reward mere competence. If you want to stand out, you must find a way to be different and get noticed in a sea of similar offerings. This is where Seth Godin's concept of the "Purple Cow" comes into play.

Imagine driving through the countryside and seeing hundreds of brown and white cows. Eventually, you stop noticing them. But if you suddenly saw a purple one? It would be impossible to ignore. That extraordinary cow would instantly grab your attention.

That's the point: in business, you must be the Purple Cow, the element that breaks the mold and leaves a lasting impression.

WHAT IS THE PURPLE COW AND WHY IS IT SO POWERFUL?

People ignore what's ordinary and predictable. To stand out, you must provide something surprising and unexpected.

The Purple Cow is:

- A product or service that breaks the mold.
- An idea so unique that it captures immediate attention.
- Something people are eager to discuss and share with others.

Practical Example: *LEGO has redefined the concept of toys by transforming simple building blocks into a creative and interactive experience that engages both children and adults, giving rise to a global community passionate about building and innovation.*

Practical Exercise: Consider your industry and ask yourself: what unique approach can you take that sets you apart from others?

IDENTIFYING YOUR UNIQUE STRENGTH

Every business has a unique strength. The challenge is to recognize it and convey it effectively.

How to discover your Purple Cow:

- **What truly makes you stand out?** (Not just better, but different.)
- **What problem do you solve in a way that no one else is addressing?**
- **Does your product have a surprising or unexpected feature?**
- **Are you challenging a long-established norm in your industry?**

Practical Example: *Dyson revolutionized the vacuum cleaner market by* *eliminating the bag and incorporating cyclone technology, transforming a typical appliance into a symbol of design and innovation.*

Practical Exercise: List three factors that set your product or service apart from the competition.

CRAFTING A STORY THAT REINFORCES YOUR DIFFERENTIATION

A Purple Cow alone is not enough; you must effectively communicate the story of your uniqueness.

Strategies for communicating your difference:

- **Share a compelling story:** What is your purpose? What is your mission?
- **Create a clear and direct message:** The audience should quickly understand what sets you apart.
- **Evoke emotions:** People remember what resonates with them.
- **Utilize social proof:** Testimonials, reviews, and success stories enhance your credibility.

Practical Example: *Airbnb didn't just offer an alternative to hotels; it narrated a tale of human connection, unique experiences, and a new way to travel.*

Practical Exercise: Create a brief message (just one sentence) that powerfully and clearly conveys what makes your brand unique.

BEING BOLD: THE COURAGE TO BE DIFFERENT

Many people are afraid to stand out too much, but the truth is that in today's market, being "normal" is the same as being invisible.

Things to remember when creating your Purple Cow:

- **Being different attracts criticism**: Not everyone will understand your idea right away, and that's okay.
- **Innovation is risky, but conformity is fatal**: The world doesn't need another product that looks just like the others.
- **It's not enough to be original; you must also be relevant**: Your uniqueness needs to solve a real problem or satisfy a deep desire of your audience.

Practical Example: *Nintendo chose not to compete directly with Sony and Microsoft in the gaming sector. Instead, it focused on developing innovative consoles like the Wii, which redefined how people play video games.*

Practical Exercise: Think of one aspect of your business where you can be bolder and more daring to distinguish yourself.

ADAPTING AND CONSTANTLY INNOVATING

Being a Purple Cow today doesn't guarantee that you will remain one forever. The market evolves, and your differentiation must evolve with it.

Strategies to keep your uniqueness alive:

- **Monitor feedback and adapt your product.**
- **Continue innovating and enhancing your offer.**
- **Never stop testing new ideas to remain relevant.**

Practical Example: *Netflix started as a DVD rental service but continued to innovate, ultimately becoming the streaming giant it is today.*

Practical Exercise: Define one action you can implement in the coming months to sustain your brand's innovation and surprise.

Being a Purple Cow means being unique, bold, and extraordinary in a world full of ordinary options.

- Identify your unique strengths and use them to stand out.

- Create a strong narrative to clearly communicate your uniqueness.
- Embrace your uniqueness: the courage to break the mold will help you shine.
- Continue innovating to stay one step ahead.

Remember: People may forget the ordinary, but they always remember extraordinary experiences.

BRINGING THE WINNING IDEA TO LIFE

An idea, no matter how brilliant, is not enough. Success doesn't come from a sudden *stroke of genius* but from the ability to turn an insight into a tangible project.

Many entrepreneurs fail not due to a lack of ideas, but because they don't know how to develop and test them effectively. The process of creating a winning idea requires strategy, validation, and ongoing adaptation.

Let's explore how to structure the journey from initial brainstorming to the concrete realization of the idea, minimizing the risk of failure and maximizing the potential for success.

GENERATING MANY IDEAS: EXPANDING CREATIVE THINKING

The first step is to avoid settling for the first idea that comes to mind. Creativity is born from exploration.

Strategies for generating innovative ideas:

- **Unfiltered brainstorming:** Write down any idea, without judging it right away.
- **Creative associations:** Combine a concept with ideas from other fields to create new perspectives.
- **Analyze existing problems:** The best ideas often come from solving a real, concrete issue.

- **Study other industries:** Inspiration often comes from completely different sectors.

Practical Example: *Spotify revolutionized the music industry by solving the problem of digital piracy. It offered a streaming service that was accessible, legal, affordable, and sustainable for users and artists.*

Practical Exercise: Generate at least 10 ideas for a new business or project, without discarding any of them right away.

EVALUATING AND SELECTING THE BEST IDEA

Not all ideas hold the same potential. You must analyze them to identify which ones are genuinely effective.
Criteria for selecting a winning idea:

- **Feasibility:** Can it be implemented with the available resources?
- **Originality:** Is it something new or a significant improvement on what already exists?
- **Market demand:** Is there an audience willing to pay for this idea?
- **Scalability:** Does it have the potential to grow and generate profits over time?

Practical Example: *Airbnb recognized a significant issue: hotels were costly and lacked personal touch. They redefined the notion of hospitality into a more genuine experience, enabling anyone to rent out their home.*

Practical Exercise: Review your list of ideas and assess them according to these criteria. Which ones appear to be the most promising?

REFINING AND DEVELOPING THE IDEA

Once you've identified the idea with the most potential, it's time to turn it into a detailed project.
How to improve the idea before launching:

- **Identify key details:** Who is your target audience? What is the appropriate price? What are the associated costs?
- **Analyze the competition:** What are others doing? How can you set yourself apart?
- **Create a business model:** What will be your primary source of revenue?

Practical Example: *Netflix started as a DVD rental service by mail but rapidly shifted its model to focus on streaming distribution in order to stay competitive.*

Practical Exercise: Compose a brief strategic plan that answers the key questions: Who? What? How? Why? When?

TESTING THE IDEA WITH A PROTOTYPE OR AN MVP (MINIMUM VIABLE PRODUCT)

Don't wait for perfection to get started. Launch a simplified version to see if the idea truly works.
Ways to test the idea without major investments:

- **Test landing page:** Create a simple webpage with a product description and a sign-up option.
- **Basic prototype:** A simplified version of the product that allows users to try it out.
- **Pre-launch campaign:** Utilize crowdfunding or pre-sales to validate market interest.
- **Focus group or beta testing:** Invite a small group of people to try the product and provide feedback.

Practical Example: *Before developing its ride-sharing platform, Uber started with a simple MVP (minimum viable product) that allowed users to request a black car via SMS. This initial test confirmed demand before committing to a full-scale app.*

Practical Exercise: Define how you could test your idea without immediately creating the final product.

REFINING AND ADAPTING THE IDEA BASED ON FEEDBACK

Success is not a straight path; it requires adapting the idea based on the data and the audience's responses.

How to adapt the idea for improvement:

- **Pay attention to early users:** Identify the strengths and weaknesses of your offering.
- **Make gradual improvements:** Address what isn't working while maintaining the original vision.
- **Be open to pivoting:** If the data indicates that a different approach could be more effective, remain adaptable.

Practical Example: *Instagram originally started as a more complex app known as Burbn, which combined geolocation and check-ins. After analyzing user data, the founders realized that photo sharing was the most popular feature. They eliminated everything else and created the photo-sharing platform we know today.*

Practical Exercise: Analyze potential weaknesses in your idea and consider alternative solutions to address them.

Bringing a winning idea to life is not an instant process. It's a journey that requires strategy, experimentation, and adaptation.

- Generate numerous ideas to expand your possibilities.

- Choose the most viable idea by evaluating feasibility, originality, and market demand.
- Develop a clear plan to implement the idea.
- Test the idea with a prototype or MVP to validate its potential.
- Refine and improve the idea using feedback while remaining open to adjustments.

Remember: There's no such thing as a perfect idea on the first attempt; real success comes to those who have the courage to adapt and improve continuously.

CREATING A BUSINESS PLAN: YOUR ROADMAP TO SUCCESS

No matter how brilliant, a business idea cannot become a real business without solid planning.

The Business Plan is a document that transforms a concept into a concrete, sustainable, and fundable project. It's an essential tool for attracting investors, securing loans, and planning business growth.

So, how do you build an effective Business Plan?

Here, we'll examine the key components of a Business Plan, common mistakes to avoid, and how to structure it for successful fundraising.

WHY IS THE BUSINESS PLAN SO IMPORTANT?

Many entrepreneurs underestimate the importance of a Business Plan, but without it, you're operating in dark.

The main benefits of a solid Business Plan:

- **Clarity and strategic vision:** Helps you define goals, strategies, and concrete actions.
- **Fundraising tool:** Investors and banks seek solid numbers before financing a project.

- **Risk management:** It enables anticipation of problems and planning of solutions.
- **Operational guide:** It provides a clear roadmap for launching and growing your business.

Practical Examples: *Spotify convinced investors with a business plan that highlighted a shift in how people consume music, proposing an innovative subscription model that revolutionized the music industry.*

Airbnb gained investor trust with a business plan focused on providing affordable and authentic lodging for travelers. With a clear and scalable strategy, it became one of the most revolutionary booking platforms in the world.

Practical Exercise: Consider how a business plan could improve your business idea and clarify your strategy.

THE KEY ELEMENTS OF A WINNING BUSINESS PLAN

A successful business plan must be clear, engaging, and based on solid data.

Essential sections:

1. **Executive Summary**
    - A concise overview of the business, its mission, and the value it offers.
    - It should capture investors' attention in just a few lines.
    - **Mistake to avoid:** Being too vague. Investors want to know exactly what your business is about and why it's likely to succeed.
2. **Business Description and Vision**
    - What problem are you solving?
    - What are your short- and long-term goals?
    - What is your unique value proposition?
    - **Mistake to avoid:** Underestimating the importance of long-term vision. An idea that seems promising today might not be viable if it is not scalable.

3. **Market and Competitor Analysis**
   - Who are your target customers?
   - What is the size of the market?
   - Who are your main competitors?
   - What's your competitive advantage?
   - **Mistake to avoid:** Ignoring the competition. Believing there is no competition is a serious mistake; there's always an alternative solution for the customer.
4. **Business Model (How You Make Profit)**
   - What are your revenue streams?
   - What are your main costs?
   - What pricing strategy will you adopt?
   - **Mistake to avoid:** Not having a clear revenue model. No investor will take it seriously if your plan doesn't clearly explain how you'll generate profit.
5. **Marketing and Sales Strategy**
   - How will you reach your target audience?
   - What channels will you use to promote yourself?
   - What will your customer acquisition strategies be?
   - **Mistake to avoid:** Believing that the product will sell itself. Without a solid marketing strategy, even the finest product can fail.
6. **Operational Plan and Logistics**
   - What are the key activities to run the business?
   - What tools, technologies, or suppliers will you use?
   - What team will be needed to manage the operations?
   - **Mistake to avoid:** Lack of a clear operations strategy. Investors want to understand how you plan to deliver your product or service.
7. **Financial Plan and Economic Forecasts**
   - How much initial capital do you need?
   - What are your projected revenues and expenses over the next 3–5 years?
   - When will you reach break-even?
   - What's the growth potential of the business?

- **Mistake to avoid:** Overly optimistic financial projections. Investors prefer realistic figures supported by trustworthy data.

HOW TO USE YOUR BUSINESS PLAN TO SUCCESSFULLY RAISE FUNDS

Investors don't fund vague ideas. They want to see concrete numbers and a clear vision strategy.

What makes your Business Plan attractive to investors?

- A growing market with a genuine problem to solve.
- A competent team with solid experience.
- A scalable business model.
- Reliable financial projections.

Mistake to avoid: Lacking knowledge about your numbers can undermine your credibility if you can't answer financial questions.

CROWDFUNDING: START YOUR BUSINESS WITHOUT UPFRONT CAPITAL

An increasingly popular way to finance a project without substantial initial investment is **crowdfunding**. It's a form of collective fundraising that allows anyone, through dedicated platforms, to contribute financially to support an idea, product, or business venture.

Even with this method, having an attractive business plan is essential.

In recent years, crowdfunding has become a true launchpad for startups, artists, innovators, and creatives across various industries. The most intriguing part? You don't need to rely on big investors or financial institutions; it's everyday people, passionate about your idea, who fund your project.

There are several types of crowdfunding:

- **Reward-based crowdfunding:** In exchange for their contribution, supporters receive a reward, such as an early version of the product or exclusive perks.
- **Equity crowdfunding:** Backers receive a small stake in the company, becoming actual investors.
- **Donation-based crowdfunding:** Based on donations with no financial return, often used for social or charitable causes.
- **Lending crowdfunding:** Also known as peer-to-peer lending, allows individuals to lend money, which is later repaid with interest.

If you have a solid idea and know how to present it effectively, crowdfunding can be a fantastic way to raise the capital you need without incurring debt or giving up equity in your company. Offer appealing rewards, create a captivating video, and keep your backers updated regularly. Additionally, always have a backup plan in case the campaign doesn't reach its funding goal.

The key to success lies in crafting a clear, engaging, and well-structured proposal that attracts the right audience and convinces them to invest in your vision.

Mistake to avoid: Launching a campaign without a defined audience, setting unrealistic goals, or neglecting communication.

COMMON MISTAKES TO AVOID WHEN CREATING A BUSINESS PLAN

Many business plans fail due to avoidable mistakes.

Most common errors:

- Being too generic: Vague statements fail to convince investors.
- Ignoring competitors: Claiming "we have no competition" raises red flags about your experience.
- No clear revenue model: An idea cannot be sustainable without revenue.

- Unrealistic financial projections: Your numbers must be supported by actual data.
- Not tailoring the plan to the audience: A business plan for a bank will differ from one intended for a private investor.

Practical Example: *Many startups in the tech sector have failed because they underestimated the time needed to acquire users and the true development costs. A realistic business plan is consistently more effective than an overly optimistic yet unrealistic one.*

Practical Exercise: Review your business plan and ask yourself: Am I avoiding these mistakes?

A well-crafted business plan is not just a document; it serves as a strategic guide to turn an idea into a successful business.

- Clearly define your business, strategy, and financial objectives.
- Analyze the market and identify your competitive advantage.
- Avoid common pitfalls to strengthen and enhance the credibility of your plan.
- Utilize your business plan to attract investors and raise funds.

Remember: An idea without a plan remains merely a dream.

HOW TO FIND YOUR CUSTOMERS

You've worked hard to develop your idea and crafted a comprehensive business plan, and now you're ready to launch your product or service. But how will you find your customers?

A business without customers cannot survive. Identifying and reaching the right audience is essential for success.

Allow me to guide you through the most effective strategies for finding, attracting, and retaining customers, optimizing your marketing efforts, and building a strong network.

DEFINING YOUR TARGET AUDIENCE: WHO ARE YOUR IDEAL CUSTOMERS?

You can't sell to everyone, but you can successfully sell to those who truly need your product.
How to identify your ideal audience:

- **Who are they?** Define their demographic characteristics (age, gender, income, location).
- **What problems do they face?** Understanding their needs and pain points helps you offer a tailored solution.
- **Where do they spend their time?** Are they active on social media, industry forums, or specific events?
- **How do they make purchasing decisions?** Do they rely on reviews, recommendations from friends, or direct contact advertising?

Practical Example: *Nike not only targets athletes; it also segments its audience into professional athletes, fitness enthusiasts, and fashion-forward consumers, tailoring its marketing strategies to each group.*

Practical Exercise: Write a detailed profile of your ideal customer (buyer persona) and consider where you might locate them.

LEVERAGING THE POWER OF DIGITAL MARKETING

Digital marketing allows you to reach your audience effectively and in a measurable way.
Key strategies to consider:

- **SEO (Search Engine Optimization):** When your website ranks high in Google search results, you will receive free organic traffic.

- **Social Media Marketing:** Utilize Facebook, Instagram, LinkedIn, TikTok, or X (formerly Twitter) to engage with your audience and enhance brand awareness.
- **Content Marketing:** Develop articles, videos, podcasts, or infographics that draw in customers without being overly promotional.
- **Email Marketing:** Create an email list and deliver valuable content to keep your audience engaged and boost customer loyalty.
- **Online Advertising (Google Ads, Facebook Ads):** Invest in targeted advertisements to quickly reach your ideal audience.

Practical Example: *Airbnb used digital marketing strategies to expand quickly, utilizing SEO, referral marketing, and captivating content to draw in new users.*

Practical Exercise: Select two digital strategies to implement immediately and begin enhancing your online presence.

CREATING A COMMUNITY AROUND YOUR BRAND

Your most loyal customers aren't just buyers; they're true ambassadors for your brand.
How to build a strong community:

- **Provide valuable content:** Guides, webinars, and tutorials that benefit your audience.
- **Create a community or forum:** A space (even online) where customers can interact with one another and your brand.
- **Engage actively:** Respond to comments, ask questions, and involve your audience in meaningful discussions.
- **Host events and webinars:** Opportunities to share knowledge and experiences while building authentic connections.

Practical Example: *Apple has built a loyal community through events such as WWDC and dedicated forums, creating a strong bond with its customers.*

Practical Exercise: Consider how to engage your audience beyond merely selling your product.

NETWORKING AND LEVERAGING WORD OF MOUTH

Relationships can be more powerful than advertising.
Where and how to network:

- **Industry events:** Attend trade shows, workshops, and conferences to connect with potential clients and partners.
- **Meetups and local groups:** If your business is local, create a direct network with entrepreneurs and professionals in your community.
- **Collaborations and partnerships:** Work with influencers, other brands, or industry professionals to extend your reach.
- **Referral marketing:** Provide incentives to your customers for referring new clients (discounts, freebies, exclusive services).

Practical Example: *Dropbox leveraged word-of-mouth and referral marketing by providing free storage to users who invited friends, which led to exponential growth.*

Practical Exercise: Identify three contacts or companies you can collaborate with to boost your visibility.

DELIVERING AN EXCEPTIONAL CUSTOMER EXPERIENCE TO BUILD LOYALTY

A satisfied customer not only returns but also brings in new ones.
How to improve the customer experience:

- **Listen to feedback:** Solicit customers' opinions and use their suggestions to improve your product or service.
- **Exceed expectations:** Delight your customers with small gestures that make their experience unforgettable.
- **Create top-notch customer service:** The speed and effectiveness of your problem-solving significantly affect your business's reputation.
- **Develop a loyalty program:** Reward your most devoted customers with exclusive perks.

Practical Example: *Amazon achieved its success through outstanding customer service, which includes free returns and personalized support.*

Practical Exercise: Think of one small detail you can enhance in your service to make the customer experience exceptional.

ADAPTING AND OPTIMIZING STRATEGIES BASED ON RESULTS

Finding customers is a dynamic process; it demands ongoing analysis and optimization.

How to continually improve your customer acquisition strategies:

- **Monitor data:** Use tools like Google Analytics, Meta Insights, or email marketing platforms to identify what works best.
- **Experiment with new strategies:** If one channel is performing poorly, explore alternatives. Test new messages, offers, and engagement methods.
- **Optimize conversions:** If many people visit your site but few make a purchase, there might be an issue with your messaging or pricing.

Practical Example: *Netflix regularly reviews user behavior to improve recommendations and make the service more engaging.*

Practical Exercise: Choose one aspect of your marketing strategy to improve and design a test to optimize it.

Finding your customers is not a random activity; it's a well-planned strategy.

- Clearly define your target audience.
- Utilize digital marketing to effectively reach more people.
- Cultivate a loyal community around your brand.
- Network and leverage the power of word-of-mouth.
- Provide an exceptional customer experience to retain and attract new clients.
- Track results and continuously adjust your strategy.

Remember: Success depends not only on the quality of your product but also on the number of people you can reach.

IN SUMMARY

Choosing the right idea is the first crucial step toward entrepreneurial success. You need to consider your passions, skills, and market needs to identify an idea with real potential. The "Purple Cow" represents the unique element that will help your idea stand out from the competition. Creating a winning idea involves brainstorming, evaluating, refining, and testing. Don't be afraid to make changes and improvements along the way. Finding your customers requires a clear understanding of your target audience and the implementation of digital marketing strategies, networking, and community building. Remember that entrepreneurial success doesn't happen overnight. It's a journey that demands dedication, perseverance, and adaptability. Be open to feedback, learn from mistakes, and continue to grow. With a solid idea, an effective marketing strategy, and a constant focus on customer satisfaction, you are well on your way to achieving success in business and life.

6 HOW TO BE A GOOD PARTNER

Success is never a solitary journey.

The people we surround ourselves with influence our way of thinking, affect our motivation, and ultimately determine our results.

If you're surrounded by ambitious, positive, and motivated individuals, your own approach to life and work will reflect those qualities. On the other hand, if your environment is filled with negative people who complain and lack belief in personal growth, you risk absorbing that energy and limiting your potential.

I've learned the hard way just how important it is to carefully choose the people with whom you spend your time and energy. In the past, I worked alongside individuals who didn't believe in their own abilities and spent more time complaining than seeking solutions. Gradually, that mindset began to affect me as well. Then I decided to make a change: I started surrounding myself with people who embraced a growth mindset. The result? An incredible boost toward new opportunities and a shift in perspective that transformed my path.

THE INFLUENCE OF THE PEOPLE AROUND YOU

Your environment reflects your future.
How those around you affect your success:

- **They can motivate or demotivate you:** When surrounded by ambitious individuals with a growth mindset, you're more likely to work hard toward your goals. Conversely, if you're among complainers who see obstacles everywhere, you may adopt that limiting perspective.
- **They can inspire or hold you back:** Engaging with people who have already achieved what you aspire to help you recognize success as attainable. In contrast, those who discourage you or lack belief in your abilities may negatively impact your self-esteem.
- **They create opportunities or obstacles:** A strong network can unlock doors that might otherwise remain closed. Influential individuals, mentors, and collaborators can provide valuable advice and opportunities you might not have considered before.

Practical Example: *Steve Jobs and Steve Wozniak mutually influenced each other, merging Jobs' entrepreneurial vision with Wozniak's technical brilliance to create Apple.*

Many great innovators found success through collaborations with individuals who challenged and motivated them to excel. The most brilliant ideas often arise when brilliant, ambitious minds surround you.

Practical Exercise: List the five people you spend the most time with and ask yourself: Are they contributing to my growth or holding me back?

CREATING A WINNING PEOPLE ENVIRONMENT

Your growth also depends on the people you choose to spend time with.

Strategies to attract and keep successful people around you:

- **Seek mentors:** Find individuals who have already achieved what you aspire to and learn from them.
- **Engage in stimulating environments:** Attend events, workshops, and conferences in your field to connect with others who share similar interests.
- **Distance yourself from toxic people:** Don't be afraid to cut ties with those who demotivate you or belittle your dreams.
- **Build your own network:** Don't wait for the right people to approach you; actively cultivate a network of valuable connections.

Practical Example: *Elon Musk has consistently aimed to surround himself with skilled engineers and innovators, building teams capable of executing ambitious projects like Tesla and SpaceX.*

Many entrepreneurs have succeeded by investing time in building a strong network, attending events, and forming relationships with like-minded individuals.

Practical Exercise: Think of someone you admire and would like to engage with more. Write a plan for how you might connect with them, such as following them on social media, attending events where they will be, or sending a thoughtful message.

THE MIRROR EFFECT: BECOME THE PERSON YOU WANT TO ATTRACT

To surround yourself with successful people, you also need to be a person of value.

How to improve yourself to attract high-quality individuals:

- **Develop useful skills:** The more skilled you are in a specific area, the more interesting people will be drawn to your expertise.
- **Maintain a positive attitude:** No one wants to be around someone who constantly complains or sees problems in every situation.
- **Offer value before asking for anything:** Help others, share your knowledge, and build relationships without expecting immediate returns.
- **Be selective:** Not everyone you meet deserves your time. Choose people who truly enrich your life and career.

Practical Example: *Oprah Winfrey became a role model for many successful people because she consistently worked on herself, improved her skills, and built genuine relationships.*

Many successful leaders have built strong, authentic connections thanks to their growth mindset and their ability to provide value before asking for anything in return.

Practical Exercise: Identify three qualities you wish to develop to become a person who attracts success, and start working on them today.

THE POWER OF COLLABORATION: SUCCESS IS NOT ACHIEVED ALONE

Even the most successful entrepreneurs and leaders have achieved their success with the support of a team.
Why collaboration is essential:

- **It increases opportunities:** A network of talented individuals can lead to new ideas, projects, and partnerships.
- **It compensates for your weaknesses:** We can't excel at

everything. A strong team allows you to focus on what you do best.
- **It encourages innovation:** Engaging with diverse perspectives generates new ideas and creative solutions.

Practical Example: *Larry Page and Sergey Brin joined forces to create Google, one of the most influential companies in the world.*

Some of the greatest successes in business and innovation have emerged through collaboration among individuals with complementary skills who enhance each other's abilities.

Practical Exercise: Identify a potential collaborator for a project and suggest a partnership idea.

MANAGING RELATIONSHIPS STRATEGICALLY

Networking isn't just about making contacts; it's about nurturing meaningful relationships over time.

How to maintain strong professional and personal connections:

- **Express gratitude:** A simple "thank you" can significantly strengthen a relationship.
- **Keep in touch:** Don't only reach out when you need something; nurture the relationship even during neutral times.
- **Give before you ask:** Offer help, advice, or connections prior to requesting favors.
- **Be consistent:** People trust those who honor their promises and demonstrate long-term reliability.

Practical Example: *Richard Branson is known for his relational approach; he maintains authentic connections and builds relationships based on trust and respect.*

Practical Exercise: Reach out today to someone you'd like to deepen your connection with, expressing genuine interest in their journey.

Success isn't just about talent or luck; it's about who you choose to have by your side.

- Build authentic connections and strategically expand your network.
- Partner with brilliant minds to enhance your opportunities for success.
- Embody the qualities you wish to attract; your worth shapes the quality of your relationships.

Remember: Your environment can either boost or obstruct your success. Choose wisely!

THE ROLE OF A PARTNER IN THE JOURNEY TO SUCCESS

Success is never a solo journey. The people we work with, exchange ideas with, and develop projects alongside play a significant role in our professional and personal growth. Among them, one of the most crucial figures is your partner, whether that's a business partner, a close collaborator, or a life partner.

I've learned firsthand how vital it is to choose the right people to collaborate with on a project. A partner can either be the best growth accelerator or the anchor that holds everything back. There have been moments when I had people by my side who helped me overcome challenges, and others when I worked with collaborators who didn't share my vision and complicated matters even more. A valuable partner is someone who encourages you to grow, offers a fresh perspective, and, most importantly, shares your ambition.

THE RIGHT PARTNER: SUPPORT OR OBSTACLE?

The people around us can either lift us up or hold us back.

Having someone who believes in your project by your side can make the difference between giving up and pushing forward with even greater determination.

How a partner can impact your journey:

- **Offers a fresh perspective:** When we become too absorbed in our own ideas, we may miss alternative solutions. A good partner helps you notice what you might overlook.
- **Supports you during tough times:** Every journey has its challenges. Having someone by your side when things get difficult is a tremendous advantage.
- **Shares the workload:** Dividing and delegating tasks is essential to prevent burnout and maximize results.
- **Strengthens skills:** No one excels at everything. A partner with complementary skills can fill in the gaps and enhance the overall project.

Practical Example: *Bill Gates and Paul Allen established Microsoft through a partnership grounded in trust and a division of skills: Gates concentrated on strategy, while Allen focused on technology.*

In the past, I've worked with people who didn't share my enthusiasm. Every small challenge became an excuse to give up. However, when I found partners who shared my mindset, everything changed: we faced obstacles as a team, and every problem turned into an opportunity for growth.

Practical Exercise: Make a list of the people you work with most frequently and ask yourself: Are they helping me succeed or holding me back?

CREATING MUTUAL AND CONSTRUCTIVE SUPPORT

A strong collaborative relationship does not develop by chance; it must be cultivated with purpose and dedication.

Strategies to value your partner:

- **Appreciate their ideas:** Everyone wants to feel heard and valued. Acknowledging another person's input fosters motivation.
- **Communicate clearly:** Misunderstandings are a major source of tension in collaborations. Being transparent and direct helps prevent complications.
- **Be supportive during tough times:** There will be ups and downs. A true partner is there not only when things are going well.
- **Define roles and responsibilities:** A clear division of tasks helps prevent overload and conflict.

Practical Example: *Larry Page and Sergey Brin founded Google by leveraging each other's strengths: Page focused on the big-picture vision, while Brin handled technological innovation.*

I've learned that a partner is not just someone with whom you share a project but also a journey. I remember a time when a project went poorly; my instinct was to find someone to blame. Instead, my partner helped me see the situation from a different perspective, and together, we turned a failure into a valuable lesson.

Practical Exercise: Ask your partner which aspects of your collaboration could be improved.

BUILDING TRUST AND RESPECT

Without trust, collaboration is impossible. Mutual respect serves as the foundation for a lasting and productive relationship.

How to build a strong partnership:

- **Always keep your word:** If you promise to do something, follow through. Credibility is crucial.
- **Provide constructive feedback:** Criticism should always include solutions.
- **Recognize your partner's achievements:** Sometimes, a simple "great job" can motivate someone to excel even further.
- **Minimize unnecessary conflict:** Disagreements are normal, but they should be managed wisely.

Practical Example: *Elon Musk frequently highlights the vital role his teams play in the success of his companies, demonstrating that valuing collaborators is essential.*

I once worked with a partner who never met deadlines. There was always an excuse, and as a result, the project suffered. When I finally decided to address the issue honestly and directly, I realized they weren't the right fit for me.

Practical Exercise: Explore methods to build trust in your relationship with your partner. Is there anything you could tackle differently?

AVOIDING COMMON MISTAKES IN COLLABORATIONS

Even the best collaborations can break down if not managed properly.
Mistakes to avoid:

- **Taking your partner's contribution for granted:** Being grateful strengthens professional relationships.
- **Poor communication:** Lack of clarity causes misunderstandings and tension.
- **Ignoring problems instead of addressing them:** Avoiding issues only makes them worse.
- **Uneven workload:** When one person feels overwhelmed, the relationship begins to deteriorate.

Practical Example: *Steve Jobs and Jonathan Ive transformed Apple into an iconic brand by merging creativity with technological innovation.*

I used to believe that the more I worked, the better the results would be. However, I realized that if my partner wasn't contributing, I ended up carrying all the weight. True success lies in finding balance.

Practical Exercise: If you have a professional partner, ask them if there are any aspects of your working relationship that could be improved.

Success is influenced by the people we choose to work with.

- A good partner acts as a growth accelerator.
- Communication and trust form the foundation of successful collaboration.
- Valuing one another fosters a productive and positive work environment.
- Avoiding common mistakes contributes to building strong, lasting relationships.

Remember: Choosing the right partner might be the key that turns an idea into a real, lasting success.

BUSINESS AND FAMILY: A FRAGILE BALANCE

For many entrepreneurs, family is the heart of life; however, the dynamic shifts completely when it comes to business. Combining business and family ties can be either a winning strategy or a ticking time bomb. I've seen companies grow thanks to collaboration among relatives, but I've also observed businesses devastated by internal conflicts and decisions made from emotion rather than logic.

After years of experience and conversations with numerous entrepreneurs, I've come to understand that keeping a distinct boundary between family and business is often the smartest choice. However, if you need to work with loved ones, it's essential to establish clear rules and a well-defined strategy.

THE BENEFITS OF INCLUDING FAMILY IN BUSINESS

There are valid reasons to involve family members in a business, and in some cases, it can be a strategic decision.

Benefits of a family-run business:

- **Trust and loyalty:** Ideally, family members should be more reliable than outsiders.
- **Shared vision:** When there is a common goal, motivation tends to be greater.
- **Long-term continuity:** A family business can last for generations.
- **Cost savings:** Relatives may be more inclined to make financial sacrifices during difficult times.

Practical Example: *Many legacy companies, such as Ferrari or Hermès, were established and evolved within family circles, creating strong and lasting brands.*

Practical Exercise: If you're thinking about involving a family member, ask yourself: Do they really have the required skills, or is this merely an emotional choice?

THE DISADVANTAGES OF MIXING FAMILY AND BUSINESS

While there are clear benefits, working with relatives can also become a nightmare.

Common problems in family businesses:

- **Lack of objectivity:** Decisions are driven by emotions rather than strategy.

- **Difficulty separating personal life from work:** Business discussions can flow into family life.
- **Conflicts of interest:** A relative might prioritize personal needs over the business's interests.
- **Compromised strategic decisions:** If relatives lack experience, they can obstruct the company's growth.
- **Difficulty firing a family member:** If a relative underperforms, terminating their position becomes emotionally complex.

Practical Example: *Many family-owned businesses have encountered crises or even failure due to internal conflicts, as seen in the case of the Gucci family, where tensions ultimately resulted in the company's sale to outside parties.*

I've seen businesses collapse due to family members disputing leadership roles or making decisions influenced by personal relationships instead of solid business practices

Practical Exercise: If you had to make a difficult decision regarding a family member in your company, would you be able to do it without letting personal ties affect you?

SEPARATING BUSINESS AND FAMILY: A STRATEGIC CHOICE

After years of experience, I firmly believe that keeping work and family separate is the best way to prevent conflict.
Reasons to keep the two spheres separate:

- **Greater professionalism:** Choosing collaborators based on skill rather than family ties ensures more efficient management.
- **Independent decision-making:** Excluding inexperienced family members allows for quicker, more autonomous actions.

- **Healthier family life:** By eliminating work-related issues at home, family relationships can remain more peaceful.
- **Avoids favoritism and internal conflict:** Conflicts or harmful competition can easily arise when multiple family members are involved.

Practical Example: *Many successful entrepreneurs, like Warren Buffett, opt not to involve their families directly in managing their companies to prevent conflicts of interest and uphold meritocracy.*

Practical Exercise: When you get home, establish a boundary: no work talk, just quality time with your family.

IF YOU INVOLVE FAMILY, TRAIN THEM PROPERLY

If you choose to involve a family member in the business, ensure they receive appropriate training for the role.

Why training is essential:

- It prevents unqualified individuals from holding key positions.
- It makes the business more professional and less vulnerable to favoritism.
- It ensures genuine growth for the company without the risk of ill-informed decisions.

Strategies for training a family member:

- Have them gain experience in other environments before joining the family business.
- Provide training courses to improve their skills.
- Assign them progressively responsible roles; no shortcuts should be taken.

Practical Example: *Successful family-owned businesses, such as Ferrero,* *have always emphasized training before giving leadership roles to family members.*

Practical Exercise: If you have a family member in the business, evaluate their level of preparation. Do they require specific training?

Mixing Business with Family Can Be Risky. Sometimes it works, but only with clear guidelines and a professional framework.

- Involving family can foster trust and stability, but it may also lead to challenges.
- Business decisions should be based on competence rather than family ties.
- Keeping work and personal life separate is essential for maintaining healthy family relationships.
- When working with family, treat them like any other employee by providing proper training and promoting a merit-based evaluation system

Remember: Success depends not only on entrepreneurial skills but also on the individuals you choose to have by your side.

SUCCESS IS A TEAM EFFORT

If there's one thing I've learned on my entrepreneurial journey, it's that success is never a solo path.

The people you choose to collaborate with can either accelerate your growth or slow you to the point of failure.

I've had fantastic collaborators who helped me bring ambitious ideas to life and others who made every step a struggle.

Finding the right partners and building an effective team is essential for turning an idea into reality. Carefully selecting your collaborators, creating a productive environment, and managing the team with smart strategies can make the difference between success and failure.

Let's examine how to select the right collaborators, develop a strong team, and enhance collaboration to achieve the best results.

HOW TO BE A GOOD PARTNER

CHOOSING THE RIGHT WORK PARTNERS

Finding the right partner involves more than just chemistry or convenience; it's a strategic choice that can shape the future of your project.

Criteria for selecting a good partner:

- **Aligned vision and goals:** Working with someone who shares your vision reduces conflict.
- **Complementary skills:** A strong partner should have skills that balance yours, fostering a winning synergy.
- **Reliability and commitment:** Honesty, dedication, and accountability are non-negotiable. Without these qualities, even the most talented individual can become ineffective.
- **Conflict management skills:** Every collaboration will encounter challenges, so it's crucial to choose someone who can handle issues maturely and without taking things personally.
- **Initiative and adaptability:** A partner should be willing to innovate, adapt, and proactively suggest solutions.

Practical Example: *In one of my earliest business experiences, I chose a partner based on friendship without assessing his actual compatibility with the project. Within a few months, our differences became unbearable, and the partnership ended poorly. I learned that while trust is important, skills and alignment of goals are even more crucial.*

Practical Exercise: If you're searching for a partner, create a list of essential qualities and compare it to the candidates you're considering. Are they genuinely the right fit for your project?

AVOIDING COMMON MISTAKES WHEN CHOOSING PARTNERS

Selecting the wrong partner can jeopardize your business or considerably hinder its progress and growth.

Mistakes to avoid:

- **Relying solely on personal relationships for decisions:** A trusted friend does not automatically make a good business partner.
- **Ignoring signs of incompatibility:** If someone has already shown themselves to be unreliable, why would they change their behavior?
- **Not clearly defining roles and responsibilities**: Without a clear division of tasks, issues are bound to arise.
- **Failing to establish written agreements:** A detailed contract helps prevent misunderstandings, even among trustworthy individuals.

Practical Example: *Many startups fail not because of market issues, but due to disagreements between partners often caused by poor communication and unclear roles.*

I know many entrepreneurs who have seen their companies collapse because of partner conflicts. Sometimes, a few written rules can prevent major problems.

Practical Exercise: If you already have a partner, assess your collaboration: are there areas that could be strengthened?

BUILDING AN EFFECTIVE TEAM

A brilliant idea isn't enough. You need a strong team to bring it to life.

The success of a project depends on its leaders and the team working behind the scenes.

While working in film and commercial production, I often had to coordinate over 300 people on set each day. I can tell you, it's no easy feat.

There's no book that can teach you how to manage the organized chaos of a production set. You learn through experience and by having a team that knows exactly what to do. If even one piece of the puzzle doesn't fit, everything else can fall apart.

The same is true for any business: without clear roles and a well-structured system, things will eventually start to unravel.

Key elements of a winning team:

- **Thoughtful selection:** Each team member should possess specific skills and align with the project's vision.
- **Open communication:** Everyone should comprehend what is expected of one another.
- **Defined roles:** Assigning clear responsibilities prevents confusion and inefficiencies.
- **Supportive work environment:** A motivated team performs better and handles challenges more effectively.

Practical Example: *Elon Musk personally chooses his closest collaborators, seeking highly skilled and motivated individuals who can perform well under pressure.*

In one of my most ambitious projects, I experienced firsthand the difference between a motivated team and a disengaged one. With the former, everything ran smoothly; with the latter, even the smallest decisions turned into battles.

Practical Exercise: Evaluate your team. Are there roles that could be adjusted to enhance productivity?

STRATEGIES FOR EFFECTIVE TEAM MANAGEMENT

Managing a team requires coordinating a variety of individuals while ensuring that everyone remains focused on common goals

Effective management strategies:

- **Clear expectations:** Each member must understand what is expected of them.
- **Collaboration and discussion:** The best ideas often arise from open exchanges.

- **Constructive feedback:** Criticism without solutions is ineffective.
- **Work management tools:** Platforms such as Trello, Asana, or Slack can improve organization.
- **Recognize achievements:** Individuals who achieve strong results should feel valued.

Practical Example: *Google is known for its innovative approach to team management, emphasizing collaboration and continuous feedback as essential drivers of productivity.*

I've been part of teams with unclear leadership, and the outcome was total chaos. A leader needs to provide direction, not simply give orders.

Practical Exercise: Establish a weekly feedback system to enhance communication and team efficiency.

OVERCOMING CONFLICTS AND TIMES OF CRISIS

Every team faces challenging moments. The key is to handle them effectively.

How to handle conflicts:

- **Listen to all parties:** Many problems arise from misunderstandings.
- **Seek reasonable compromises:** You can't always win, but you can achieve balance.
- **Avoid favoritism and hasty decisions:** Team management must be impartial.
- **Regularly evaluate the organization:** If something isn't working, it's time to change it.

Practical Example: *Many successful companies have overcome internal crises thanks to effective leadership and their ability to adapt to change.*

In the past, I tried to ignore conflicts within the team, hoping they would resolve on their own. That never worked. The best approach is always to tackle them early.

Practical Exercise: If there are tensions within your team, arrange a meeting to openly address the issue.

Choosing the right partners and managing a team effectively are crucial to success.

- A good partner brings complementary skills, reliability, and a clear vision.
- It is essential to avoid making decisions based solely on personal relationships.
- An effective team is well-structured, motivated, and managed with clarity.
- Conflicts must be addressed immediately with honest and transparent communication.

Remember: Success isn't achieved alone. Surround yourself with the right people, and the results will follow!

IN SUMMARY

Success cannot be achieved alone; it requires the support and collaboration of those around us.

Valuing your life partner and involving family in your professional journey can create valuable balance in your life. Choosing the right work partners and managing your team effectively is essential for achieving meaningful results.

Working with motivated and competent individuals who share your vision and values can be the driving force that propels you toward your goals. Never underestimate the power of relationships.

Investing in your connections, both personal and professional, can be the key to unlocking doors and opportunities that might otherwise remain closed.

Remember that success isn't just about talent and hard work; it also involves the meaningful relationships that support and inspire us on our journey.

7 HOW TO COMMUNICATE WELL

Communication is a powerful tool for success in life. It acts as the bridge that connects people, allowing them to understand each other, collaborate, and achieve remarkable results together.

Let's explore the importance of listening to others, the essential techniques of communication, and the topics to avoid or carefully consider when speaking with someone you don't know or when working in a team.

We've already noted how crucial it is to know how to listen. However, I now want to explore a key aspect: applying active listening in relationships with clients, business partners, and vendors. In a world where everyone wants to speak and few genuinely want to listen, mastering this skill provides a significant advantage.

From personal experience, I've seen entrepreneurs fail not because their ideas were poor but because they never truly listened to their audience. I've also witnessed salespeople turn a conversation into a successful sale simply because they valued the customer's words. Listening is an art, and those who master it have a noticeable edge.

ACTIVE LISTENING: THE SUPERPOWER NO ONE USES

Active listening involves more than just hearing words; it requires understanding, interpreting, and responding appropriately.
Why is active listening so powerful?

- It builds trust and credibility with clients and collaborators.
- It helps you better understand the needs and expectations of others.
- It enables you to solve problems more quickly and effectively.
- It prevents misunderstandings, thereby reducing conflict.
- It enhances the quality of negotiations and sales.

Practical Example: *Richard Branson, the founder of Virgin, attributes much of his success to his ability to listen. He has always appreciated feedback from customers and employees, using it to continuously improve his businesses.*

I was confident I knew exactly what my potential clients wanted, but when I started asking questions and truly listening, I discovered their needs were completely different. I tailored my service accordingly, and sales soared

Practical Exercise: Next time you talk to a client or collaborator, avoid interrupting until they've finished speaking. Make a mental note of what they say, and respond only afterward.

TECHNIQUES FOR EFFECTIVE ACTIVE LISTENING

Active listening is a skill you can develop through simple techniques:

1. **Maintain eye contact:** This shows interest and engagement.
2. **Use non-verbal cues:** Nod, smile, and demonstrate your involvement.

3. **Ask specific questions:** Request clarification to delve deeper.
4. **Paraphrase what you've heard:** Restate in your own words to ensure understanding.
5. **Don't interrupt:** Allow the speaker to complete their thought.
6. **Avoid distractions:** Phones, emails, notifications… they can be distracting.

Practical Example: *I once faced a tough negotiation with a supplier. Instead of pushing back right away, I decided to listen. After ten minutes, he finished speaking, and I clearly understood where we could find common ground. The result? I achieved better terms without having to push harder.*

A salesperson who listens carefully to a client can identify their true needs and suggest the most suitable solution, increasing the chance of closing the deal.

Practical Exercise: After an important conversation, write a brief summary of what you heard. Are you sure you captured all the key points?

LISTENING TO CLIENTS: THE KEY TO BETTER SALES

A client who feels heard is a client who returns. How can you achieve this?

- **Allow the client to speak first.** Don't rush to offer solutions before fully understanding the problem.
- **Ask open-ended questions.** For example: "What are your main challenges with this product?"
- **Grasp the emotions behind the words.** Are they seeking a technical fix, or do they require reassurance?
- **Avoid contradicting immediately.** Even if you believe they're mistaken, listen first, then guide the conversation with facts and information.

Practical Example: *A successful restaurateur doesn't just take orders; they listen to customer feedback. A small detail, like a more comfortable chair or a clearer menu, can make the difference between a one-time guest and a loyal customer.*

Practical Exercise: Refrain from speaking for at least 60 seconds while a client shares their problem. Only then should you respond with a focused solution.

LISTENING TO A BUSINESS PARTNER: BUILDING STRONG RELATIONSHIPS

In business, relationships frequently determine the difference between success and failure. Listening is crucial for establishing a solid rapport with partners.

- **Understand their priorities:** A good partner has their own goals, not just yours.
- **Show empathy and genuine interest:** Make them feel like an essential part of the project.
- **Find a balance between your ideas and theirs**: Compromise often leads to the best outcomes.
- **Give them space to express themselves:** Don't always hurry to impose your own view.

Practical Example: *Many significant business deals have been finalized not because one side dominated the other, but because both parties listened to each other's needs and reached a win-win agreement.*

Practical Exercise: Next time you discuss a strategy with a partner, listen to their perspective without interrupting and try summarizing it before you respond.

LISTENING TO A SALESPERSON: SMART BUYING

Listening is essential to making informed decisions, even as a customer. A good buyer is also a good listener.

Here's how to listen to a salesperson without being unduly influenced:

- **Allow the salesperson to explain their point completely.** The more information you gather, the easier it will be to make a smart choice.
- **Ask specific questions**, such as, "What are the differences between this product and its competitor?"
- **Recognize sales tactics, but don't give in to pressure.**
- **Take time before deciding:** A serious salesperson respects an informed customer.

Practical Example: *Over time, I learned that better conditions in negotiations often arise simply from listening carefully to the salesperson first. Understanding their perspective is half the strategy.*

An entrepreneur who listens to salespeople can negotiate better deals and choose the best suppliers.

Practical Exercise: The next time you talk to a salesperson, listen carefully and summarize the key points before deciding.

Listening is a powerful yet underrated skill in business and life.

- Active listening enhances communication, minimizes conflict, and fosters better decision-making.
- Listening to customers leads to improved sales and loyalty.
- Engaging with a business partner strengthens valuable relationships and enables strategic choices.
- Listening to a vendor facilitates wiser purchasing decisions.
- Those who listen gain an advantage over those who talk too much.

Remember: Next time you find yourself in an important conversation, take a moment to ask yourself, "Am I truly listening or simply waiting for my turn to speak?"

COMMUNICATION: THE BRIDGE TO SUCCESS

I'll never tire of saying that communication is the foundation of success. Whether you're selling a product, persuading an investor, motivating a team, or building professional relationships, the quality of your communication will determine your results. A brilliant idea is worthless if it isn't communicated effectively.

In the past, I learned the hard way how poor communication can lead to misunderstandings, slow down a project, or even result in missed opportunities. Fortunately, I soon realized that communication isn't just a natural talent; it's a skill that can (and should) be refined.

COMMUNICATION AS A TOOL FOR SUCCESS

The ability to articulate yourself clearly and effectively is what sets successful leaders apart.

Why is communication so important?

- **Enhances persuasion:** Being persuasive aids in selling ideas, products, and projects.
- **Improves team management:** A good leader knows how to communicate clearly and motivate others.
- **Facilitates negotiation**: Strong communication skills enable you to secure better terms.
- **Minimizes conflict:** Clarity and empathy reduce misunderstandings and tension.
- **Fosters strong relationships:** People trust those who communicate well.

Practical Example: *Steve Jobs was a master communicator. His speeches weren't merely informative; they were emotional, persuasive, and inspirational. This skill contributed to making Apple an iconic brand.*

More than once, I lost a job opportunity simply because I couldn't clearly explain the value of my project. I had the perfect solution for the client but presented it in a confusing, disorganized way. The result? They opted for a competitor with a lesser offer but better communication.

Practical Exercise: Next time you present an idea, ask yourself: *Am I communicating clearly? Does my audience understand the value of what I'm saying?*

THE 3 RULES OF EFFECTIVE COMMUNICATION

To improve your communication skills, you need to master three key principles.

1. Clarity

- Avoid complicated words or ambiguous ideas.
- Get to the point and use clear examples.
- If a message can be conveyed with fewer words, do it.

2. Engagement

- Use a dynamic tone of voice and vary your speech rhythm.
- Incorporate stories or anecdotes to make your message more compelling.
- Pay attention to body language to support your words.

3. Adaptability

- Tailor your communication style to fit the context and your audience.
- When interacting with a client, be clear and reassuring.
- In discussions with a business partner, be straightforward and professional.

- When addressing a team, be encouraging and inclusive.

Practical Example: *A good communicator knows how to adjust their language based on the audience: technical with specialists, inspiring with the public, and strategic with potential investors.*

Practical Exercise: When speaking with different people, consider adjusting your language and approach to discover what works best.

TALKING IS EASY. COMMUNICATING IS AN ART

Communication doesn't simply mean speaking; it involves delivering your message effectively.

Common Mistakes to Avoid:

- **Providing too much information at once:** Overloading your listener causes them to tune out.
- **Not engaging with the other person**: Communication is a dialogue, not a monologue.
- **Failing to adjust to the context:** Using overly technical language with a non-expert only creates confusion.
- **Overlooking non-verbal cues:** Tone of voice, eye contact, and posture affect how your message is perceived.

Practical Example: *A good leader not only provides instructions but also observes the team, listens to concerns, and adjusts their communication strategy according to the needs of those they lead.*

Practical Exercise: Record one of your speeches or presentations and listen to it. Does it sound clear and effective? If you were the audience, would you be convinced?

WRITING TO COMMUNICATE BETTER

Beyond verbal communication, the ability to write clearly and effectively is essential.

How to write persuasive messages, emails, and texts:

- **Be clear and direct:** Avoid long, complex sentences.
- **Use natural language:** Write as if you're speaking directly to the reader.
- **Highlight key points:** Utilize bullet points, bold text, or subheadings to enhance readability.
- **Always include a call to action:** Clearly indicate what you want the reader to do after reading.

Practical Example: *A well-written email can open doors and opportunities. A confusing email can jeopardize important collaborations.*

Practical Exercise: *Review your previous work email and ask yourself: Is it clear, concise, and impactful? If you received it, would you respond immediately?*

LEARNING FROM GREAT COMMUNICATORS

Studying great communicators can help you improve your own skills.
Examples of outstanding communicators:

- **Martin Luther King Jr.:** His effective use of pauses, repetition, and evocative language made his speeches incredibly impactful.
- **Oprah Winfrey:** Demonstrates empathy and fosters emotional connections with the audience.
- **Jeff Bezos:** Explains with clarity and simplifies complex concepts effectively.
- **Tony Robbins:** Exhibits energy and motivational power.

Practical Example: *By studying the communication techniques of great leaders, we can strengthen our own messages and make them more memorable.*

Practical Exercise: *Watch a speech by one of these speakers and* analyze how they use their voice, body language, and pauses to emphasize key points.

Communication is the foundation of success in any field.

- Those who communicate better gain more opportunities.
- Clarity, engagement, and adaptability are essential for effective communication.
- Talking is easy, but conveying your message with impact is a true art.
- Enhancing your written and verbal communication can lead to significant results in both life and business.
- Learning from great communicators helps you develop more effective skills.

Remember: The way you communicate determines how others see you. Improve your communication, and you'll enhance your success.

IMPROVING COMMUNICATION: TECHNIQUES AND STRATEGIES

Effective communication isn't just about words; it's a skill that combines listening, expression, and body language.

There are specific techniques that can help you improve your communication skills, making conversations more fluid, persuasive, and productive. Whether you're speaking with a client, a business partner, or a larger audience, the way you communicate will influence the outcome of the conversation.

I'll admit it: early in my career, I believed that speaking well meant confidently delivering ideas. Later, I realized that the true secret lies in listening and adapting to your audience. I've seen presentations fail because the speaker didn't notice the audience's body language, and negotiations collapse because no one truly took the time to listen.

Now, I would like to share some practical strategies for improving communication using psychological and behavioral techniques.

THE POWER OF OPEN-ENDED QUESTIONS

Open-ended questions are among the most powerful tools in communication.

Why are they so effective?

- They encourage others to express themselves freely, resulting in deeper conversations.
- They help you gathering more information, steering clear of closed and superficial answers.
- They foster interactive, engaging dialogue, boosting empathy and connection.

Examples of effective open-ended questions:

- "What are the main challenges you're facing right now?"
- "What's your opinion on this solution?"
- "How do you envision the future of your industry?"

Practical Example: *An experienced salesperson doesn't just ask, 'Do you need this product?' Instead, they ask, 'What features are you looking for in a product like this?' This approach makes the client feel involved and increases the likelihood of a purchase.*

Practical Exercise: Next time you talk to someone, try replacing closed (yes/no) questions with open-ended ones, and notice how the conversation changes.

THE PARAPHRASING TECHNIQUE: REPHRASING TO SHOW UNDERSTANDING

Restating or rephrasing what the other person said enhances clarity and trust.

How does it work?

- Confirms that you've correctly understood the other person's message.
- Prevents misunderstandings, providing an opportunity to clarify or correct.
- Demonstrates active listening and engagement, making the person feel valued.

Examples of effective paraphrasing:

- **Speaker:** "I find the project intriguing, but I have some concerns about the timeline."
- **Paraphrased response:** "So your biggest worry is whether we can meet the deadlines, correct?"

Practical Example: *In a business negotiation, a skilled negotiator doesn't merely say, 'Okay, I understand.' Instead, they rephrase: 'If I understand correctly, your primary objective is to reduce costs without compromising quality, right?' This ensures that both sides are aligned.*

Practical Exercise: In your next important conversation, consider summarizing what the other person said before responding.

BODY LANGUAGE: COMMUNICATING BEYOND WORDS

Words are just one aspect of communication; body language plays a fundamental role.

Key elements of body language:

- **Eye contact:** Maintain a proper balance; neither staring nor completely avoiding it.
- **Open posture:** Avoid crossing your arms or leaning back, as these can indicate disinterest or defensiveness.
- **Natural movements:** Use gestures to emphasize key points.

- **Facial expressions:** A smile, when appropriate, communicates confidence and positivity.

Practical Example: *In a job interview, a candidate who avoids eye contact, slouches, and answers hesitantly will appear insecure, regardless of what they say.*

Practical Exercise: Next time you speak with someone, pay attention to your posture and gestures. Does your body reinforce your message or contradict it?

THE IMPORTANCE OF TONE OF VOICE

How you express something is often more important than what you say.
How to use your tone effectively:

- **Vary your pace**: A monotone voice quickly loses the listener's attention.
- **Emphasize keywords**: Use strategic pauses to highlight important ideas.
- **Adjust volume and intonation**: A confident, dynamic tone makes your speech more engaging.

Practical Example: *The best speakers don't use a monotonous tone; they incorporate variations in pitch and pace to maintain interest and engage their audience.*

Practical Exercise: The next time you give a speech or presentation, record yourself and listen to it later. Is your tone flat, or does it express energy?

Effective communication is a trainable skill.

- Open-ended questions enhance conversations, making them more engaging and productive.

- Paraphrasing demonstrates active listening and minimizes misunderstandings.
- Body language expresses confidence and builds credibility.
- Tone of voice serves as a powerful tool for creating impact and conveying emotion.
- Enhancing your communication improves your success in both life and business.

Remember: The way you communicate shapes how others perceive you. Enhancing your communication skills will give you a significant advantage in every area of life.

COMMUNICATION AND THE ART OF CHOOSING THE RIGHT TOPICS

Communication is an art; like any art, it requires sensitivity and context awareness. I've learned the hard way that when speaking with someone you don't know well, the risk of stumbling into inappropriate topics is high. Some subjects can create tension, misunderstandings, or awkward situations, compromising the first impression and the opportunity to build a positive connection.

I've found myself more than once in conversations that, within seconds, took a wrong turn. Like the time at a networking event when I made what I thought was an innocent political joke, only to discover that my conversation partner had very strong, opposing views. The result? The conversation ended within minutes, and I lost a valuable opportunity.

Let's explore the topics you should avoid when speaking to someone you've just met and the alternatives you can use to keep the conversation engaging and constructive.

TOPICS TO AVOID IN A FIRST CONVERSATION

There are certain subjects that are best avoided, particularly when you're not closely acquainted with the other person yet.

1. Politics

- Politics is the ultimate divisive topic. Differing opinions can quickly escalate into heated debates, especially if the other person holds strong beliefs.
- Even if you have a clear stance, avoid political discussions until you know the person better.

Alternative: If the topic arises organically, guide the conversation toward broader subjects, such as technological innovations or economic trends.

2. Religion and Faith

- Similar to politics, religion is deeply personal and sensitive. Everyone is entitled to their beliefs, but it can become a contentious topic if your views differ.
- Even seemingly innocent questions like "Do you believe in God?" can seem intrusive.

Alternative: If the conversation shifts to values and life philosophy, remain general and discuss universal concepts such as gratitude, personal growth, or the significance of kindness.

3. Health and Physical Appearance

- Commenting on someone's appearance, even if well-intentioned, can be uncomfortable or offensive.
- Do not inquire about health or personal habits related to diet and lifestyle unless the other person brings up the topic.

Alternative: If you're discussing wellness, focus on general topics like sports or travel, and avoid giving unsolicited advice or making judgments.

4. Financial Situation and Salary

- Asking someone about their salary or financial situation is one of the most inappropriate questions you can ask.
- Even if you're curious about someone's profession, avoid digging into personal details.

Alternative: If the topic is work-related, you can ask, "What do you do for a living?" or "How did you get into your field?" This allows for a more discreet response.

5. Romantic Life and Family Choices

- Inquiring about someone's marital status, children, or reasons for being single can come off as intrusive.
- Questions such as "Why are you still single?" or "When do you plan to have kids?" can make the other person feel uncomfortable.

Alternative: If you're sharing personal experiences, keep it light by discussing hobbies, travel, or personal interests.

NEUTRAL TOPICS FOR A PLEASANT CONVERSATION

If you aim to establish a friendly and low-risk dialogue, here are some great alternatives:

a) Hobbies and Passions

- Inquiring about someone's hobbies is always a safe choice.
- It provides an opportunity to connect and reveal shared interests.

b) Travel and Favorite Destinations

- Travel is a captivating and universal topic that encourages people to share positive experiences.

- You can ask, *"What's the most beautiful place you've ever visited?"*

c) Movies, Music, and Books

- Discussing culture is an excellent way to discover common ground and explore new perspectives.
- Sample questions include: *"Have you seen any good movies lately?"* or *"What's your favorite book?"*

d) Sports and Physical Activities

- Even if you're not a sports fan, discussing sports events or outdoor activities serves as a good conversation starter.
- Questions like *"Do you play any sports?"* or *"Do you follow any teams?"* can help break the ice.

e) Curiosities and Trending Topics

- New technologies, global events, and interesting facts are always excellent conversation starters.
- You could ask: *"Have you heard about the new technology they're developing?"*

HOW TO HANDLE A CONVERSATION THAT'S GOING SOUTH

Sometimes, a conversation might drift into uncomfortable or sensitive territory despite your best intentions.

What can you do in these situations?

- **Change the subject naturally.** If someone begins a heated political rant, you might say, *"I understand your point. By the way, have you seen that new documentary on Netflix?"*
- **Use humor.** A light joke can defuse tension and shift the conversation to safer ground.

- **Stay respectful.** If you disagree with the other person's words, avoid direct confrontation and respect their viewpoint.

Practical Example: *Once, I was in a conversation that was about to turn into a heated political debate. I smiled and said, 'You know, we could argue about this for hours... but in the meantime, do you know where to find the best pizza in town?' We both laughed, and the conversation quickly shifted to a lighter, more enjoyable topic.*

Practical Exercise: The next time you find yourself in an uncomfortable situation, consider three topics that can help you smoothly transition the conversation.

Choosing the right conversation topics can make all the difference.

- Avoid controversial topics like politics, religion, finances, and romantic relationships.
- Opt for neutral, uplifting subjects such as hobbies, travel, sports, and culture.
- If a discussion becomes tense, change the subject smoothly and diplomatically.
- The aim is to foster a harmonious and engaging dialogue without unnecessary conflict or tension.

Remember: A meaningful conversation involves more than just words; it requires sensitivity and respect for the person in front of you.

COMMUNICATION IN TEAMWORK: THE TRUE KEY TO SUCCESS

A well-organized, cohesive team is the engine that turns an idea into reality. However, to make it truly work, you need to establish clear rules and address some fundamental topics from the beginning. I've seen teams fail due to a lack of direction and others thrive due to a few crucial best practices. Without a solid team by your side, everything becomes more difficult, slower, and frustrating.

Let's explore the essential ingredients that make a team truly successful.

SETTING GOALS: EVERYONE NEEDS TO KNOW WHERE THEY'RE GOING

Imagine being on a boat where the crew has no idea where the destination is. Some row left, some row right, and some don't row at all. A team without clear goals operates just like that; energy is wasted, time is lost, and no one knows if they're on the right track.

Why is this so important?

- **Clarity:** Every team member must understand their objectives and the timeline.
- **Alignment:** When everyone pulls in the same direction, you'll achieve the goal much quicker.
- **Motivation:** A clear purpose makes work more engaging and fulfilling.

How do we address goals effectively?

- Set clear and measurable objectives. For example, instead of saying, "Let's improve customer service," say, "Let's reduce response times by 20% within the next three months."
- Use tracking tools like project management software to monitor progress.
- Regularly review and adjust goals as needed.

Practical Example: *A tech company developing a new product must ensure that development, marketing, and sales teams are aligned on the same goals to ensure a successful launch.*

Practical Exercise: Ask yourself: Does your team have clear goals? If not, schedule a meeting to align right away.

ROLES AND RESPONSIBILITIES: EVERYONE MUST KNOW WHAT TO DO

One of the most common mistakes within teams is confusion about roles. When two individuals perform the same task, they risk overlapping efforts and wasting time. If no one takes responsibility because everyone assumes someone else will, it leads to disaster

Why is this important?

- **Prevents overlap and conflict.** Clear roles help eliminate situations where multiple people are working on the same task or, worse, where no one is addressing it at all.
- **Increases efficiency** because everyone understands their job. Well-defined roles enhance workflow.
- **Encourages accountability.** When responsibilities are clear, there's no longer an excuse of, "I thought someone else was handling it."

How to assign responsibilities?

- Use the **RACI matrix** to clearly define who is **Responsible (R)**, **Accountable (A)**, **Consulted (C),** and **Informed (I)** for each task.
- Ensure that each **individual's skills** align with their assigned role. Avoid assigning tasks to people who lack the capabilities to manage them efficiently.
- **Allow space for personal growth** by broadening responsibilities to assist team members in developing new skills.

Practical Example: *In a project I was involved in, marketing and technical development were in constant conflict because no one understood who had the final say on changes. After we clarified roles and responsibilities, our workflow improved, and we reduced downtime.*

Practical Exercise: Examine your team's roles. If you identify any ambiguities or overlaps, resolve them promptly.

COMMUNICATION: WITHOUT IT, THE TEAM FALLS APART

Communication is the oxygen of any team. When it is absent, problems arise: errors, misunderstandings, and tensions. I've witnessed teams fall apart simply because no one truly understood what the others were doing.

Common communication mistakes:

- Excessive irrelevant emails or unclear messages.
- Lack of constructive feedback.
- Long, unproductive meetings.

How to improve communication?

- **Establish clear communication channels.** Use productivity tools for collaborative sharing and organized group discussions.
- **Minimize unnecessary meetings.** If information can be conveyed in a message, skip the meeting. Be clear and concise; clarity reduces errors and accelerates work.
- **Conduct brief, regular check-ins** (e.g., 10-minute stand-up meetings) to stay aligned without wasting time.

Practical Example: *When working with a remote team, it was chaos at first. Everyone was using WhatsApp, emails, and personal calls; no one quite understood anything. Everything dramatically improved once we established clear guidelines regarding when and how to communicate.*

Practical Exercise: Observe how your team communicates. If there are excessive interruptions or disorganization, propose new guidelines.

TRUST AND RESPECT: WITHOUT THESE, THE TEAM FALLS APART

I've seen individuals leave high-paying jobs solely because of a toxic environment. On the other hand, I've observed teams achieve remarkable results thanks to their mutual support and trust.

Why is trust essential?

- It boosts collaboration and productivity. People are more at ease sharing ideas and feedback.
- It alleviates stress and conflict. A positive environment supports the mental well-being of team members.
- It fosters creativity and innovation. When individuals feel free to express themselves, more creative ideas surface.

How to build a climate of trust:

- **Provide constructive feedback.** Avoid destructive criticism and concentrate on growing together.
- **Acknowledge achievements.** A simple "thank you" or public recognition can boost motivation.
- **Encourage transparency.** If issues arise, address them openly rather than behind closed doors.

Practical Example: *In a startup team, founders who communicate openly with employees and value their contributions create a healthier, more productive work environment.*

Practical Exercise: Consider how trust is handled within your team. If you notice tension or a lack of transparency, tackle the issue before it becomes a ticking time bomb.

A successful team isn't built by chance but rather through intention and strategy:

- **Clear goals** to prevent wasting energy.

- **Defined roles** to maximize efficiency.
- **Effective communication** to reduce errors and misunderstandings.
- **Mutual trust** to improve collaboration and maintain motivation.

Remember: A strong team is not composed of the most talented individuals but of those who collaborate effectively.

Now the question is: Does your team possess these elements? If the answer is "no," you know what steps to take.

IN SUMMARY

Effective communication is a key factor in life success. Active listening, employing appropriate communication techniques, avoiding sensitive topics with unfamiliar people, and selecting relevant subjects in teamwork can all enhance the quality of interpersonal relationships and result in more meaningful outcomes. Improving your communication skills is an investment in your personal and professional success.

8 HOW TO CREATE AN IMPACT

Although success in life may seem like an ambitious or even intangible goal, there is a crucial factor that is often overlooked: the audience. Regardless of your field, understanding your audience and target customers is essential for achieving excellence and lasting success. In this chapter, we will explore the importance of knowing your audience, effective promotional strategies, and ways to create buzz so people talk about you or your product.

One of the most common mistakes I made early in my entrepreneurial journey was trying to speak to everyone. I believed that the more people I reached, the more successful I would be. However, the truth is that when you attempt to speak to everyone, you end up reaching no one. The message becomes generic, lacks impact, and fails to engage people.

To succeed, you need to know exactly who you are addressing. Who are your customers, readers, or followers? What are their needs, preferences, and challenges? The better you know your audience, the easier it will be to attract, engage, and retain the right people.

WHY IS IT CRUCIAL TO KNOW YOUR AUDIENCE?

Without a clear understanding of your target, you risk wasting time, energy, and resources on ineffective strategies.

- **Personalization:** A targeted message results in higher engagement and conversions.
- **Efficiency:** Avoid spending money on marketing campaigns that don't yield results.
- **Better positioning:** You'll discover how to stand out from competitors by meeting specific needs.
- **Increased loyalty:** An audience that feels understood is more likely to return and recommend your products or services.

Practical Example: *When I first began offering my advertising services, I tried to convince everyone. It was only when I recognized that my true audience was small to medium-sized businesses wanting to stand out without large budgets that I started seeing real results.*

Practical Exercise: Write one sentence that defines your ideal audience and the main problem they seek to solve.

CREATING YOUR IDEAL CUSTOMER PROFILE (BUYER PERSONA)

A buyer persona is a comprehensive representation of your ideal customer based on real data and market insights

Key elements of a buyer persona:

- **Demographics:** Age, gender, location, education, profession, income.
- **Behaviors and habits:** Where do they spend time online? Which social media platforms do they use? What are their interests?

- **Pain points and needs:** What challenges do they encounter? What solutions are they looking for?
- **Goals and desires:** What do they hope to achieve? What motivates them?
- **Decision-making process:** How do they choose a product or service? What influences their purchasing decisions?

Practical Example: *An online personal trainer selling workout programs might create a buyer persona like this:*
- *Name: Marco, 35 years old, office worker, living in a large city.*
- *Problem: Wants to get back in shape but has limited time for the gym.*
- *Goal: Work out at home with flexible programs.*
- *Habits: Uses Instagram and YouTube to find fitness and nutrition tips.*
- *Decision factors: Seeks easy-to-follow programs with guaranteed results and authentic testimonials.*

Practical Exercise: Develop a detailed profile of your ideal customer, incorporating all the elements mentioned above.

HOW TO COLLECT DATA TO UNDERSTAND YOUR AUDIENCE

The more information you gather, the easier it becomes to refine your message and offer.

Tools for audience analysis:

- **Website analytics:** Monitor your website traffic, where visitors originate, and your most popular pages.
- **Social media insights:** Identify who interacts with your content and what generates the most interest.
- **Surveys and interviews:** Ask your customers directly what they desire and what improvements they would suggest.
- **Feedback and reviews:** Evaluate customer opinions to understand what they value most.

Practical Example: *When I launched a new promotional video service, I noticed that most inquiries came from the tourism and real estate sectors. This made me realize I should create targeted offers for hotels, tour operators, and real estate agencies rather than spreading my efforts across less interested industries.*

Practical Exercise: Use one of the tools above to collect data about your audience and uncover at least one valuable insight to enhance your strategy.

ADAPTING YOUR MESSAGE TO YOUR TARGET AUDIENCE

Every audience possesses its own language, communication style, and preferences.

- **Tone of voice:** Is it formal or informal? Direct or motivational? Friendly or professional?
- **Communication channels:** Young people typically use TikTok and Instagram, professionals prefer LinkedIn, while book lovers prefer blogs and newsletters.
- **Types of content:** Should you use videos, short posts, long articles, webinars, or eBooks? Choose based on your audience's preferences.
- **Personalized calls to action:** What do you want your audience to do, buy a product, subscribe to a newsletter, or engage with a post? The CTA must be clear and targeted.

Practical Example: *If your audience consists of young creatives, an effective strategy could be to create engaging, quick, and practical visual content. Short videos featuring instant tips are likely to generate more engagement and collaboration requests than long articles.*

Practical Exercise: Analyze your current communication style and determine if it aligns with your target audience.

CONTINUOUSLY IMPROVING YOUR AUDIENCE UNDERSTANDING

Markets shift, and audience needs evolve. Studying your target once isn't enough; you must update your strategy regularly.

- **Review your data regularly:** Every 3 to 6 months, assess whether your audience has changed.
- **Test new strategies:** Experiment with a different tone, modify your content formats, and try out various platforms.
- **Listen to feedback:** Comments, private messages, and client emails provide valuable insights.
- **Monitor the competition:** Study how they interact with their audience and pinpoint their most effective practices

Practical Example: *A friend of mine who owns a restaurant noticed that an increasing number of customers were ordering through delivery apps instead of dining in. He adjusted his marketing strategy for these digital customers by enhancing his online presence and offering exclusive promotions through the app.*

Practical Exercise: Choose a specific date each quarter to review your data and revise your communication strategy.

Knowing your audience is the foundation of any winning strategy

- Clearly define your target audience and create detailed profiles.
- Collect data to make informed decisions.
- Customize your communication to meet your audience's needs and preferences.
- Regularly refresh your strategy based on market trends.

Remember: Success isn't just about luck; it's about knowledge and strategy!

HOW TO PROMOTE YOUR PRODUCT OR SERVICE EFFECTIVELY

Having a great product or service isn't enough; if no one knows about it, it can't succeed. I learned this firsthand when I launched my first online tourism promotion project. I assumed that quality alone would attract clients, but I was wrong. Promotion is the bridge between your work and the right audience.

A winning strategy doesn't depend on just one channel; instead, it relies on a combination of tools and techniques customized to your audience's needs. The goal is to establish a consistent and memorable presence by using the appropriate channels and maintaining effective communication over time.

CHOOSING THE RIGHT PROMOTION CHANNELS

Every audience has different preferences for how they consume information. Choosing the right channels can make the difference between an ignored message and one that converts.

Promotion Strategies:

- **Social Media Marketing:** Utilize Instagram and TikTok to engage younger, visual audiences; leverage Facebook for community building and structured promotions; use LinkedIn for networking and professional content; rely on YouTube for educational or promotional videos.
- **Email Marketing:** Ideal for fostering loyalty, providing exclusive offers, and ensuring consistent communication.
- **Online Advertising:** Ads on digital platforms enable you to reach individuals actively seeking your product or service.
- **Events and Networking:** Engage in trade shows, conferences, workshops, or webinars.
- **Partnerships and Influencer Marketing:** Collaborating with strategic partners or influencers can enhance your message.

Practical Example: *When selling training courses for entrepreneurs,*

LinkedIn and YouTube are likely to be more effective than TikTok or Instagram.

Practical Exercise: Choose three main channels to focus on and develop a tailored strategy for each.

CREATING ENGAGING AND VALUABLE CONTENT

Promotion is not only about advertising; providing valuable content is the most effective way to attract and retain your audience.

Types of effective content:

- Blog articles featuring practical tips
- Tutorial or demonstration videos
- Educational and inspirational social media posts
- Case studies and customer testimonials
- E-books or downloadable reports in exchange for email addresses

Content strategy tips:

- **Be consistent:** Publish regularly to keep your audience's attention.
- **Be authentic:** Honesty and sincerity build trust.
- **Be interactive:** Reply to comments, conduct polls, and involve your audience.

Practical Example: *An author promoting their book might share free excerpts, start discussions on related topics, and create behind-the-scenes videos about their writing process.*

Practical Exercise: Create a content calendar for the upcoming month, incorporating at least three distinct content formats.

OPTIMIZING YOUR PROMOTIONAL MESSAGE

How you communicate your message is essential to attracting the right people audience.

Define a clear value proposition:

- What problem do you solve?
- What makes your product/service stand out?
- What benefits do customers gain by choosing you?

Use effective Calls-to-Action (CTAs):

- "Download the free guide" → Promotes email subscriptions.
- "Book a free consultation" → Encourages prompt action.
- "Sign up now and get 20% off" → Instills a sense of urgency.

Practical Example: *A business software vendor might use a CTA such as: 'Reduce administrative management time by 50% with our software. Schedule a free demo today!*

Practical Exercise: Revise your existing promotional message to enhance clarity and engage your audience effectively.

INTEGRATING MULTIPLE STRATEGIES TO MAXIMIZE IMPACT

There isn't a one-size-fits-all method: the key is to combine different strategies to achieve the best results.

Example of an integrated strategy:

1. Write a blog article featuring valuable content.
2. Promote it through a social media post.
3. Create a YouTube video to explore the topic in depth.
4. Run a sponsored ad to expand reach.
5. Include the link in your email newsletter for your subscribers.

Practical Example: *If you're promoting an online course, consider combining a free webinar, a series of informative emails, and social media promotions. This mix of strategies boosted sales by 40%.*

Practical Exercise: Identify three complementary strategies to incorporate into your promotional plan.

MONITORING RESULTS AND OPTIMIZING STRATEGIES

An effective strategy relies on data-driven. Analyze your performance and keep improving.
Tools for tracking performance:

- Analyze website traffic and conversions.
- Monitor social media interactions.
- Evaluate email open and conversion rates.
- Use A/B testing to compare different ad versions.

Practical Example: *If you notice your audience interacts more with videos than with written posts, it might be time to boost your video content production.*

Practical Exercise: Review your recent promotional efforts and determine one strategy to improve.

An effective promotional strategy requires careful planning, creativity, and adaptability.

- Choose the most suitable channels for your audience.
- Create valuable content that engages and builds loyalty.
- Refine your message and incorporate clear CTAs to encourage action.
- Integrate multiple strategies to maximize impact.
- Track results and continuously optimize your promotional efforts.

Remember: Having a great product or service isn't sufficient; if no one knows about it, it can't thrive.

GETTING NOTICED AND GETTING PEOPLE TALKING

We live in a world where everyone is shouting for attention; if you don't find a way to stand out, you risk fading into the background. I learned this early on when I started promoting my own projects. I believed that having a great product or service was enough, but the reality is that quality alone isn't sufficient. You must capture the public's interest and spark conversations around your offering.

The key is to break the mold and surprise people, not with forced provocation but with fresh ideas and a strong, recognizable identity.

STANDING OUT FROM THE CROWD: WHAT MAKES YOU UNIQUE?

If you want to attract attention, you need to offer something unique. Identifying what sets you apart is the first step to getting people to talk about you.

Find your unique element:

- Do you have an innovative product?
- Do you offer a service with unique added value?
- Does your brand have a strong, revolutionary message?

Focus on originality:

- Tell your story in an unexpected way.
- Use a unique, recognizable tone of voice.
- Be bold in your design, packaging, or messaging.

Practical Example: *When I launched a new project, instead of doing a traditional promotion, I introduced it with an unexpected event. I created a mysterious teaser video that revealed nothing about its purpose. The result? Curiosity took over, and people began sharing it spontaneously.*

Tesla didn't just sell electric cars; it redefined sustainable mobility with futuristic design, high performance, and a groundbreaking user experience.

Practical Exercise: Write down three things that make your product or service unique compared to your competitors.

CREATING A CAMPAIGN THAT SPARKS WORD OF MOUTH

People talk about what surprises, excites, or entertains them. If you want others to talk about you, you must create content embodying these qualities.

Strategies to Generate Word of Mouth:

- **Experiential marketing:** Provide your customers with an engaging and unforgettable experience.
- **Unexpected gestures:** A surprise, an exclusive gift, or a creative action can make a significant impact.
- **Challenges and trends:** Develop a viral challenge that encourages participation and sharing.
- **Emotional storytelling:** Tell a story that resonates with the audience and compels them to share it.

Practical Example: *Apple turned its product launches into major media events, generating extraordinary anticipation within the tech industry. Through innovative marketing strategies and captivating presentations, it transformed each product release into a global phenomenon, strengthening audience loyalty and desire.*

Practical Exercise: Consider a campaign that might astonish your audience and inspire them to share it enthusiastically.

LEVERAGING INFLUENCERS AND THOUGHT LEADERS

People tend to trust those with an established following. Partnering with influencers and industry experts can enhance your influence message.

How to choose the right influencers:

- Their audience should align with your target.
- They must be authentic and credible.
- Their communication style should reflect your brand.

Types of collaborations:

- Product reviews and unboxings.
- Co-created content.
- Guest appearances at events, interviews, or podcasts.

Practical Examples: *I contacted an expert in my industry and proposed a collaboration. Rather than just asking them to promote my work, I offered value by sharing something useful for their audience. This method made the partnership genuine and resulted in tangible outcomes.*

"Nike partners with world-renowned athletes to promote its products, leveraging their charisma and credibility to strengthen the brand's identity."

Practical Exercise: Compile a list of three influencers or experts in your field with whom you could collaborate to boost visibility.

USING SURPRISE AND MARKETING PSYCHOLOGY

People remember what affects them unexpectedly. Use surprise as a tool to create a strong impact impression.

Techniques to leverage the surprise factor:

- **Unconventional launches:** Announce your product in a distinctive way to spark curiosity.
- **Wow factor in packaging or purchase experience:** Extraordinary unboxings or innovative designs enhance memorability.
- **Disruptive marketing:** Challenge your competitors to stand out.

Practical Examples: *I introduced a new service without making a direct announcement. Instead, I created a series of clues that guided participants to the final reveal. This mystery sparked anticipation and engagement, making the launch far more effective.*

IKEA has developed immersive shopping experiences, including pop-up stores and temporary showrooms that feature interactive activities, generating excitement and curiosity among customers.

Practical Exercise: Create a method to unexpectedly delight your customers.

MAINTAINING HIGH INTEREST OVER TIME

Gaining attention once isn't sufficient; you need to sustain audience interest through long-term strategies.

- **Create recurring events:** Challenges, promotions, new initiatives.
- **Interact with your community:** Reply to comments, start conversations, engage your audience.
- **Consistently refresh your brand:** Keep innovation at the center of your identity.

Practical Example: *Netflix maintains high audience interest by consistently releasing new series and engaging actively on social media.*

I've learned that a major launch followed by silence isn't sufficient.

Each week, aim to create engaging content so your audience doesn't forget about you or your product.

Practical Exercise: Develop a long-term strategy to maintain audience engagement over time.

Getting people talking is not about luck; it's about strategy and creativity.

- Identify what makes you unique and leverage it to stand out.
- Develop campaigns that surprise and engage your audience.
- Partner with influencers and key voices in your field.
- Use surprise and marketing psychology to capture attention.
- Maintain the momentum with long-term engagement strategies.

Remember: The world is loud, but those who have the courage to be different are heard.

BUILDING A CONSISTENT AND AUTHENTIC BRAND

In business and marketing, innovation gains attention, but trust is earned through consistency and authenticity.

I learned this the hard way. When I started promoting my projects, I believed that having a brilliant idea was enough to succeed. Then I realized that without clear and consistent communication, people wouldn't form a connection with what I offered. I made mistakes and changed direction multiple times, trying to follow every new trend. The result? Confusion. Eventually, I understood the key: staying true to my values and communicating authentically.

A recognizable and respected brand goes beyond simply promoting a product; it reflects and consistently expresses your values over time. The public is more aware than ever and can distinguish between genuine messaging and attention-seeking gimmicks.

WHY ARE CONSISTENCY AND AUTHENTICITY SO IMPORTANT?

A brand that is inconsistent or inauthentic quickly loses credibility.

- **Consistency builds trust:** When your audience knows what to expect, they develop familiarity and a sense of security.
- **Authenticity fosters connection:** People relate to those who are genuine rather than just trying to sell something.
- **A clear identity strengthens positioning:** A brand that communicates a consistent message becomes more recognizable and memorable.

Practical Example: *Apple has established its image through simplicity, innovation, and design. Each product, advertisement, and marketing strategy embodies these values, creating a solid and cohesive identity.*

When I started working in advertising, I attempted to accommodate every client request, even when it contradicted my style and values. I recognized that the results were mediocre and my work lacked a distinct identity. I started attracting the right clients when I focused on what I did best and communicated consistently.

Practical Exercise: Write down three core values of your brand or project and check whether your communication truly reflects them.

MAINTAINING CONSISTENT COMMUNICATION ACROSS ALL CHANNELS

Your message must be recognizable across all platforms, including your website, social media, and even customer service.

Build a clear brand identity:

- **Tone of voice:** Will you be formal or informal? Motivational or technical?

- **Visual style:** Ensure that colors, fonts, logos, and imagery are consistent.
- **Key messages:** Which phrases and concepts do you want your audience to associate with you?

Apply consistency to all your content:

- Your website should convey the same tone and visual identity as your social media.
- Marketing emails should align with the style of your advertising campaigns.
- Your interactions with customers should reflect your company's values.

Practical Example: *If your brand promotes sustainability yet relies on polluting packaging, your audience will recognize the inconsistency and lose trust in you.*

Practical Exercise: Review all your communication channels to ensure your tone, design, and messaging are consistent.

BEING AUTHENTIC: SHOW YOURSELF AS YOU ARE

Authenticity cannot be faked; people can sense when a brand is genuine or just pretending.

How to be authentic in business:

- **Share your story:** Talk about your journey, the challenges you've faced, and your values.
- **Don't try to please everyone:** It's better to connect with the right audience than to attempt to appeal to everyone.
- **Own your mistakes:** If something goes wrong, confront it openly instead of hiding it.

Show your brand's human side:

- Share behind-the-scenes content.
- Discuss both your successes and the challenges you've encountered.
- Engage with your audience genuinely, not just to make a sale.

Practical Example: *Patagonia is an outdoor clothing brand focused on sustainability. It doesn't just talk the talk; it walks the walk by rejecting fast fashion, repairing garments for free, and donating a percentage of profits to environmental causes. This commitment is what makes it authentic and credible.*

Practical Exercise: Identify three elements that make your project authentic, and ensure you're clearly communicating them to your audience.

CONSISTENCY OVER TIME: DON'T CHANGE DIRECTION TOO OFTEN

A brand that frequently shifts its message, values, or identity risks confusing its audience.

How to maintain consistency over time:

- **Define a long-term vision:** Where do you want to be in 5 to 10 years?
- **Avoid following every trend:** Stay aware of market changes without compromising your identity.
- **Hold on to your values:** Even as your business evolves, your core principles should remain clear and strong.

Practical Example: *Coca-Cola has always maintained a positive message centered on happiness and sharing. While it has refreshed its design and marketing strategies, the core message has remained consistent.*

Practical Exercise: Evaluate whether your brand has stayed consistent over time or if you frequently changed direction and messaging.

BUILDING A RELATIONSHIP OF TRUST WITH YOUR AUDIENCE

Consistency and authenticity lead to trust, which is the foundation of a loyal and engaged audience.

Strategies to strengthen trust:

- **Keep your promises:** If you make a statement or commitment, follow through with it.
- **Listen to your audience:** Engage sincerely and address their needs.
- **Provide genuine value:** Don't just aim to sell; help your audience with meaningful, useful information and content.

Practical Example: *A small artisan brand that takes the time to personally respond to customer messages and shares the story behind each product establishes much stronger trust than a company with impersonal communication.*

I've noticed that brands that actively respond to comments and customer messages build much stronger relationships than those that don't communicate impersonally.

Practical Exercise: Analyze how you communicate with your audience and pinpoint one area where you can improve trust and engagement.

Consistency and authenticity are not abstract concepts but powerful tools for building a strong, enduring brand.

- Maintain consistent communication across all channels.
- Be genuine and transparent in your actions and messaging.
- Avoid abrupt changes in direction that may confuse your audience.
- Build trust by providing real value and actively listening to your community.

Remember: A consistent and authentic brand doesn't need to shout to be heard; audience trust is its loudest megaphone.

CREATING A COMPELLING STORY FOR YOUR PRODUCT

People don't just buy products or services; they purchase emotions, experiences, and stories. I learned this the hard way when I first started promoting my projects. I thought saying, "Here's my product; it's amazing, buy it!" would be enough. But no one was interested.

Then, I realized that I needed to tell a story instead of selling.

A well-crafted story grabs attention, creates connection, inspires trust, and makes your brand memorable. It's the reason some products become iconic while others fade away.

If you want your audience to connect with your brand, you need to share a compelling, authentic story that evokes emotion.

WHY IS STORYTELLING SO POWERFUL?

Stories activate the emotional part of the brain, making a message more effective and memorable than simple data or technical features.

- **Creates an emotional connection:** People remember more about how you made them feel than what you said.
- **Helps you stand out from the competition:** A compelling story can make even an ordinary product feel unique.
- **Enhances perceived value:** A product with a strong narrative holds greater meaning and desirability.
- **Encourages sharing:** People enjoy sharing interesting, relatable stories.

Practical Example: *Nike doesn't just sell shoes, it sells the story of athletes pushing beyond their limits, embodied in the iconic slogan 'Just Do It.'*

Practical Exercise: Think of a product or service you use daily and ask yourself: does it have a story behind it? If so, what makes it memorable?

HOW TO CREATE A CAPTIVATING STORY FOR YOUR PRODUCT

A good story follows a clear, engaging structure.

When I launched a new service, instead of doing a traditional promotion, I shared my story: why I created it, the mistakes I made, the challenges I overcame, and the results I achieved. This approach made everything feel more authentic, and people felt like a part of my journey.

Key elements of an effective story:

1. **The Protagonist:** Who is the main character? It could be the founder, a customer, or even the product itself.
2. **The Problem:** What challenge or obstacle does the protagonist face?
3. **The Transformation:** How does your product or service help overcome that problem?
4. **The Emotion:** What feelings do you want to evoke in your audience?

Practical Example: *Airbnb has established its brand around the concepts of belonging and connection between travelers and hosts. Their campaigns highlight stories of individuals finding a 'home away from home' in every part of the world.*

Practical Exercise: Draft your story by following these four steps.

INTEGRATING YOUR STORY INTO MARKETING

Storytelling should be consistent with your communication and applied across all channels.

I noticed that simply presenting a product didn't generate much engagement. When I prepared campaigns for other companies, I encouraged them to share customer stories, including their successes, struggles, and how the product helped them. This built greater trust and increased sales.

How to integrate your story into marketing:

- **Website:** Share your mission and brand story in the "About Us" section.
- **Social Media:** Use posts, videos, and stories to highlight key moments and behind-the-scenes content.
- **Packaging and Promotional Materials:** Incorporate a narrative element that adds value to your product.
- **Advertising and Branding Campaigns:** Develop emotional ads or testimonials that emphasize the brand's story.

Practical Example: *"The brand 'Dove' revolutionized the beauty industry with its 'Real Beauty' campaign, sharing authentic stories of real women and redefining the concept of beauty."*

Practical Exercise: Choose one channel (website, social media, packaging) and consider how to incorporate your story into it.

MAKING YOUR STORY SHAREABLE

The most powerful stories are those that people want to share.

Strategies to create a viral story:

- **Tap into emotions:** surprise, move, or inspire your audience.
- **Create a movement:** associate your brand with a larger cause or message.
- **Invite participation:** motivate your audience to share their own experiences with your product.
- **Use the right format:** videos, images, and engaging text enhance the impact of your story.

Practical Example: *GoPro developed its brand by allowing customers to* *share their adventures through breathtaking videos, turning users into enthusiastic brand ambassadors.*

Shared stories have an incredible impact: greater credibility, increased engagement, and more word-of-mouth.

Practical Exercise: Consider how to make your story easily shareable for your audience.

AUTHENTICITY IS THE KEY TO SUCCESS

A made-up or forced story will never have the same impact as an authentic one.
How to ensure authenticity in your story:

- **Incorporate genuine experiences, testimonials, or real events.**
- **Avoid excessive self-praise** or overly promotional language.
- **Highlight your struggles**, not just your successes.
- **Maintain consistency over time:** your story should truly reflect who you are.

Practical Example: *LEGO overcame tough moments in its corporate history and has been transparent in sharing that story, strengthening the emotional bond with its audience.*

Practical Exercise: Reflect on how your story can be told in a transparent and authentic way.

Stories sell more than products. A compelling narrative can turn an idea into a global phenomenon.

- Identify the protagonist, the problem, the transformation, and the emotion in your story.
- Integrate storytelling into your marketing to enhance brand recognition.

- Create a compelling, shareable story that sparks conversations.
- Maintain authenticity and consistency to foster trust and connection with your audience.

Remember: A product may be forgotten, but a compelling story lingers in people's minds.

ENGAGING YOUR AUDIENCE: FROM INTEREST TO ACTIVE PARTICIPATION

If there's one thing I've learned throughout my career, it's that people don't just want to buy a product or follow a project; they want to be a part of it. We live in an age where interaction is everything. Anyone can launch something on the market, but only those who truly engage their audience create lasting impact.

I've faced both situations: launching an idea and watching it go unnoticed, and later, with a more focused strategy, turning a disinterested audience into an engaged community. It's not magic; it's the result of genuine engagement.

WHY IS AUDIENCE ENGAGEMENT SO IMPORTANT?

An engaged audience isn't merely a collection of customers or viewers; it transforms into an ally for your brand's growth. Interaction nurtures connection, trust, and even new opportunities.

When I launched an online project, I initially expected people to take an interest on their own. Then, I realized I had to involve them actively. I started asking questions, requesting opinions, and creating interactive moments. The result? People began to feel like they were part of the project and shared it spontaneously.

- **Increases interest and engagement** – When your audience participates, they're more likely to remember and support you.

- **Generates organic word of mouth** – People love sharing their passion.
- **Provides valuable feedback** – You can enhance your offer through direct input from your audience.
- **Builds trust and connection** – When people feel heard, their bond with the brand grows stronger.

Practical Example: *Netflix leverages social media to actively engage its audience through polls, open-ended questions, and personalized content, making each user feel like part of a larger conversation.*

Practical Exercise: Evaluate your level of audience engagement and pinpoint one area for improvement.

CREATING OPPORTUNITIES FOR ONLINE INTERACTION

Digital platforms provide countless opportunities to engage your audience directly and interactively.

Once, I launched a contest inviting the audience to share their experiences with a client's product. The result? It not only gained greater visibility but also garnered numerous authentic stories that made the brand feel more relatable.

Effective strategies for creating online engagement:

- **Interactive polls and quizzes:** Solicit your audience's opinions on topics relevant to your brand.
- **Contests and giveaways:** Encourage participation by offering prizes related to your product.
- **Live streams and Q&As:** Utilize platforms like Instagram Live, Facebook Live, or YouTube for real-time interaction.
- **Viral challenges and hashtags:** Design a fun challenge and invite your audience to participate.
- **User-Generated Content (UGC):** Motivate users to share their experiences with your brand.

Practical Example: *LEGO created the LEGO Ideas platform, allowing fans to propose new set concepts and vote on others, transforming customers into genuine co-creators of the product.*

Practical Exercise: Choose one of the strategies mentioned above and implement it for your brand by introducing an engaging initiative for your audience.

ENGAGING THE AUDIENCE AT LIVE EVENTS

Even in today's digital world, face-to-face interaction remains a powerful way to build genuine connections.
Ways to engage your audience during events:

- **Workshops and masterclasses:** Offer hands-on experiences that deliver real value.
- **Meetups and community gatherings:** Host informal events to strengthen relationships.
- **Immersive experiences:** Design interactive events where participants can engage with your brand firsthand.
- **Networking and discussion panels:** Encourage exchange and sharing of ideas.

Practical Example: *Red Bull organizes extreme events and sports competitions that attract thrill-seekers, turning the brand into a genuine lifestyle.*

Practical Exercise: Think of a live event or experience that you could organize to enhance audience engagement.

COLLECTING FEEDBACK AND MAKING THE AUDIENCE PART OF THE PROCESS

People love feeling like they're part of something. Giving them a voice makes them more emotionally invested in your brand.
Ways to involve your audience in your brand's growth:

- **Ask for feedback on new ideas or products:** Use polls or beta testing to collect direct input.
- **Reward participation:** Acknowledge and celebrate your most engaged community members.
- **Create content based on your audience's needs:** Pay attention to their challenges and provide targeted solutions.
- **Respond to comments and interact regularly:** Don't just publish; build a genuine dialogue.

Practical Example: *Spotify introduced personalized playlists designed to fit user preferences, showing how addressing feedback can greatly enhance the customer experience.*

Practical Exercise: Create a brief survey to find out what your audience wants to improve or see next from your brand.

BUILDING AN ACTIVE AND LOYAL COMMUNITY

Engagement should not be a one-time action but rather a continuous process that strengthens your community.

How to build a strong community:

- **Give your community an identity:** A name, hashtag, or exclusive group can help unite your audience.
- **Encourage member interaction:** Create dialogue spaces like forums, Facebook groups, or private communities.
- **Organize regular interaction moments:** Plan weekly livestreams, recurring events, or scheduled meetups.
- **Create a sense of belonging:** Help your audience feel part of something bigger.

Practical Example: *Harley-Davidson doesn't merely sell motorcycles; it has created an entire culture around the brand, with rallies, exclusive clubs, and a profound sense of belonging among its customers.*

You can establish a private group for your most loyal clients, providing exclusive content and direct interaction. This strengthens the bond and turns members into true brand ambassadors.

Practical Exercise: Think of an initiative that can engage your audience and make them feel like part of an exclusive community.

The audience isn't just a group of clients or followers; it's a community that can become the driving force of your brand.

- Create online interaction opportunities with engaging content.
- Host live events to strengthen connections with your audience.
- Request feedback to make people feel involved in your brand's growth.
- Cultivate a strong, active community that can support your project long-term.

Remember: Engagement turns spectators into participants, customers into advocates, and ideas into movements.

BUILDING AUTHENTIC RELATIONSHIPS WITH YOUR AUDIENCE

Success depends on the quality of your product or service and your ability to build genuine, lasting relationships with others.

I learned this when I started promoting my projects. I thought that offering something good would be enough and that people would simply show up. However, I soon realized that the audience desires more: to feel seen, heard, and appreciated. People don't just want to be customers or followers; they want to be part of a community where their voice is valued.

To build a loyal and engaged audience, you must invest time and energy into creating genuine relationships based on trust and sincere communication.

WHY ARE AUTHENTIC RELATIONSHIPS SO IMPORTANT?

Loyalty is more valuable than acquisition; a loyal audience is more likely to support you over time.

- **Builds trust and credibility:** People trust those who are authentic and consistent.
- **Boosts engagement:** An audience that feels valued is more likely to interact with you.
- **Drives word of mouth:** Happy customers recommend your brand to friends and family.
- **Gives you a competitive advantage:** In a crowded market, your connection with the audience is what sets you apart.

Practical Example: *Starbucks doesn't just sell coffee; it creates an experience that makes customers feel welcomed, with their names on the cups and a familiar environment that strengthens the emotional bond.*

Practical Exercise: Consider how your brand or project might provide a more personal experience for your audience.

LISTENING TO YOUR AUDIENCE AND RESPONDING MEANINGFULLY

Audience interaction shouldn't be superficial; it should be genuine dialogue.

How to improve listening and communication:

- **Respond to comments and messages:** A simple "thank you" demonstrates that you care.
- **Ask for opinions and feedback:** Utilize polls and open-ended questions to engage your audience.
- **Show empathy and availability**: Be mindful in responding to concerns and questions.

- **Personalize communication:** Addressing people by name or acknowledging loyal customers makes a significant difference.

Practical Example: Ritz-Carlton is renowned for its outstanding customer service, empowering every employee to take initiative in delivering an extraordinary guest experience that fosters lasting loyalty and an emotional connection with the brand.

Practical Exercise: Dedicate 10 minutes each day to thoughtfully and personally respond to your audience's messages.

BEING PRESENT AND ACCESSIBLE

An audience that recognizes your consistent presence is more inclined to feel connected to you.

Strategies to increase your presence:

- **Post regularly:** Avoid vanishing for weeks only to show up unexpectedly.
- **Participate in comment threads and groups:** Show interest and involvement.
- **Create direct interaction opportunities:** Live sessions, webinars, and Q&A sessions strengthen the bond.
- **Show your authentic self:** Share experiences, behind-the-scenes content, and genuine moments.

Practical Example: Gary Vaynerchuk regularly replies to comments and messages from his followers, creating a sense of direct connection with his audience, even with a massive following.

Practical Exercise: Schedule at least one piece of content per week that directly engages your audience (live, Q&A, replies to comments).

CREATING A SENSE OF BELONGING

People want to be part of something bigger. Give them a reason to feel part of your community.

Ways to strengthen belonging:

- **Give your community a name:** Creating a shared identity reinforces the bond.
- **Reward audience loyalty:** Offer exclusive perks to your most active followers.
- **Involve them in key decisions:** Ask for feedback on new products or ideas.
- **Share audience stories:** Show appreciation by highlighting your customers or readers.

Practical Example: *Apple has built a loyal user community that identifies with the brand through exclusive events, dedicated forums, and a unique user experience.*

Practical Exercise: Consider how to make your audience feel like they're part of a unique community connected to your brand.

BUILDING AUTHENTIC RELATIONSHIPS OVER TIME

Strong relationships aren't built in a day; they require consistency, authenticity, and dedication.

How to maintain trust over time:

- **Keep your promises:** If you make an announcement or commitment, always follow through.
- **Avoid being overly commercial:** Balance promotional content with real value.
- **Show appreciation:** Thank your audience for their support and attention.
- **Evolve while maintaining your identity:** Grow and innovate, but stay true to your values.

Practical Example: *IKEA has built strong customer relationships by promoting sustainability and accessibility. Through its 'IKEA Family' program and furniture reuse/recycling initiatives, it's created a loyal community that shares its brand values.*

Practical Exercise: Identify three ways to demonstrate to your audience that you genuinely appreciate their loyalty.

Nurturing authentic relationships is the key to building a loyal, passionate audience.

- Listen to your audience and interact sincerely.
- Be present and accessible, not just a digital shadow.
- Create a sense of belonging and involve people in your initiatives.
- Build trust over time with consistency and authenticity.

Remember: People recall the feelings you evoked more than the products you offered.

IN SUMMARY

Understanding your audience and target customers is essential for success in life and achieving your goals. Implement targeted promotional strategies, challenge the norm, and create an impact that gets people talking about you or your product. Maintain consistency, stay authentic, craft a compelling story, actively engage your audience, and nurture genuine relationships. These are the key ingredients for building lasting success based on public attention and interest.

9 HOW TO MANAGE TIME

"Time is money." How many times have I heard this phrase in my life? Too many. And for years, I actually believed it to be true. I worked non-stop, convinced that the more hours I dedicated to my business, the more money I would earn and the more successful I would become. But over time, I came to understand that mindset was fundamentally flawed.

Time is not money! Money can be earned, lost, and regained. However, time, once it's gone, is lost forever. That's why true wealth doesn't come from accumulating money but from learning how to use it to create more time for what truly matters.

THE PARADOX OF WORK AND WEALTH

At the beginning of my career, I found myself caught in an endless cycle:

- The harder I worked, the more I earned.
- The more I earned, the more I wanted to work to increase my earnings further.
- But the more I worked, the less time I had for myself.

I remember a time when I barely slept, worked seven days a week, and was always chasing new clients and opportunities. I kept telling myself: *"I'm building my future; I need to sacrifice now to enjoy life later."* But when exactly was that "later" supposed to arrive? If I hadn't changed my mindset, it probably never would have.

The turning point came when I started observing people who had already achieved success. I realized that truly wealthy people didn't trade time for money. They built systems, made investments, and created income streams that worked without their direct involvement.

That was my first real lesson in financial freedom: it's not about working harder; it's about working smarter.

BUILDING PASSIVE INCOME: THE SECRET TO FREEDOM

Early on, one of my biggest mistakes was thinking that to earn more, I had to work more. Many people fall into this trap. The truth is, real financial success comes when money works for you instead of you working for money.

When I understood this, I started building **passive income streams**. I invested in projects that could generate earnings even without my daily involvement.

Here are a few strategies I adopted:

- **Real estate investments** – I purchased rental properties to create a steady income stream.
- **Automated businesses** – I developed systems and delegated tasks that could operate without my constant supervision.
- **Intellectual property** – I write books, scripts, and TV formats, which are assets that continuously generate value over time.
- **Online income** – I created digital products and services that generate revenue without fixed commitments.

Thanks to these strategies, I began to free up my time. It didn't happen overnight, but every small step brought me closer to freedom.

DELEGATING AND RECLAIMING TIME

One of the hardest moments in my career was realizing I was trying to do everything on my own. I believed no one could do things as well as I could. I thought delegating meant losing control.

But the day I finally decided to entrust some responsibilities to trusted collaborators, I discovered something amazing:

Not only did my business still function, but it often ran better than when I was doing everything myself!

If we want to maximize our time, we must learn to delegate.

Here's what I began to delegate:

- **Repetitive tasks** – I employed assistants for administrative duties and communications.
- **Content production** – I partnered with writers and creatives to develop my projects.
- **Investment management** – I consulted with experts to maximize returns on my financial assets.

Every delegated task gave me precious hours to dedicate to what matters: my family and friends, my hobbies, and my creative passions.

THE REAL GOAL: FREE TIME AND QUALITY OF LIFE

In the end, the real question isn't, "How much money do I have?" It's, "How much free time do I have to enjoy my life?"

I've met wealthy people who didn't have a single minute for themselves. They lived to work, constantly stressed and always in a hurry. On the other hand, I've encountered individuals with less money who are much happier and more balanced lives.

I decided that my wealth wouldn't be measured solely in money but in the freedom to choose how I spend my time. Time is the most precious resource we have, and once it's gone, we can't get it back.

If I could give one piece of advice to anyone pursuing success, it would be this:

Don't just work to accumulate wealth. Work to create a system that gives you more time to truly live.

TIME IS AN OPPORTUNITY: DON'T WASTE IT!

Every day is an opportunity. Every hour is an investment. The difference between those who succeed and those who remain stuck lies in how they use their time.

Here are some questions I ask myself every day to ensure I'm not wasting it:

- Am I dedicating my time to what truly matters?
- Am I building something that will provide me with more freedom in the future?
- If today were my last day, would I be satisfied with how I spent it? If the answer to any of these is "no," then I know it's time to make a change.

Don't wait to be "rich enough" to start enjoying life. Start creating a system today that allows you to spend time on the things you love. Use money as a tool to buy time, not as a goal in itself.

Because, in the end, true success isn't measured by how much you've earned but by how much you've lived.

Remember: Time is not money. It is so much more. It's freedom, life, and opportunity.

STRUCTURING YOUR DAY

One of the most common mistakes I made early in my career was believing that, in order to succeed, I had to work as much as possible, cramming every minute of my day with tasks and commitments. It felt like a race against time: an illusion that made me think I was productive, but in reality, it only drained me.

Then, I discovered a concept that completely changed my

approach: it's not working more that makes you wealthy, but working better.

The book *"The 4-Hour Workweek"* by Timothy Ferriss was eye-opening. Not because I think everyone can truly work only four hours a week (although that would be amazing), but because it taught me that how we structure our time determines the quality of our lives. Ferriss emphasizes that efficiency and delegation matter more than the sheer number of hours worked, which was fundamental to me.

TIME IS THE MOST PRECIOUS RESOURCE

Many believe that money is the most important resource, but the truth is that time is the one thing we can never get back.

Strategically organizing your day means:

- Avoiding chaos and improvisation.
- Making the most of every moment.
- Eliminating the stress of last-minute deadlines.
- Dedicating more time to what truly matters.

Practical Exercise: Take a sheet of paper and write down everything you do during the day. Analyze how much time you spend on truly important activities. You may discover that many hours are wasted on distractions and non-essential tasks.

CREATING A SUCCESSFUL MORNING ROUTINE

The way you start your day sets the tone for the hours ahead. I've tried various routines over the years and learned that certain elements truly make a difference:

- **Waking up early** – Getting up before others gives you a huge advantage: more time for yourself and to focus on your goals without distractions.
- **Avoid using your phone right away** – Checking emails and

social media as soon as you wake up overloads your mind with unnecessary information and distracts you.
- **Meditation or conscious breathing** – Even just 5 minutes help reduce stress and improve focus.
- **Physical activity** – A short morning workout activates both body and mind.
- **Defining daily goals** – Take 5 minutes to write down 2–3 key goals for the day. This helps you stay focused.

Practical Exercise: Create a list of things you want to include in your ideal morning routine. Begin with small changes and gradually add new habits.

PLANNING TECHNIQUES TO MAXIMIZE PRODUCTIVITY

To effectively organize your day, you can use some proven techniques.

1. The 3 Priorities Method

Each morning, identify three key tasks that, if accomplished, would ensure your day is successful.

- Write down the three priorities on paper or in a note-taking app.
- Tackle them during the early hours of the day, when you have the most energy.
- Avoid distractions until you've completed them.

2. Time Blocking Technique

This method involves dividing your day into blocks of time dedicated to specific tasks.

- Set aside time for work, learning, physical activity, and leisure.
- Avoid multitasking: focus on one activity at a time.
- Use a timer to stick to the scheduled blocks.

Practical Exercise: Try planning your day into 60–90 minute segments focused on specific tasks. After each segment, take a 5–10 minute break to recharge.

3. *The Pomodoro Technique*

If you tend to procrastinate or get easily distracted, the Pomodoro method can help. It works like this:

- Work intensely for 25 minutes.
- Take a 5-minute break.
- Repeat the cycle 4 times, then take a longer break of 15–30 minutes.

Practical Exercise: Set a timer and try the Pomodoro technique for one work session. Observe how it impacts your productivity.

ELIMINATING TIME WASTERS

One main reason people don't reach their goals is the time they spend on useless activities.

Here are a few habits to avoid in order to reclaim valuable time:

- **Scrolling through social media aimlessly** – Limit your social media use and set a daily maximum.
- **Constantly checking emails** – Allocate specific times of the day for handling emails instead of checking them continuously.
- **Saying "yes" to too many requests** – Learn to say "no" to commitments that don't contribute to your goals.
- **Watching too much TV or endless shows** – Allow yourself time to relax, but don't overdo it.

Practical Exercise: Make a list of your main distractions and find ways to reduce or eliminate them.

THE IMPORTANCE OF REST AND LEISURE TIME

A common mistake is believing that working more hours means being more productive. In reality, the quality of the time spent working is far more important than the quantity. Breaks and leisure time are not a waste; they are essential for maintaining high levels of energy and creativity.

Here are some practices for effective rest:

- **Sleep at least 7–8 hours per night** – Sleep is essential for physical and mental well-being.
- **Disconnect from work before bedtime** – Avoid screens and emails in the evening to improve sleep quality.
- **Dedicate time to hobbies and passions** – Pursuing interests outside of work helps maintain mental balance.

Practical Exercise: Schedule at least one hour each day for an activity that relaxes and recharges you.

Organizing your day doesn't mean filling it with tasks, but giving it meaning and clear direction.

I've learned the hard way that productivity isn't measured by hours worked but by results achieved. As Ferriss states in his book, the secret isn't working more; it's working smarter.

Remember: The goal isn't just to do more but to focus on what truly matters. If we learn to manage our time wisely, we can achieve remarkable results without compromising our personal well-being.

ORGANIZING YOUR WORK TIMELINE

Having big goals is essential, but without a clear plan, we risk getting lost in confusion or falling into procrastination. I know this well because I've experienced it firsthand. In my early years as an entrepreneur, I had countless ideas and projects in mind, but without a solid strategy, I often found myself chasing time, working late, and not achieving the results I hoped for. That's when I understood the importance of organizing an effective work timeline.

Time management isn't a cage that limits our creativity; it's a tool that gives us more freedom and control over our work and our life.

A well-structured timeline allows you to:

- Have a clear vision of the steps required to achieve your goals.
- Allocate time more efficiently, avoiding waste and distractions.
- Prevent overload and reduce stress from excessive work.
- Focus on what is truly important and urgent.

BREAKING DOWN GOALS INTO SPECIFIC TASKS

A goal without a strategy is merely a wish. I learned this lesson the hard way when I decided to write my first book. Initially, I thought I could write freely, without a clear structure, but I soon realized that I was wasting time without making real progress. It was only when I broke the project down into concrete steps with specific deadlines that I was able to complete it successfully.

> **Practical Example:** *Goal: Write a 200-page book in six months. Breakdown:*
>
> - *Research and outline the book's structure (1 week)*
> - *Write the first chapter (2 weeks)*
> - *Complete the remaining chapters, one at a time (4 months)*
> - *Conduct final revisions and editing (1 month)*

Practical Exercise: Write down your primary goal and divide it into detailed sub-tasks, assigning an estimated completion time to each one.

CREATING A REALISTIC TIMELINE

Once we have broken down the goals, we need to arrange the tasks into a manageable timeline.
To do this effectively:

- **Prioritize** – Which tasks are most urgent or have fixed deadlines? Start with those.
- **Be realistic about time** – Avoid overloading yourself. Give each task the time it needs to be completed effectively.
- **Include strategic breaks** – Schedule moments of rest to prevent burnout and maintain high productivity.
- **Stay flexible** – Prepare for the unexpected and leave room for adjustments to the plan.

Weekly Timeline Structure:

- **Monday:** Plan and set weekly goals
- **Tuesday–Thursday:** Tackle the most important and challenging tasks
- **Friday:** Review completed work and finalize tasks
- **Saturday and Sunday:** Recharge and get ready for the upcoming week

Practical Exercise: Create a weekly timeline for your current project, assigning specific tasks to each day.

USEFUL TOOLS FOR TIMELINE MANAGEMENT

There are numerous digital tools, including free apps and software, that can assist us in better organizing our work timeline:

- **A personal planner** – Whether paper or digital, it's essential for planning your days and commitments.
- **A well-structured calendar** – Creating events with deadlines and reminders helps keep goals in sight.

- **A task management system** – Breaking work into clear steps helps maintain focus and avoid procrastination.

Practical Exercise: Choose a time management method that suits your lifestyle and start using it to organize your work schedule.

AVOIDING WORK OVERLOAD

One of the most common mistakes is overloading your timeline with activities without leaving room for breaks or unexpected events. This results in stress, inefficiency, and a loss of motivation.

Here are some strategies to prevent overload:

- **Learn to say NO** – If a task isn't a priority, postpone or delegate it.
- **Leave space between tasks** – A jam-packed schedule leaves no room for creativity or reflection.
- **Monitor your mental and physical well-being** – If you feel overwhelmed, take a break.

Practical Exercise: Analyze your current workload. Are there tasks you can eliminate or delegate to improve your productivity without risking burnout?

FOCUS ON HIGH-IMPACT ACTIVITIES

Not all activities have the same value. Some directly impact our goals, while others are just busy work that gives us the illusion of being productive.

The 80/20 Rule (Pareto Principle)

20% of our daily activities generate 80% of the results. The key to excellent timeline management is identifying and focusing on the small percentage of high-impact tasks that yield the best results.

Practical Exercise: Analyze the activities you perform daily and ask yourself: "Which of these bring the greatest results with the least effort?" Focus on those.

Effective time management improves productivity and allows us to work less stressed and more satisfied.

The goal is not to fill every minute of the day with activity but to plan intelligently and maintain balance, leaving space for personal growth and well-being. I've learned that the key to lasting success is not working endlessly but working more intelligently and strategically.

Remember: Organizing your work timeline is essential for turning goals into tangible results.

Start creating your work timeline today, and you'll see how much your efficiency and success can improve!

THE ART OF DELEGATING: HOW TO FREE UP TIME AND BOOST PRODUCTIVITY

One of the most common mistakes among entrepreneurs, managers, and professionals is thinking they have to do everything themselves. This approach often leads to work overload, stress, and inefficiency. Learning to delegate is one of the most powerful strategies for saving time and increasing productivity.

Delegating does not mean losing control, it means optimizing available resources and freeing up valuable time to focus on the most strategic and high-value tasks. Moreover, delegating allows others to grow and develop their skills, creating a more efficient and collaborative environment.

WHY IS DELEGATING IMPORTANT?

Those who know how to delegate accomplish more with less effort
Handing off the right tasks brings many benefits:

- **Time savings** – You free up precious hours in your day.

- **Increased productivity** – You focus on high-value tasks while others handle secondary activities.
- **Less stress and more balance** – You reduce your workload and improve your quality of life.
- **Team and business growth** – Delegating gives others the chance to develop new skills.

Practical Exercise: Write down all the activities you do daily. Which of these could be assigned to others?

WHAT TO DELEGATE AND WHAT TO KEEP FOR YOURSELF

Not all tasks can be delegated. The key to a good balance is understanding what to hand off to others and what to keep under your control.

Tasks to Delegate:

- **Repetitive and operational tasks** – Emails, admin, social media management, system updates.
- **Tasks others can do better than you** – If someone else is more skilled in an area, let them handle it.
- **Low-value tasks** – Tasks that take time but don't directly contribute to achieving your goals.

Tasks to Keep for Yourself:

- **Strategic decisions** – Business vision and key choices should remain under your control.
- **Creative and innovative tasks** – As the driving force behind your business, maintain focus on what truly makes an impact.
- **Relationships and networking** – Building meaningful connections is a responsibility that should not be delegated.

Practical Exercise: Review your work and split the tasks into two columns: "To Delegate" and "To Handle Personally."

HOW TO DELEGATE EFFECTIVELY

Delegating means more than simply assigning a task to someone; it involves doing so strategically to ensure the best outcome.

Here are the steps for effective delegation:

1. **Identify the right person.** Assign the task to someone with the appropriate skills, and if necessary, invest in their training.
2. **Communicate clearly** – Provide detailed instructions, specify the goals, and set clear expectations.
3. **Give autonomy and trust** – Avoid micromanagement; allow the person to find their own method to complete the task.
4. **Monitor without over-controlling** – Set checkpoints to evaluate progress without constant interference.
5. **Provide feedback and support** – Help people improve over time by offering constructive suggestions.

Practical Exercise: Start by delegating a simple task this week, following these five steps.

TOOLS FOR DELEGATING EFFICIENTLY

Thanks to technology, delegating is now easier than ever. Digital tools enable teams to organize tasks, manage projects, and effectively track progress.

Some useful tools include:

- **Project management platforms** to break down tasks and assign responsibilities among team members.
- **Cloud storage solutions** for sharing documents and collaborating in an organized manner.

- **Internal communication tools** to facilitate remote collaboration and improve information flow.
- **Freelance marketplaces** for locating specialized professionals from across the globe.

Practical Exercise: Select a digital tool that meets your needs and start using it to delegate a task.

OVERCOMING THE FEAR OF DELEGATING

Many people struggle to delegate because they fear losing control or because they believe "no one can do it as well as I can."

If you identify with this mindset, try changing your perspective:

- "Delegating means losing control" → "Delegating means achieving more with less effort."
- "No one will do the job like I do" → "Others might do it better, freeing up time for what matters more."
- "I can't trust anyone" → "I can train others to work effectively."

Practical Exercise: Think about a time when you chose not to delegate tasks because you were afraid of losing control. How might you have approached it differently?

Delegation is one of the most powerful skills for saving time and improving efficiency.

The more we learn to delegate effectively, the more time we have to concentrate on what truly matters.

Remember: It's not just about offloading tasks but about building an effective system in which everyone contributes at their highest level.

Start delegating today and you'll discover how much your productivity and quality of life can improve.

INVESTING TIME IN WHAT BRINGS THE GREATEST RETURN

I may sound repetitive, but I'll never stop emphasizing that time is the most precious resource we have, and how we use it largely determines our success and happiness. Over the years, I've learned this lesson through mistakes, periods of stagnation, and poor decisions that helped me realize how crucial it is to dedicate ourselves only to what truly matters.

We often fall into the trap of filling our days with urgent but unimportant tasks. We respond to unnecessary emails, attend unproductive meetings, or spend hours on social media without a real purpose.

To make the most of our time, we must identify the activities that yield the greatest results and commit to them with discipline and consistency.

THE DIFFERENCE BETWEEN BEING BUSY AND BEING PRODUCTIVE

For a long time, I also believed that being constantly busy was a sign of success. I thought that working late and filling every minute of my day meant I was making progress. But the truth is different: being busy does not equate to being productive.

Being busy means:

- Filling your day with insignificant activities.
- Constantly being in motion without a clear direction.
- Multitasking without completing anything effectively.

Being productive means:

- Focusing your time on high-impact activities.
- Removing distractions and working with intention.
- Saying "no" to what does not serve your goals.

Practical Exercise: Write down all the activities you accomplished today. Then ask yourself: "Which of these truly contributed to my goals?" You might discover that several were unnecessary or low-value tasks.

SUCCESS ISN'T JUST WEALTH: FINDING WORK-LIFE BALANCE

Throughout my career, there were moments when I was so focused on work that I overlooked everything else: friends, family, and personal well-being until I realized that true success isn't defined solely by money or professional achievements.

Dedicating our time to what truly matters also means balancing work with:

- **Personal relationships** – Spending time with family and friends is essential for a fulfilling life.
- **Personal growth** – Engaging in reading, learning, and continuously improving ourselves contributes to our fulfillment.
- **Health and well-being** – Without physical and mental health, no amount of success is meaningful.

If we work nonstop without ever pausing, we may one day find ourselves with money in the bank but lacking energy, real relationships, and a sense of fulfillment.

Practical Exercise: Reflect on how much time you dedicate each week to the people you love, focusing on your personal growth and well-being. If you are neglecting these aspects, it's time to realign your priorities.

IDENTIFYING HIGH-YIELD ACTIVITIES

To optimize our time, we must distinguish between high-impact and low-impact activities.

High-impact activities:

- Generate significant results toward our goals.
- Bring us closer to long-term success.
- Are strategic, not just operational.

Low-impact activities:

- Represent repetitive tasks that don't add real value.
- Act as distractions that divert us from our goals.
- Make us feel "busy" without providing real benefits.

Practical Exercise: Make a list of your weekly activities and classify them based on their impact. Then try to reduce or remove low-impact tasks and dedicate more time to the most productive ones.

ELIMINATING DISTRACTIONS

A major barrier to productivity is a lack of focus. We often find ourselves distracted by notifications, emails, social media, or other people's requests.

Here are some strategies to protect your time:

- Turn off your phone notifications during work hours.
- Avoid constantly checking emails: set specific times for it throughout the day.
- Say NO without feeling guilty to commitments that don't add value to your life.
- Set time limits on low-productivity activities like watching TV or browsing social media.

Practical Exercise: Today, focus on working for one hour without interruptions by turning off notifications and removing distractions. You'll be surprised by how much more you can achieve in less time.

DISCIPLINE: THE SECRET TO TIME OPTIMIZATION

Sometimes we already know which tasks are most important, yet struggle to put them into action. Personal discipline is the key to staying focused and resisting procrastination.

Here are a few ways to build more self-discipline:

- Start your day with a clear plan – Knowing exactly what to do reduces the chance of wasting time.
- Apply the "work first, reward later" method – Complete the most important tasks first, then allow yourself a break.
- Cultivate strong habits – Focusing on what matters should become a habit, not an occasional choice.
- Monitor your progress – Observing your advancement toward your goals increases motivation.

Practical Exercise: Choose one productive habit to develop and dedicate yourself to practicing it daily for a week.

Time is our most limited resource. Each day that goes by is one less day available to us. If we want to succeed, we must act with urgency and make the most of every moment.

Practical Exercise: Before bed each night, reflect on your day and ask yourself, "Did I use my time productively and meaningfully?" If the answer is no, commit to doing better tomorrow.

Remember: Time is our most valuable resource; let's not waste it.

IN SUMMARY

Dedicating your time to what brings the highest return means thoughtfully selecting activities that enhance your life.

True success involves more than just money; it encompasses a balance between work, personal growth, and relationships.

10 HOW TO NEGOTIATE

Many people tend to confuse selling with negotiating, but in reality, they are two distinct processes.

Selling means convincing a client of the value of a product or service by showing how it can solve a problem or meet a need. The focus is on communication, building trust, and highlighting the offer's benefits.

Negotiating, on the other hand, is about reaching an agreement that satisfies both parties. It's not just about persuading; it's about finding a balance between different needs, managing compromises, concessions, and alternative solutions.

Although sales and negotiation share some common elements, such as active listening and the ability to create value for the counterpart, selling is often the first step. Negotiation comes into play when there are more variables to define, like price, conditions, or contract details.

In short, *you can sell without negotiating, but you can't negotiate without knowing how to sell.*

UNDERSTANDING THE CLIENT'S NEEDS: THE POWER OF LISTENING

In negotiation and sales, too much emphasis is often placed on what we want to say, while the most crucial aspect is neglected: listening. Truly understanding the client's needs allows us to offer relevant solutions and build trust.

The most common mistake is approaching a negotiation with a pre-packaged idea of what the client should want instead of discovering it directly from them. Only through active listening can we gather valuable information to personalize our offer in a convincing and effective way.

ACTIVE LISTENING: HEARING IS NOT ENOUGH; YOU MUST UNDERSTAND

Active listening involves more than just hearing the client's words; it requires being fully engaged in the conversation, understanding not only the explicit meaning of what is said but also the emotions and intentions behind it.

Elements of active listening:

- **Fully focusing on the speaker** – Avoid distractions and don't interrupt.
- **Observing non-verbal communication** – Facial expressions, gestures, and tone of voice often reveal more than words.
- **Paraphrasing and confirming understanding** – Summarizing what the client said shows that you truly understood.

Practical Example: *"I think finding a solution that reduces management time while maintaining quality is very important to you. Is that correct?"*

Practical Exercise: Do not express your opinion immediately during your next client conversation. Instead, listen to the speaker for at least one full minute and summarize what you understand in your own words.

IDENTIFYING THE CLIENT'S TRUE NEEDS

Clients often fail to express their true needs clearly. Instead, they concentrate on superficial details or immediate concerns. An effective salesperson or negotiator knows how to look beyond words and uncover the genuine motivations behind the client's choices.

How to identify real needs:

- **Ask open-ended questions** – These encourage the client to share more information.
- **Ask "Why?"** – Whenever a client says they want something, ask why they want it.
- **Observe their priorities** – Their main concerns will reveal what truly matters to them.

Practical Example: *"I'd like to know what matters most to you in this solution: flexibility, cost, or speed of execution?"*

Practical Exercise: Consider a typical client request and ask yourself what underlying need may be motivating it.

SILENCE AS A COMMUNICATION TOOL

Silence is one of the most underrated techniques in negotiation. Many people feel uncomfortable with silence and try to fill it by talking more. However, those who understand how to use silence strategically can gain valuable insights.

Why silence is effective:

- **It gives the client time to reflect** – A pause often leads to more thoughtful responses.
- **It prevents rushed answers** – A moment of silence before replying demonstrates thoughtfulness.

- **It can draw out additional information** – Many clients will elaborate to fill the silence.

Practical Example: *"After asking a key question, pause for a few seconds before saying anything. You may be surprised by what the client discloses."*

Practical Exercise: In your next conversation, silently count to five before responding to the client's statements.

ADAPTING YOUR LANGUAGE TO THE CLIENT

Every client has a different communication style, and adapting to their way of speaking significantly increases your chances of closing a deal.
How to adapt to the client's language:

- **Pay attention to their communication style** – Are they direct or prefer detailed explanations?
- **Use key words that the client has used** – This strengthens the connection.
- **Match their tone and pace** – If the client speaks slowly and calmly, avoid being too fast or aggressive.

Practical Example: *"You mentioned that ease of use is essential to you. This product was designed specifically for individuals seeking an intuitive and user-friendly interface."*

Practical Exercise: Consider repeating some of the client's key words in a conversation. Notice if this builds more rapport.

THE IMPORTANCE OF EMOTIONS IN THE DECISION-MAKING PROCESS

Purchasing decisions are not entirely rational; emotions significantly impact them. Effective listening helps identify the emotional triggers that influence the client's decisions.
How to identify the emotions behind a decision:

- **Observe facial expressions and tone of voice** – Do they convey enthusiasm, concern, or uncertainty?
- **Ask what excites or worries them most** – This reveals the true buying motivators.
- **Show empathy** – If a client expresses doubt, acknowledge it before responding.

Practical Example: *"I understand that you want to feel confident before making a decision. It's an important choice, and it's perfectly fine to take your time."*

Practical Exercise: Identify the dominant emotion a client expresses during a conversation and try to mirror it with empathy.

Understanding clients' needs isn't just about listening to their words; it's about comprehending what they're truly seeking. Active listening, strategic silence, adapting your language, and emotional awareness are essential tools for building meaningful customer experience.

Remember: A client who feels truly understood is a client who will trust you.

THE STAGES OF NEGOTIATION: FROM FIRST CONTACT TO CLOSING

Negotiation is not an improvised confrontation but a structured process following clear stages. Understanding each phase helps improve the effectiveness of the negotiation, avoid mistakes, and ensure a mutually beneficial outcome.

I learned this the hard way. Early on, I thought negotiation was simply about convincing the other party to accept my offer. Then I realized the key to success was something else: listening, preparing, and building an agreement on solid ground.

Every negotiation is different, but it follows a logical path from initial preparation to closing the deal. Knowing and mastering these stages allows you to approach negotiations with confidence and flexibility.

PREPARATION: BUILDING A SOLID FOUNDATION

Preparation is the cornerstone of a successful negotiation. Entering a negotiation without a clear plan puts you at a disadvantage. I have experienced firsthand how disastrous jumping into a negotiation without a strategy can be. Once, I had to completely revise a deal because I hadn't studied the other party thoroughly, which cost me weeks of work.

What to do in this phase:

- **Define your objectives** – What is the minimum acceptable outcome? What would be the ideal deal?
- **Study the other party** – What are their interests, strengths, and weaknesses?
- **Identify alternatives** – What other options do you have if the negotiation fails?
- **Anticipate possible objections** – What arguments might they raise, and how will you respond?

Strategy: Prepare a negotiation framework outlining key points to address and possible scenarios.

Practical Exercise: Before a negotiation, write down your main objectives and a strategy for achieving them. Analyze the other party's perspective to prepare for an effective response.

OPENING: CREATING A CLIMATE OF TRUST

The initial interaction between parties is crucial in establishing the tone for the negotiation. A thoughtfully managed opening fosters constructive dialogue and reduces initial tension or bias.

I've witnessed negotiations fail within the first five minutes simply because one party approached with an overly aggressive or defensive attitude.

Goals of the opening phase:

- Create a climate of mutual respect.
- Clearly establish the ground rules for the discussion.
- Show openness to dialogue without immediately revealing all your cards.

How to set a positive initial tone:

- Start with a neutral and professional approach.
- Observe the other party's body language to pick up useful cues.
- Find common ground to ease any tension.

Practical Example: *"I appreciate the time we're dedicating to this conversation. I'm confident we'll find a solution that benefits both of us."*

Practical Exercise: In your next negotiation, consider starting with a phrase that shows openness and collaboration.

INFORMATION EXCHANGE: UNDERSTANDING THE REALITIES AT PLAY

Once a positive atmosphere is established, it's time to gather and share information strategically. This phase focuses on better understanding the other party's position while uncovering their needs, expectations, and constraints.

How to handle the information exchange:

- **Ask targeted questions** – Try to obtain details that will help you build a compelling offer.
- **Avoid revealing your final position right away** – Share information gradually while assessing the other party's reactions.

- **Listen more than you speak** – The information you collect is more valuable than what you share.

Practical Example: *"I would like to understand better which factors are most important to you in this collaboration. Could you please share some insights regarding your priorities?"*

Practical Exercise: During your next negotiation, prioritize listening over speaking in the initial phase of information exchange.

SOLUTION BUILDING: CREATING A WIN-WIN AGREEMENT

An effective negotiation isn't about winning or losing; it's about finding mutually beneficial solutions. I've learned that a small, strategic concession can often unlock a whole negotiation.

Strategies for identifying common ground:

- **Focus on interests, not positions** – Often, both parties want the same thing but express it differently.
- **Be flexible with alternatives** – Sometimes, a small concession can lead to a broader agreement.
- **Use concrete data** – Offering numbers and objective references strengthens your arguments.

Practical Example: *"If your main concern is delivery speed, we can develop a plan that guarantees quicker timelines in return for a greater volume commitment."*

Practical Exercise: Next time you negotiate, try proposing at least two alternatives to the initial offer to increase your chances of a successful outcome.

CLOSING: FORMALIZING THE AGREEMENT

The final stage is where the agreement is finalized, and the definitive terms are confirmed. Although it may seem like the simplest step, closing properly is crucial to avoid misunderstandings or second thoughts.

How to close successfully:

- **Summarize the main points of the agreement** to ensure both parties are aligned.
- **Clarify the next steps.** Define clearly what concrete actions will follow.
- **Ensure the agreement is formalized** clearly and transparently.

Practical Example: *"We've agreed that the service will be activated within 30 days, and support will be provided for one year. Shall we proceed with signing the contract?"*

Practical Exercise: Following your next negotiation, ensure that both parties understand the agreement by requesting immediate feedback.

Negotiation is a logical process that requires preparation, active listening, and the ability to find balanced solutions. Each phase matters; skipping any of them could jeopardize the final outcome.

Remember: A good negotiator isn't someone who imposes their will but knows how to guide the process toward a solid and lasting agreement.

VALUING THE CLIENT: BUILDING A RELATIONSHIP BEYOND THE SALE

Through experience, I've learned that selling is not just about closing a deal; it's about building a relationship.

I've seen companies obsessed with acquiring new clients neglect the ones they already had, only to wonder why their business was stagnating. The secret? Treat every client as if they're the most important because they are.

A client who feels appreciated returns and tells others about you. And there's no better advertisement than positive word of mouth. But how do you turn a one-time buyer into a brand advocate? It takes a mix of attention, personalization, and authentic communication.

UNDERSTANDING THE CLIENT BEYOND THE TRANSACTION

Early in my career, I believed my job was to sell a product or service as effectively as possible. Then, I realized that my true goal was to solve a client's problem, and that changed everything.

How to do it:

- **Truly listen** – Clients don't always directly communicate what they want, but you can pick it up between the lines.
- **Personalize the offer** – Tailoring the solution to their needs is what turns a sale into a relationship.
- **Make them feel unique** – A client who feels like a priority is more likely to trust and stay loyal to you.

Practical Example: *"I've noticed that in your industry, speed is crucial. We can design a tailored service that guarantees maximum efficiency without compromising quality."*

Practical Exercise: Next time you interact with a client, try to learn more about their work context and what truly matters to them.

CREATING A SUPERIOR EXPERIENCE

While the quality of the product or service is important, the overall experience is what the client will truly remember. I've seen clients remain loyal for years, not because the product was flawless but because they felt treated with respect and care.

How to enhance the customer experience:

- **Clarity and transparency** – No one wants unpleasant surprises.
- **Ease of communication** – People value fast and accurate responses.
- **Post-sale support** – Clients shouldn't feel abandoned after making a purchase.

Practical Example: *"We understand the importance of post-sale support. That's why we've created a dedicated channel where you can receive immediate assistance without wasting time."*

Practical Exercise: Examine your existing customer interaction process and pinpoint one area where you can improve the overall experience.

SHOWING GRATITUDE AND CARE

We often assume that a good product is enough to keep a client loyal, but the small gestures make the biggest difference.

I've learned that a simple "thank you" can be more powerful than a discount.

Ways to show client appreciation:

- **Personalized follow-ups** – Sending a message after a purchase to request feedback demonstrates that you care.
- **Loyalty rewards** – Providing exclusive benefits to returning clients strengthens the relationship.
- **Listening to suggestions** – A client who feels appreciated is more likely to remain loyal.

Practical Example: *"We value your feedback, and thanks to your suggestions, we've improved some features of our service."*

Practical Exercise: After a sale, send a personalized message to thank the client and request honest feedback on their experience.

BUILDING A LONG-TERM RELATIONSHIP

Closing a sale alone isn't enough; the real goal is to establish a lasting relationship. A client who feels cared for won't feel the need to seek alternatives.

Key elements to maintaining the relationship:

- **Consistency over time** – Service must always remain at a high standard.
- **Non-sales-related contact** – A message sharing updates or offering free value can make a significant impact.
- **Adapting to their needs** – If you anticipate their needs before they do, they're more likely to stay with you.

Practical Example: *"The market is evolving, and this new strategy might catch your interest. Would you like to talk about how it could benefit you?"*

Practical Exercise: Develop a contact plan for key clients, incorporating regular updates to maintain the relationship even after the sale.

COMMUNICATION AS A TOOL FOR CLIENT VALUE

Every interaction with a client provides an opportunity to strengthen the relationship. An overlooked email or hasty reply can harm that connection.

How to improve communication:

- **Be clear and direct** – Avoid using unnecessary jargon.
- **Show empathy** – The client should feel that you understand their perspective.

- **Be responsive** – Prompt replies demonstrate respect and professionalism.

Practical Example: *"I completely understand your need for quick service. I can assure you that we can deliver within 48 hours at no extra cost."*

Practical Exercise: Examine your responses to clients and consider how to improve your communications by being clearer, more empathetic, and more direct.

Valuing a client involves more than just delivering a product or service; it's about making them feel part of an experience.

I've learned that business success depends on the quality of your offering and your ability to build strong, lasting relationships.

Remember: A client who feels valued becomes your best ambassador. Treat them like people, not numbers, and your business will grow naturally and sustainably.

WINNING A NEGOTIATION: CREATING VALUE FOR BOTH PARTIES

Winning a negotiation doesn't mean forcing your will on the other party; it means finding a meeting point that brings value to everyone involved.

Over time, I've learned that the best negotiations are not those where one side wins and the other loses but those in which both sides feel they've gained something valuable. That's the secret to building lasting relationships and successful collaborations.

THE WINNING MINDSET IN NEGOTIATION

The first step to achieving results is having the right attitude. Early in my career, I approached negotiations with the mindset that I needed to win at all costs. Then, I realized that true success lies in collaboration and creating mutually beneficial solutions.

Key aspects of a winning mindset:

- **Flexibility** – Being open to alternative solutions while keeping your goals in sight.
- **Collaboration** – Viewing negotiation as an opportunity to create value rather than a competition.
- **Focus on interests, not positions** – Redirect your attention from what you want to what both parties truly need.

Practical Example: *"If your goal is to reduce the price, and my aim is to guarantee high quality, we can agree on a service package that maintains value while fulfilling your expectations."*

Practical Exercise: The next time you negotiate, analyze your attitude. Are you more defensive or open to collaboration?

STRATEGIES FOR CONDUCTING A SUCCESSFUL NEGOTIATION

During the negotiation, it's essential to manage the conversation wisely to reach a beneficial agreement.

Effective techniques:

- **Ask open-ended questions** – They help gather information without revealing too much.
- **Use silence to your advantage** – After making an offer, wait for the other side's response without rushing to fill the silence.
- **Break down the problem** – If a point is difficult to resolve, divide it into smaller, manageable parts.

Practical Example: *"What is the most important factor for you in this negotiation? If we can meet that priority, we can discover a solution that benefits both sides."*

Practical Exercise: Next time you negotiate, consider pausing for a few seconds before responding to an offer. Pay attention to how the other person reacts.

IDENTIFYING AND LEVERAGING COMMON INTERESTS

While parties may appear to have opposing goals, a closer examination often uncovers shared interests.

How to find common interests:

- **Ask about the other party's priorities** – You may discover unexpected points of alignment.
- **Understand underlying motivations** – A request for a lower price may arise from a need to reduce operating costs.
- **Propose solutions that benefit both sides** – The goal is to create an agreement where everyone gains something.

Practical Example: *"If your goal is to achieve faster delivery and mine is to maintain a healthy profit margin, we can reach a compromise by accelerating production for a slight additional cost."*

Practical Exercise: In your next negotiation, identify a shared value element that can lead to a win-win outcome.

FLEXIBILITY AS A COMPETITIVE ADVANTAGE

Being rigid about every negotiation point often leads to deadlock. The key to winning without conflict is knowing when to concede on less critical matters in exchange for more important concessions.

How to use flexibility to your advantage:

- **Distinguish between essential and secondary points** – Focus on what truly matters.
- **Offer alternative options** – Suggest a different solution if one request is unacceptable.

- **Leverage concessions to gain something in return** – Every concession should come with mutual benefit.

Practical Example: *"I'm willing to accept installment payments if we can agree on a long-term contract."*

Practical Exercise: During your next negotiation, identify one point where you can be flexible and use it to gain a more significant concession.

Winning a negotiation involves creating a mutually beneficial outcome, building trust, and fostering long-term collaborations.
Preparation, targeted strategies, and flexibility are essential ingredients for maximizing every negotiation.

Remember: A well-conducted negotiation has no winners or losers, only opportunities smartly seized.

THE BENEFITS OF KNOWING HOW TO LOSE A NEGOTIATION

When people think of negotiation, most assume the only acceptable outcome is to win. But what if I told you that knowing how to lose, in some cases, can be even more valuable?

I've learned this the hard way through various experiences. Over time, I realized that not every deal must end in an immediate win. Sometimes, accepting an "apparent loss" is the smartest move to open up future opportunities.

THE STRATEGIC VALUE OF AN APPARENT LOSS

The party that gets the "better" deal immediately doesn't always truly win.
There are situations where walking away can lead to much greater gains in the long run.
I've experienced negotiations where the requested compromise was

too burdensome or the terms too unfavorable. If I had insisted on closing the deal, I might have ended up with a harmful commitment or an unhappy client.

Why is it sometimes wise to lose a negotiation?

- Avoid unfavorable deals that may hurt you in the long term.
- Preserve long-term relationships with the other party.
- Show foresight and openness, gaining credibility.

Practical Example: *I once negotiated with a client who wanted unreasonable payment terms. I could've accepted to close the deal quickly, but I knew it would hurt my business. I chose to walk away, and months later, that same client returned with a much fairer offer, fully respecting my terms.*

BUILDING TRUST AND CREDIBILITY THROUGH LETTING GO

One of the biggest mistakes in negotiation is forcing a deal solely to win. Often, demonstrating your willingness to walk away makes you appear more trustworthy to the other party.

How to turn a loss into an advantage:

- Maintain a professional and respectful attitude.
- Avoid forcing an agreement at all costs.
- Always leave the door open for future collaboration.

Practical Example: *During a meeting with a potential partner, I realized we weren't on the same page. Instead of trying to persuade him insistently, I acknowledged that it wasn't the right time to collaborate. A few years later, that partner reached out to me again, recalling my professionalism, and we closed a much more favorable deal.*

MANAGING EMOTIONS IN DEFEAT

Accepting a loss in a negotiation is never easy, but allowing emotions to take over can make things worse. I've witnessed negotiators lose control, react with anger or frustration, and completely ruin their relationship with the other party.

Strategies for handling defeat with maturity:

- Accept the loss calmly; don't take it personally.
- Analyze the reasons behind the failed agreement to learn something.
- Avoid impulsive reactions or pride-driven moves.

Practical Example: *Once, a major client told me that they preferred working with a competitor. I could have insisted or attempted to discredit the other company, but instead, I inquired about what influenced their decision. I discovered it was a detail I could improve in my service. Six months later, the client returned, dissatisfied with the competitor, and I closed the deal on my terms.*

THE POWER OF "NO" AS A TOOL OF STRENGTH

Saying "no" might seem like a loss, but it's actually one of the most powerful tools in negotiation. Accepting any condition just to close a deal can be a costly mistake.

When to say "no" in a negotiation:

- If the required compromise is too damaging.
- If the terms jeopardize the sustainability of your business.
- If you have better alternatives.

Practical Example: *I once declined an offer from a distributor who proposed overly aggressive terms. At the time, it seemed like a missed opportunity, but a few months later, another partner offered me much more favorable conditions.*

TURNING FAILURE INTO OPPORTUNITY

Every unsuccessful negotiation presents an opportunity for growth.

Mistakes teach more lessons than victories and help you create better strategies for the future.

How to turn a loss into an opportunity:

- Analyze what went wrong and consider what you could have done differently.
- Study the other party's strategy and extract valuable insights.
- Build an improvement plan for future improvement negotiations.

Practical Example: *After losing an important deal, I took detailed notes on how it unfolded. I realized that my biggest mistake was not having solid alternatives to propose. Since then, I always arrive at the table with at least two options in every negotiation.*

IN SUMMARY

Understanding how to lose a negotiation is just as crucial as knowing how to win one.

Intelligently accepting defeat, managing emotions, and maintaining a strategic mindset can turn a failed negotiation into a springboard for future success.

Not every win is immediate; sometimes, the true victory lies in knowing when to wait for the right moment and being prepared for the next round.

11 HOW TO SELL

When I began my entrepreneurial journey, I never took the time to appreciate the power of a simple smile. I thought success was based entirely on preparation, strategy, and flawless execution. However, as time passed, I understood that a positive attitude, even a sincere smile, could open more doors than any diploma or business card.

THE POWER OF A SMILE IN RELATIONSHIPS

One of the first lessons I learned when I started working in advertising and film was that "People don't just buy a product; they buy you." This statement could not be truer. First impressions are crucial, and nothing fosters empathy and trust like a genuine smile.

I recall a particular anecdote: I was trying to close a deal with an important client, but he seemed distant, even annoyed. I realized my approach was too formal and stiff. Instead of continuing with my usual pitch, I made a light-hearted joke and smiled. The tension instantly vanished. From that moment on, the conversation felt more natural, and in the end, we sealed the deal.

That day, I understood that a smile is a universal language capable of profoundly connecting people.

SMILING AND PROFESSIONAL SUCCESS

Over the years, I've met numerous successful entrepreneurs and professionals, and nearly all share a common trait: the ability to smile, even in stressful situations.

A smile conveys confidence, leadership, and openness.

At a networking event in London, I found myself talking with a prominent investor. I felt nervous, aware that it was a rare opportunity. However, instead of diving straight into numbers and statistics, I began with a smile and a relaxed approach. At the end of our conversation, he remarked, *"I like your attitude; it's evident you truly believe in what you're doing."*

That marked the start of a fruitful collaboration.

THE HEALTH AND WELLNESS BENEFITS OF SMILING

Smiling isn't just good for business but also for your health.

I've experienced periods of overwhelming stress, such as looming deadlines, bills to pay, and projects that wouldn't take off. In those moments, my face reflected what I felt: tension, worry, and fatigue.

One day, when I was lost in negative thoughts, a friend said, *"Try smiling, even if you don't feel like it."*

It sounded like a cliché, but I decided to give it a try. The simple act of smiling triggered a chain reaction in my brain: I felt less tense, more focused, and better equipped to handle challenges with a fresh perspective. From then on, I began using smiling as a tool to maintain control, reduce stress, and enhance my overall well-being.

SMILING EVEN IN DIFFICULT TIMES

Don't get me wrong; I'm not saying you should ignore problems or pretend everything is fine when it's not. Yet, I've learned that facing challenges with a positive attitude helps you overcome them more easily.

Years ago, when one of my businesses wasn't going as planned, I had to attend a meeting with some unhappy clients. I could have walked in with a stern face, ready to defend myself, but I chose a different approach: I smiled, listened, and offered solutions instead of excuses.

That day, I realized that how we confront difficulties determines our success and the respect we earn from others.

HOW TO MAKE SMILING A HABIT

Smiling shouldn't be a once-in-a-while act but an essential part of who we are. I've adopted a few techniques to help me stay positive:

- **Start the day with a smile** – Every morning, look in the mirror and smile. It might feel silly, but it genuinely helps.
- **Find humor in situations** – Even during tough times, there's always something to laugh about.
- **Surround yourself with positive people** – Avoid constant complainers and seek out those who radiate positive energy.
- **Share your smiles with others** – Smiling is contagious. The more you smile, the more smiles you'll receive in return.

If there's one thing I've learned in my career, it's this: a smile is a powerful tool that can transform situations, create opportunities, and improve your quality of life.

It costs nothing yet is worth so much. So why not use it more often?

THE FIRST MEETING WITH A CLIENT: HOW TO CREATE A REAL CONNECTION

I've always believed that the first meeting with a client is a defining moment. It's not just about selling a product or service; it's about building a relationship based on trust. I learned this lesson firsthand after several unsuccessful meetings early in my career.

I often focused too much on my offer, on the numbers and product features, without realizing that what truly matters is the human connection.

The client wants to feel understood, heard, and valued. If we can create a genuine bond, the sale will naturally follow.

CREATING A CLIMATE OF RAPPORT AND TRUST

Once, I met with a client I just couldn't connect with.

I talked and explained my proposal, but he seemed distant. Then, I changed my approach: instead of discussing the product, I asked about his experiences in the industry. That simple shift was enough to make him open up and develop a more natural relationship.

How to create rapport with a client:

- **Show genuine interest** – Ask questions to understand their perspectives and needs.
- **Find common ground** – Even a small detail can create empathy.
- **Be authentic** – Avoid using canned phrases. People can quickly sense whether you're being sincere.

Practical Exercise: The next time you meet a client, try to learn at least one thing about their life that you can relate to.

USING OPEN-ENDED QUESTIONS

One of the most effective techniques for engaging a client is asking open-ended questions. I've seen the difference myself. When I used to ask, *"Are you interested in this product?"* I often got short, closed responses. But when I said, *"Tell me more about your needs and what you're looking for,"* the conversation became much richer and more constructive.

Examples of open-ended questions:

- "What motivates you to seek this solution?"
- "What is most important to you in this situation?"
- "Please share more about your experience in the industry."

Practical Exercise: During your next meeting with a client, avoid closed-ended questions and use open-ended questions to encourage dialogue.

ACTIVE LISTENING: THE KEY TO WINNING THE CLIENT

The first time I understood the importance of active listening was during a meeting with a particularly skeptical client. Instead of interrupting or trying to persuade him immediately, I simply listened attentively, nodding and asking focused questions.

At the end, he said, "I appreciate how well you listen. You're one of the few who doesn't try to sell me something right away." That phrase resonated with me.

How to practice active listening:

- **Avoid interrupting** – Let the client fully express themselves.
- **Repeat and summarize** – This confirms you understood correctly.
- **Ask targeted questions** – Show that you got the point.

Practical Exercise: In your next interaction, repeat the client's key phrase and inquire if you understood it correctly.

NON-VERBAL COMMUNICATION: BODY LANGUAGE MATTERS

Body language is powerful. I've learned that maintaining good eye contact, smiling, and keeping an open posture can greatly affect how others perceive us.

Key elements:

- **Genuine smile** – Creates instant empathy.
- **Eye contact** – Shows confidence and attention.
- **Open posture** – Avoid crossing arms or looking stiff.

- **Positive tone of voice** – How you speak matters as much as what you say.

Practical Exercise: The next time you meet with a client, pay attention to your body language and observe how the client responds.

THE FIRST MINUTE IS CRUCIAL

They say first impressions matter, and it's true. I've had meetings where I lost everything in the first 30 seconds due to a rushed or insecure approach.

How to create a strong impact in the first seconds:

- **Stay relaxed and confident** – Anxiety is noticeable.
- **Show enthusiasm** – The client needs to feel that you genuinely want to help.
- **Use their name** – Personalize the conversation from the start.

Practical Exercise: In your next meetings, focus on the first 60 seconds and aim to make them as welcoming and positive as possible.

HOW TO HANDLE DIFFICULT CLIENTS

Not every client is straightforward. I recall a time when one client was particularly skeptical and distrustful. I remained calm, listened attentively to his concerns, and addressed them with facts. Ultimately, he was convinced.

Strategies for dealing with difficult clients:

- **Don't react emotionally** – Stay calm and professional.
- **Ask questions to understand better** – Resistance often comes from a negative past experience.
- **Show empathy** – Let the client know you understand them.
- **Offer concrete solutions** – Demonstrate the value of your offer with facts.

Practical Exercise: If you encounter a challenging client, consider using these techniques and see if their attitude shifts.

ENDING THE FIRST MEETING WITH A MEMORABLE EXPERIENCE

First impressions matter, but final impressions are just as important. I've learned that ending the meeting right can be the difference between a client who comes back and one who forgets about us.
How to conclude effectively:

- Always thank them for their time.
- Summarize the key points of the conversation.
- Suggest the next step: a follow-up or a clear action.

Practical Exercise: At the end of your next client interaction, summarize the main points and leave a positive impression with a friendly closing gesture.

The first approach with a client can define the entire business relationship.
The key ingredients for a successful meeting are creating rapport, listening actively, using effective communication, and conveying trust.
A satisfied client won't just buy from you; they'll speak well of you and return with confidence. The quality of your first interactions shapes the future of your relationship.

Remember: A happy client is your business's best ambassador. Start every interaction on the right foot!

PRESENTING THE PRODUCT: THE DEFINING MOMENT

After establishing a connection with the client and building trust, the crucial moment arrives: presenting your product or service. This is the point at which the client needs to understand the real value of what you offer and see how it can solve their problems or improve their lives.

Early in my career, I made the classic mistake many people make: I got lost in the product's technical features, listing them as if they were the most important thing in the world.

The truth? Clients don't care how many megabytes, inches, or algorithms are behind a product. They want to know how it can simplify their life, save them time, or increase their income. I realized that selling isn't about explaining; it's about telling a story the client can relate to.

SELL BENEFITS, NOT FEATURES

One of the most common mistakes is focusing on technical specifications instead of highlighting the real benefits for the client.
Practical Example:

- *"This camera features a 50-megapixel sensor."*
- *"With this camera, you can capture sharp, detailed images even in low light, turning every moment into a perfect memory."*

Practical Exercise: Choose a product or service you offer and rewrite its description by turning features into benefits for the client.

TELLING A COMPELLING STORY

People don't remember facts and figures; they remember stories and emotions. Here's how to structure an effective presentation:

- **The problem:** Describe a situation your client might face.
- **The solution:** Show how your product solves that problem.
- **The positive result:** Explain the benefit the client will gain from your product.

Practical Example: *"Have you ever missed an important opportunity* *because you didn't have a ready presentation? With our software, you can design professional slides in just minutes, no graphic design skills required."*

Practical Exercise: Write a short story that highlights a typical client issue and how your product resolves it.

PERSONALIZING THE PRESENTATION

Every client is different and has specific needs. To make your presentation more effective:

- **Listen before you speak** – Understand the client's true needs before presenting the product.
- **Customize your pitch** – Avoid generic explanations and tailor your presentation to their specific situation.
- **Use concrete examples** – Mention similar cases that demonstrate how your product has helped others.

Practical Exercise: The next time you present a product, begin by asking the client about their main challenges. Then, customize your explanation accordingly.

USING CLEAR AND ACCESSIBLE LANGUAGE

Salespeople often use technical jargon that confuses instead of persuading. The rule is simple: **speak as you would to a friend**.

Rules for effective communication:

- **Avoid technical jargon** – Use simple, understandable language.
- **Use practical examples** – Help the client visualize how to use the product.
- **Be direct and concise** – Too many details are boring and confusing.

Practical Exercise: Consider explaining your product or service to a 10-year-old. If you can do it clearly, your communication is effective.

ENGAGING THE CLIENT WITH A DEMONSTRATION

Observing the product in action is the most effective way to show its value.

Ways to engage the client:

- **Live demo** – If possible, show the product in use.
- **Free trial** – If you offer a service, let them test it risk-free.
- **Testimonials** – Share examples of satisfied customers.

Practical Example: *"Let me show you in 30 seconds how our software can save you an hour of work every day. You'll see the difference immediately!"*

Practical Exercise: Find a way to let clients try your product without requiring a major initial commitment.

ANTICIPATING OBJECTIONS AND RESPONDING WITH CONFIDENCE

When you introduce a product, it's natural for the client to have doubts. Instead of avoiding them, address them with confidence and transparency.

Common objections and how to respond:

- **"It's too expensive"** → "Considering the money you might lose without this solution, it's an investment that pays off in the long run."
- **"I'm unsure if it's right for me"** → "I totally understand! That's why we offer a free trial; you can test it with no risk."
- **"I don't have time to learn how to use it"** → "It only takes 5 minutes to get started, and we'll guide you through it step by step."

Practical Exercise: Make a list of the most common objections your clients might have and prepare clear, convincing responses for each one.

ENDING WITH A CLEAR CALL TO ACTION

After presenting the product, it's essential to guide the client toward the next step, don't leave them wondering what to do next.

How to close your presentation effectively:

- **Recap the key benefits** – Remind the client why this product is the ideal solution for them.
- **Give a clear call to action** – Ask directly for what you want them to do: "Would you like to try it now?"
- **Create a sense of urgency** – Offer a limited-time incentive, such as a discount or bonus.

Practical Example: *"This exclusive offer is valid only until tomorrow. Would you like to take advantage of it now?"*

Practical Exercise: Rewrite your sales closing to include a clear and motivating call to action.

Presenting a product the right way isn't just about describing it; it's about helping the client perceive its value and understand how it can improve their life.

If we learn to tell a compelling story, personalize the pitch, and actively involve the client, we significantly increase our chances of success.

Remember: Don't sell a product. Sell a result, an emotion, a solution.

PERSUADING WITHOUT PRESSURE

After introducing the product, the crucial moment arrives: helping the client feel that it's the right choice. Persuasion doesn't come from pressure; it comes from showing, with concrete facts, that what you offer can improve one's life.

Early in my career, I made a common mistake: I was so excited about my product that I overwhelmed clients with words and technical details. It was clear that my offer was great, but I didn't realize that selling is never merely logical. People want to feel that they're making the right choice, not being pushed into one. Only when I started focusing on how my product could truly help them, without pressure or unnecessary jargon, did I notice a significant improvement in results.

CREATING A VALUABLE EXPERIENCE FOR THE CLIENT

The client should feel that their decision isn't just a purchase but an investment in their well-being or success.

Instead of focusing only on the product, I learned to shift the attention to the overall experience it creates.

Strategies to create value:

- **Get them involved in the conversation** – Help them imagine what life will be like after using your product.
- **Show real examples** – Talk about other clients who have benefited from making the same choice.
- **Appeal to emotion** – People decide more based on emotion than logic.

Practical Example: *Once, I sold a service to a client simply by saying: 'Imagine managing your business promotion with less stress and more efficiency. This tool is designed to give you more free time without sacrificing work quality.'*

That was exactly what he needed to hear, articulated in a way that helped him visualize the outcome, rather than just the functionality.

REMOVING CLIENT DOUBTS

Many clients hesitate due to unresolved doubts. Addressing those doubts directly will help them decide, demonstrating that you have already considered their concerns.

How to overcome hesitation:

- **Anticipate common questions** – Provide answers before customers ask them.
- **Offer quality guarantees** – A satisfaction policy, return options, or post-sale support can build trust.
- **Be transparent** – Avoid exaggerated promises; stick to honest facts.

Practical Example: *One client once told me, 'I'm afraid this service might not be right for me.' Instead of arguing, I said: 'I understand your concern, that's why we offer a full 30-day money-back guarantee. We want you to be 100% satisfied.'*

To be honest, I improvised that; it wasn't part of the original deal. But in that moment, the client realized they had nothing to lose and agreed to it.

CREATING A SENSE OF URGENCY

Sometimes, the client may be convinced yet still postpone the decision because they feel no urgency. You can gently encourage immediate action without being pushy.

Strategies to inspire action:

- **Limited-time offers** – Bonuses or incentives for immediate decisions.
- **Exclusivity** – Emphasize if the product is in limited supply.

- **Highlight the cost of inaction** – Clarify what the client could lose by waiting.

One trick I've learned over time is to set a deadline without making it sound like a marketing gimmick: "This offer is valid for 48 hours. If you want to maximize your benefits, now is the perfect time to act!"

It's not pressure; it's a genuine opportunity that motivates the client to take action.

REINFORCING THE CLIENT'S CONFIDENCE

Even when a client is about to say yes, they may require one final confirmation to feel fully secure.

How to reinforce decision-making confidence:

- Offer a no-risk option – If possible, include a free trial or guarantee.
- Emphasize it's more than just a transaction – Assure them that support will continue after the sale.
- Personalize the closing – Customize your final message to meet their specific needs.

Practical Example: *Once, a client asked me, 'What if I have questions after I buy?' I replied, 'I'm always available to support you, even after the purchase. If you have any doubts or questions, you can count on me.'*

That straightforward detail provided him the reassurance he needed, allowing him to close the deal without hesitation.

Convincing a client doesn't mean pushing them; it means helping them make the best decision for themselves.

When you can convey trust, address doubts, and encourage action, you create the ideal conditions for an informed and confident choice.

Remember: A client who is convinced today becomes a loyal customer tomorrow. In the long run, a loyal customer is worth significantly more than a one-time sale.

THE CLOSE: FROM INTEREST TO DECISION

Closing a sale doesn't simply mean finalizing a transaction. It's the moment when the customer chooses to trust you, your product, and the value you've communicated. I've learned that closing is much more than a commercial act; it's the beginning of a relationship. When handled correctly, it leads to satisfied customers who return and speak highly of you.

At the beginning of my career, I was afraid of "pushing" the customer. I thought that insisting meant applying pressure and that the customer should make their own decision. However, I came to realize that passively waiting is not a winning strategy. People need guidance, reassurance, and support to make the final step. If you don't take action, chances are no one else will.

THE RIGHT TIME TO CLOSE

Knowing when to close is crucial. There are signals that indicate the customer is ready:

- They ask specific questions about price, guarantees, or purchasing options.
- They show genuine interest in how the product can help them.
- They express excitement or make positive comments about the value of your offer.

If you notice these signals, don't wait for the customer to ask how to buy. Take the initiative and close the sale naturally and confidently.

Practical Example: *"I can see that this product perfectly meets your needs. Would you like to proceed with the basic version, or would you prefer the advanced package?"*

OFFERING CLEAR AND PERSONALIZED OPTIONS

People tend to postpone decisions when faced with too many options or when it's unclear what's best for them. However, customers are more likely to say "yes" when presented with clear and well-defined choices.

How to structure your purchase options:

- Present two or three alternatives with different features and prices.
- Offer personalized solutions based on the customer's specific needs.
- Make the purchase simple and straightforward by avoiding complex steps.

Practical Example: *"You can choose the standard plan, ideal for getting started, or the premium option, which provides additional features to maximize the benefits. Which one do you prefer?"*

USING THE RIGHT LANGUAGE TO REINFORCE THE DECISION

Words significantly influence the customer's final decision. Positive and engaging language helps customers feel confident in their choice.

Effective closing phrases:

- "Imagine how this product will improve your daily life."
- "We're confident this solution will deliver excellent results."
- "By choosing this option, you've taken a step forward toward your goal."

Avoid uncertain expressions such as "I hope you like it" or "If you'd like to think about it," as they may create doubts in the buyer's mind.

OVERCOMING FINAL HESITATIONS

Even when everything appears to be going well, some customers hesitate before making their final decision. Your role is to reassure them without putting any pressure on them.

Strategies to handle last-minute doubts:

- **Ask what's holding them back** – Understanding the obstacle allows you to address it directly.
- **Emphasize the benefits** – Remind the customer of the key advantages.
- **Offer a guarantee or post-sale support** – This removes any perceived risk.

Practical Example: *"I understand that you want to be sure about your choice. Just a reminder, we offer free assistance, and if you ever need support, we're always here for you."*

MAKING THE PURCHASE A POSITIVE EXPERIENCE

The sale doesn't end with the payment. It's the first step in building a relationship with the customer. An effective close should leave a positive impression and reinforce the customer's confidence that they made the right choice.

What to do after the close:

- Thank the customer for their trust.
- Offer clear guidance on what to expect next.
- Reassure them that you will be available for any future inquiries or concerns.

Practical Example: *"Thank you for choosing our product! If you need any support, feel free to contact us. We'll send you all the necessary information shortly."*

Closing a sale is more than just the conclusion of a transaction; it's the start of a trust-based relationship with the customer.

When customers feel value, security, and a positive experience, they are more inclined to return and recommend you to others.

Remember: Closing a sale isn't about being aggressive; it's about guiding the customer to make the best decision. When this process is handled with care, the customer doesn't just make a purchase; they become a spontaneous promoter of your product or service.

IN SUMMARY

Learning always to smile, establishing a positive initial approach with the customer, introducing the product, persuading effectively, and closing with confidence are key elements for succeeding in sales interactions.

Building genuine connections, communicating effectively, and positively influencing customer decisions are essential skills for achieving great results. Always remember: a smile is a key that opens many doors, and caring for the customer is priority number one. Master these skills, and you'll be able to forge successful relationships that help you achieve your goals.

12 HOW TO MANAGE MONEY

Effective money management is a crucial skill for achieving success in life. In this chapter, we'll explore three essential aspects of financial management: how to handle your finances, the importance of saving money, and how to use the most advantageous financial tools, such as credit cards, wisely.

HOW TO MANAGE YOUR MONEY SMARTLY

One of the most common mistakes I see people make, and that I've made myself, is believing that earning money alone ensures financial security. In reality, the true challenge begins after you receive your income: how you manage it, invest it, and grow it over time.

For years, I underestimated the importance of strategic money management. I made poor investments, overspent on low-return projects, and at times, had to roll up my sleeves to recover. However, those mistakes taught me valuable lessons that I now want to share.

SETTING CLEAR FINANCIAL GOALS

An effective financial plan always begins with well-defined goals.

- **Short-term goals** – For example, building an emergency fund or saving for a trip.
- **Mid-term goals** – Accumulating capital for a real estate investment or growing a business.
- **Long-term goals** – Building wealth, securing a safe retirement, or achieving financial independence.

Practical Example: *When I decided to launch my first company, I knew I'd need startup capital. I set a clear goal: save €50,000 in two years by cutting unnecessary expenses and diversifying my income streams.*

Practical Exercise: Write down three financial goals (one short, one mid, and one long-term), and define an immediate action to get started.

CREATING A FUNCTIONAL BUDGET

One of the best decisions I've ever made was to start tracking my income and expenses. Before then, each month felt like a mystery: I was earning well but had no idea where my money went.

Here's an effective method to manage your budget:

- **Track your income and expenses**: Knowing where your money goes is the first step to better control.
- **Apply the 50/30/20 rule:**
  - 50% for essential expenses (rent, bills, food).
  - 30% for personal spending (hobbies, travel, leisure).
  - 20% for savings and investments.
- **Cut unnecessary expenses**: If it doesn't add value to your life or future, it's likely not worth it.

Practical Example: *I once realized I was spending over €500 a month on* *breakfasts and meals out. After reviewing my budget, I halved that amount and redirected those funds toward more productive investments.*

Practical Exercise: Review your expenses from the last three months and identify three categories where you can cut costs without sacrificing quality of life.

DIVERSIFYING INVESTMENTS TO MINIMIZE RISK

One mistake I've made repeatedly is investing too much money in a single opportunity. One time, I put all my spare capital into one project without exploring alternatives. When that project faced delays, I found myself without liquidity.

Here are some asset classes to consider:

- **Stocks** – Good long-term returns, but volatile.
- **Bonds** – Safer, but with lower yields.
- **Real Estate** – Great for passive income but requires upfront capital.
- **Precious Metals** – A safe haven during economic uncertainty.
- **Cryptocurrencies** – High potential returns, but very risky.

Practical Example: *After my unfortunate experience with a single investment, I decided to diversify. Now, the majority of my investments are in intellectual property rights, some are in real estate, and I have a small budget allocated to innovative startups.*

Practical Exercise: Review your current portfolio to ensure you have adequate diversification across various asset classes.

MONITORING AND OPTIMIZING YOUR PORTFOLIO

A common misconception is that investing is a one-time action. However, the market changes, opportunities evolve, and your strategy should, too.

What to do:

- **Check performance regularly** – At least once a month.
- **Rebalance your portfolio as needed** – If one asset increases significantly compared to others, consider rebalancing.
- **Stay updated on financial news** – A good investor stays informed at all times.

Practical Example: *If the stock market is booming and your portfolio is overly concentrated in stocks, think about selling a portion of it and reallocating to bonds to balance the risk.*

Practical Exercise: Set a monthly reminder to review your portfolio and make adjustments as needed.

PROTECTING YOUR CAPITAL AGAINST THE UNEXPECTED

While no one can foresee the future, you can shield yourself from unexpected financial challenges with straightforward strategies:

- **Emergency funds:** Maintain a liquid account with at least 3 to 6 months' worth of expenses.
- **Insurance:** Protect your assets with appropriate coverage.
- **Avoid overly speculative investments:** Always calculate your risk carefully.

Practical Example: *A close friend of mine invested all his money in crypto without having an emergency fund. When the markets crashed, he had to sell at a loss to cover unexpected expenses. I, however, had a separate fund and was able to ride out the downturn without panicking.*

Practical Exercise: Check if your emergency fund is enough to cover at least three months of essential expenses.

Money management is not just about earning; it's about strategy.

I've learned firsthand that without a solid financial plan, even a high income can vanish quickly.

- Set clear goals and track your progress.
- Create a budget to maintain control over your spending and increase your investable capital.
- Diversify your portfolio to mitigate risks and maximize opportunities.
- Protect your capital so you can face the unexpected without stress.

Remember: Money works for those who manage it wisely. Be ready to make it work for you!

MONEY SAVED IS MONEY EARNED

Many people believe financial success depends solely on income. Early in my career, I was convinced that increasing my earnings was the only way to be financially secure. But I learned the hard way that earning a lot isn't enough; you also need to know how to manage that money.

Saving doesn't mean living in deprivation; it means making smart choices to optimize spending and grow your capital. One euro saved today can turn into ten euros tomorrow if invested wisely.

BUILDING AN EMERGENCY FUND FOR FINANCIAL SECURITY

One of the biggest mistakes I made early on was not having an emergency fund. When a client left me hanging with a large unpaid invoice, I found myself in a tight spot and had to take underpaid jobs just to cover my expenses.

How much should you set aside?

- Minimum 3–6 months of essential expenses (rent, bills, food, insurance).

- If you have variable income or are self-employed, aim for a 6–12 months cushion.

Where to keep your emergency fund?

- **High-liquidity savings account** – Easily accessible in case of urgent needs.
- Low-risk instruments like certificates of deposit or money market funds.

Practical Example: *If your monthly living expenses are €2,000, you should build an emergency fund of at least €6,000 to €12,000 to handle unexpected situations without worry.*

Practical Exercise: Determine your average monthly expenses and set your emergency fund goal.

CUTTING UNNECESSARY SPENDING AND STOPPING MONEY WASTE

It's not about how much you earn but how much you keep that truly matters. I speak from experience: for years, I spent money without realizing it on things I didn't need, and by the end of the month, I'd wonder where all my income had gone.

- **Review your monthly budget** – Identify recurring expenses and spot the ones you can cut.
- **Avoid impulse purchases** – Wait 24 hours before making non-essential purchases.
- **Reassess subscriptions and unused services** – Cancel what you don't use or find more affordable alternatives.
- **Replace costly habits with smarter alternatives** – Cook at home instead of dining out, use public transportation whenever possible, and invest in quality items that last longer.

Practical Example: *By eliminating two €2 coffees a day at a café, you can save approximately $1,460 a year. If you invest that amount, it could grow to €15,000 over the course of ten years.*

Practical Exercise: Create a list of your unnecessary expenses and choose three items to reduce or eliminate this month.

AUTOMATING SAVINGS TO BUILD WEALTH EFFORTLESSLY

The key to consistently saving is to resist the temptation to spend everything you have. One trick I adopted was setting up an automatic monthly transfer from my checking account to a savings account.

Practical Example: *If you transfer €200 to a savings fund each month, in five years, you'll have saved €12,000 almost without realizing it.*

Practical Exercise: Set up an automatic transfer to your savings account today.

WATCH OUT FOR SMALL EXPENSES: THE DRIP EFFECT

Regular small expenses accumulate and can secretly drain your budget.

- **Track all expenses for a month** – Analyze your habits and spot unnecessary spending.
- **Avoid daily micro-spending** – Coffee, snacks, and impulse buys are hidden costs.
- **Look for cheaper alternatives** – Buy in bulk, use loyalty cards, and compare prices before making a purchase.

Practical Example: *If you spend €5 a day on unnecessary items, that's more than €1,800 wasted in a year, money you could invest or use for more meaningful experiences.*

Practical Exercise: Track every small expense for one week and calculate how much you could save by eliminating unnecessary ones.

SAVING DOESN'T MEAN SACRIFICING QUALITY

- Many supermarkets and stores offer rewards and discounts to loyal customers.
- Many retailers and platforms run special promotions that can significantly lower purchase costs.
- Black Friday, end-of-season sales, Prime Day, plan your purchases to maximize savings.

Practical Example: *If you buy a new laptop at 40% off during Black Friday, the money you save could allow you also to purchase professional software to improve your work.*

Practical Exercise: Download a cashback app or compare prices for what you need to buy to find the best deal.

Saving is the foundation of financial freedom. Every euro you save and invest today can work for you in the future.

- Build an emergency fund to protect yourself from the unexpected.
- Cut unnecessary expenses and become more aware of your spending habits.
- Automate your savings to build wealth effortlessly.
- Be conscious of small expenses and take advantage of every opportunity to save.

Remember: Saving doesn't mean depriving yourself; it means investing in your future. Let your money work smarter!

TAKE ADVANTAGE OF LOYALTY PROGRAMS, CASHBACK, AND REWARDS

Using credit cards strategically can help you earn money through rewards and benefits.

Most common types of rewards:

- **Cashback:** A percentage of your spending is refunded directly to your account.
- **Loyalty points:** Accumulated through purchases and redeemable for gifts or discounts.
- **Airline miles:** Perfect for frequent travelers; they can earn free flights or upgrades.
- **Exclusive discounts:** Some cards provide access to events, special deals, or free insurance.

How to maximize the benefits:

- Use your card for daily expenses (bills, groceries, fuel).
- Choose a card that provides benefits that match your lifestyle.
- Check your card's exclusive offers and partnerships to maximize value.

Practical Example: *If your card offers 3% cashback on grocery shopping and you spend €400 a month, you'll earn €12 in cashback each month, which totals €144 a year in automatic savings.*

Practical Exercise: Check your current card's cashback and reward options to discover how you can maximize their benefits.

HOW TO USE CREDIT CARDS TO YOUR ADVANTAGE

Credit cards are often seen as risky debt tools, but they can become powerful financial allies when used strategically. They can help you manage cash flow, earn rewards, boost your credit score, and even save money through cashback and perks.

However, using them without a clear strategy can lead to high-interest charges, overwhelming debt, and poor financial decisions. When I received my first credit card, I thought I could use it freely without consequences until I found myself with a balance that I struggled to repay. That experience taught me discipline and how to transform a credit card from a liability into a valuable tool.

CHOOSING THE RIGHT CREDIT CARD

Not all credit cards are equal. The best card for you depends on your lifestyle and financial objectives.

What to consider when choosing a credit card:

- **Interest rate (APR)** – This becomes a critical factor if you don't pay your full balance monthly.
- **Annual fees** – Some cards offer exclusive perks but charge high annual fees.
- **Rewards and cashback programs** – Choose cards that reward you based on your typical spending.
- **Insurance and perks** – Some cards include travel insurance, purchase protection, or airport lounge access.
- **Credit limit and flexibility** – Consider interest-free installment plans' spending limit and options.

Practical Example: *If you travel frequently, a card that earns miles and offers lounge access might be more beneficial than a standard cashback card. If you shop online regularly, a card with purchase protection and fraud reimbursement will provide enhanced security.*

Practical Exercise: Review your monthly expenses and choose a card that optimizes your benefits according to your spending habits.

USING CREDIT CARDS RESPONSIBLY

A credit card can be a double-edged sword. However, using it with discipline can help you avoid financial trouble and improve your money management.

Rules for responsible use:

- Always pay the full balance each month to avoid high-interest charges.
- Avoid using the card for non-essential expenses unless you have the funds to cover them.
- Maintain a low credit utilization ratio: use less than 30% of your available limit to ensure a good credit score.
- Don't use your card for cash withdrawals: credit card cash advances incur much higher fees than standard ATM withdrawals.

Practical Example: *If your card has a €5,000 limit, try to keep your usage below €1,500 to enhance your credit score and show responsible financial management.*

Practical Exercise: Set a weekly reminder to check your card balance and prevent any unpleasant surprises at the end of the month.

MONITORING TRANSACTIONS AND UNDERSTANDING YOUR CARD TERMS

Ineffective credit card management can be expensive. Regularly monitoring your transactions helps you to prevent problems.

Habits to adopt:

- Check your balance at least once a week.
- Always read your card's terms to avoid hidden fees.
- Set spending alerts to track your activity and be notified of any suspicious transactions.

- If you use your card abroad, always verify the exchange rate. Some cards charge high fees for international transactions.

Practical Example: *If you notice a suspicious transaction on your card, contact your bank immediately to prevent any fraud and ask for a refund.*

Practical Exercise: Enable spending alerts on your account today to receive notifications for every transaction made with your card.

AVOIDING OVER-INDEBTEDNESS AND CREDIT RISK

The biggest danger of credit cards is the risk of racking up more debt than you can afford.

Strategies to avoid financial trouble:

- Don't spend more than you earn: only use the card for purchases you can pay off right away.
- Avoid having more credit cards than necessary: too many cards can encourage overspending.
- If you struggle to pay off your balance, reduce card use and reassess your budget.
- Don't use the card to consolidate other debts without a clear repayment strategy.

Practical Example: *If you accumulate €5,000 in debt on a card with a 20% interest rate and only make minimum payments, it could take you years to pay it off and cost you significantly more in interest.*

Practical Exercise: Examine your credit card usage and, if necessary, reduce spending to prevent accumulating debt.

Credit cards can be powerful financial tools if used wisely.

- Choose a card that suits your lifestyle and financial needs.
- Use it responsibly and steer clear of unnecessary debt.

- Maximize rewards and perks to gain extra value from your spending.
- Keep an eye on transactions and always read the fine print to avoid hidden fees.

Remember: When used responsibly, a credit card can be a powerful tool for managing finances.

IN SUMMARY

Financial management is a crucial pillar of success in life. Learning to manage your portfolio, save money, and use the best financial tools provides a solid foundation for achieving your goals.

Remember that managing your finances requires planning, discipline, and consistent attention. Set clear financial goals, create a budget that allows you to save, and diversify your investments to maximize your profit potential.

Money saved is money earned. Use automation to save consistently and reduce unnecessary expenses. Pay attention to daily small costs, and take advantage of deals and coupons to get the most value out of your money.

When it comes to credit cards, choose the one that suits your needs and use it responsibly. Leverage rewards and loyalty programs, keep a close eye on your transactions, avoid excessive debt, and maintain a healthy credit utilization ratio.

Take the time to understand basic financial concepts and proactively apply them in your daily life. Financial management is an ongoing process that requires continuous commitment, but the results are well worth the effort.

Stay determined, focused, and disciplined in your pursuit of financial success. By practicing strong financial management, you'll create a stable foundation for achieving your dreams and thriving in life.

13 HOW TO INVEST MONEY

Financial challenges are a constant in everyone's life, but we can overcome them and achieve success through smart investments and intelligent strategies. In this chapter, we'll explore key topics that will help you understand which investments are the most profitable and secure, how to assess risk, the importance of diversification, and the opportunities offered by both passive and active investing. We'll also examine how bank credit can be used to generate profit rather than just to purchase a home to live in.

Investing is one of the most effective ways to build wealth and ensure long-term financial stability. However, I've learned the hard way that it's not enough to jump into the promising first investment. I've made mistakes and taken wrong turns, but I've also had successes that taught me valuable lessons.

If there's one thing I've learned, it's that achieving high returns requires a clear strategy, diversification, and the wisdom to know when to take risks and when to wait. Let's explore some of the most profitable investment options and how to identify the best opportunities while minimizing risk.

INVESTING IN REAL ESTATE

When done right, real estate offers security and steady returns. When purchasing a property to rent out, avoid common mistakes. Don't underestimate maintenance costs, carefully consider the location, and never ignore taxes, which, if calculated later, could significantly impact your returns. Invest with awareness.

Types of real estate investments:

- **Residential rentals** for consistent passive income.
- **House flipping**: buying, renovating, and reselling properties.
- **Investing in land** in developing areas.

Practical Example: *I purchased a property in a growing city and rented it out to generate a steady income. Over the years, the property's value increased, and now I can sell it for a significant profit.*

Practical Exercise: Examine the real estate market in your city or an area you are familiar with, and identify a neighborhood with considerable growth potential.

NEW TECHNOLOGIES AND EMERGING MARKETS

One sector that intrigues me is emerging technology. I've witnessed unknown startups transform into global giants in just a few years.

Where to invest today:

- **Artificial intelligence and automation**: have applications in every industry.
- **Blockchain and cryptocurrencies**: still an opportunity despite their volatility.
- **Renewable energy**: set for growth during the ecological transition.

Practical Example: *If I had invested in a solar energy company ten years* ago, my capital would have tripled thanks to the increasing demand for sustainable energy sources.

Practical Exercise: Identify an emerging technology and investigate its potential over the next five years.

INVESTING IN YOURSELF: THE BEST INVESTMENT YOU CAN MAKE

Before investing in real estate, new technologies, or cryptocurrencies, prioritize investing in yourself.

Ways to do it:

- Take training courses to improve your skills.
- Start your own business.
- Expand your network to increase opportunities.

Practical Example: *Reading books, listening to real-world stories and advice about finance and investing helped me avoid costly mistakes. "If I had invested in my education earlier, I would have earned significantly more.*

Practical Exercise: Choose one area you wish to improve and invest in a course or learning experience.

ASSESSING RISK

Investing means putting your money to work with the goal of generating a return. However, every investment carries risk, and properly assessing that risk is essential for making informed decisions and protecting your capital.

There are no returns without risk, but understanding how to balance risk and reward can make the difference between a smart investment and a reckless gamble.

Main investment categories by risk level:

- **Low risk, low return** – Savings accounts, long-term real estate, and established passive income activities.
- **Moderate risk, medium return** – Investing in businesses, franchises, and commercial properties.
- **High risk, high return** – Startups, new ventures, and emerging sectors like new technologies.

Practical Example: *If I want to invest for stable, long-term income, I might choose low-risk investments such as real estate or established businesses. If I aim for higher returns, I could consider investing in an innovative startup.*

Practical Exercise: Analyze three different investments and classify them according to their risk level and potential return.

DEFINING YOUR RISK TOLERANCE

Not everyone approaches risk the same way. Understanding your personal risk tolerance is essential to avoid impulsive, stressful decisions.

Factors that influence risk tolerance:

- **Age and time horizon** – The more time you have, the more risk you can afford to take on with your investments.
- **Personal financial situation** – If you have solid financial stability, you can consider taking bolder investment risks.
- **Personality and emotional management** – If dealing with risk makes you anxious, it's wiser to adopt more conservative strategies.

Practical Example: *A young entrepreneur with fluctuating income may possess a higher risk tolerance than a retiree who requires financial stability.*

Practical Exercise: Briefly describe your risk profile and specify the types of investments that best align with your characteristics.

ANALYZING INVESTMENT RISK FACTORS

Every investment has variables that can affect its profitability. Knowing and evaluating these factors can help you reduce risk and make better-informed decisions.

Key risk factors to consider:

- **Market risk** – Economic and financial fluctuations can affect investment values.
- **Liquidity risk** – Certain investments, like real estate, can be hard to sell quickly.
- **Company or industry-specific risk** – Internal or external events can impact a business or market's performance.

Practical Example: *When I invest in an innovative startup, I must consider market risk, competition, and how quickly the sector evolves.*

Practical Exercise: Choose one investment and identify at least three risks that could impact its performance.

STRATEGIES TO REDUCE RISK

Although risk can never be completely eliminated, there are strategies that can help manage and reduce it.

Ways to mitigate risk:

- **Diversification** – Spreading capital across different assets mitigates the impact of a single failure.
- **Gradual investment plan** – Investing periodically rather than all at once can buffer against market fluctuations.
- **Research and analysis** – Studying markets, trends, and historical data reduces the risk of impulsive decisions. Don't let emotions drive your choices.

Practical Example: *If I have €10,000 to invest, rather than putting it all* *into one business, I can spread it across various sectors to minimize overall risk.*

Practical Exercise: Review your investment portfolio and assess whether it is adequately diversified.

Maintaining diversified investments helps limit losses during a market crisis. If you invest all your funds in a single asset, you risk losing a significant portion of your capital.

Investing isn't merely about finding the best deal; it's about developing the knowledge and discipline necessary to manage your capital over time.

Remember: The key isn't finding shortcuts, but having a strategy, staying informed, and learning from mistakes. If you want to build wealth, start today with small, concrete steps.

KNOWING WHEN AN INVESTMENT IS TOO RISKY

Not every investment is suitable for everyone. Sometimes, the risks are too high, making it wise to take a step back.

Warning signs of overly risky investments:

- **Promises of high, guaranteed returns** – No legitimate investment can guarantee profits without risk.
- **Lack of transparency** – If you don't understand how it works, it's better not to invest.
- **High volatility without solid fundamentals** – If the value fluctuates excessively without clear reasons, it could be a speculative bubble.

Practical Example: *If an investment looks too good to be true, it likely is. It's wise to conduct thorough research before committing your money.*

Practical Exercise: Investigate an investment you're interested in and look for signs of excessive risk.

Evaluating risk doesn't mean avoiding investments; it means making smart, informed choices.

The key to achieving satisfying returns lies in finding the right balance between risk and opportunity, supported by careful analysis and risk mitigation strategies.

Remember: Smart investing involves understanding risks, preparing to confront them, and transforming them into opportunities for financial growth.

THE SAFEST INVESTMENTS

Investing safely doesn't mean giving up on returns; it's about finding a balance between stability and growth. Before making any investment, it's essential to understand your personal risk tolerance and choose financial instruments that protect your capital while still offering opportunities for profit.

Many people rush into stock market investments simply because they think it's trendy or because they've heard stories of others who got rich from trading. However, investing in stocks can be like playing the lottery, and if you don't know exactly what you're doing, you risk losing more than you gain. It's a field that requires specific knowledge, experience, and, above all, the ability to manage your emotions during uncertain times.

What I find curious is how many people entrust their money to bank advisors, convinced that these "experts" will help them get rich. But think about it: if they were really that good at investing, wouldn't they be rich themselves instead of working for a fixed salary at a bank?

Personally, I prefer to invest in markets I know well, ones that generate steady cash flow. I'm not interested in playing the stock market, hoping a share will rise, especially when it's influenced by unpredictable socio-economic events. Instead, I focus on assets with real value that can provide long-term stability and consistent returns.

If you look around, you'll see investment opportunities everywhere, but you need to learn how to recognize them, from real estate to gold to selected cryptocurrencies like Bitcoin. Yes, they're volatile, but those who believed in Bitcoin and held onto it for years experienced significant value growth. And this wasn't by chance; it's because there's a solid project and technology with immense potential behind it.

If you believe the government will protect your savings, you're on the fast track to losing everything you've accumulated. No financial system is designed to make you wealthy; you need to take control of your money and choices.

Stop viewing investments through the perspective of those who advised you to "keep your savings in the bank and sleep well at night." Safety isn't just about letting your money sit idle; it's about making it work for you in the right sectors. Banks use your money to generate profits for themselves.

Here are some investment options considered safer than others.

GOLD: THE ULTIMATE SAFE HAVEN

Due to historical, economic, and financial factors, gold has long been considered the ultimate safe haven. It is a globally recognized asset that safeguards wealth during times of economic and geopolitical uncertainty.

Since ancient times, gold has been used as both currency and a store of value. Unlike paper currencies, which can be devalued or lose value due to inflation, gold preserves its purchasing power over time.

When central banks print more money, currency value drops, and prices rise (inflation). Gold, however, has a limited supply and cannot be printed or artificially manufactured, which is why it generally maintains or even increases its value during inflationary periods.

National currencies can rapidly lose value during economic crises, wars, and political instability or become entirely worthless. Gold, however, is recognized worldwide as a medium of exchange and consistently has an active market.

Gold is also used in industry, jewelry, and technology. This ongoing demand guarantees its liquidity and facilitates easy conversion into cash when necessary. In contrast to fiat currency, which is controlled by governments and central banks, gold is a tangible asset that cannot be arbitrarily manipulated or devalued by political or economic decisions.

Why invest in gold?

- Protection against inflation and economic uncertainty.
- Stability during financial crises.
- Portfolio diversification to reduce risk.

Ways to invest in gold:

- **Physical gold** (bars, coins): Long-term protection, but with storage costs.
- **Gold ETFs**: Invest in gold without physically holding the metal.
- **Gold mining stocks**: More speculative, but potentially higher returns.

Practical Example: *If you had invested €10,000 in gold in 2000, it would be worth around €91,611 today, which is more than eight times your original investment. Its consistent growth over time demonstrates that it's an excellent tool for protecting wealth.*

Practical Exercise: Examine gold prices from the past 20 years and assess their performance in comparison to other types of investments.

BONDS: FIXED-INCOME INVESTMENTS

Bonds are among the most popular low-risk investment options. They are debt securities issued by governments or companies that provide periodic interest until maturity.

Types of safer bonds:

- **Government bonds** – Issued by national governments, generally considered the safest option.
- **Highly rated corporate bonds** – Issued by strong, reliable companies and associated with low risk.

- **Inflation-linked bonds** – Designed to protect against the loss of purchasing power.

Practical Example: *If I want to invest €10,000 with low risk and achieve a steady return, I could opt for government bonds from a stable country.*

Practical Exercise: Compare returns from different bonds and determine which ones align best with your risk profile.

LOW-RISK MUTUAL FUNDS

Low-risk mutual funds are managed by professionals and invest in a combination of secure assets, including government bonds and high-quality securities.

Advantages:

- **Automatic diversification** to mitigate risk.
- **Professional management** without requiring direct experience.
- **Accessibility and liquidity** for straightforward market entry and exit.

Types of safe mutual funds:

- **Bond funds** – Invest in low-risk bonds.
- **Money market funds** – Invest in short-term, highly liquid instruments.
- **Bond index ETFs** – A cost-effective way to diversify fixed-income investments.

Practical Example: *If I prefer not to monitor the market daily, a bond fund can offer predictable returns with low risk.*

Practical Exercise: Identify three low-risk mutual funds and compare their performance over the past five years.

SAVINGS ACCOUNTS AND FIXED-TERM DEPOSITS

If you don't want to take any risks but still want to earn money, high-yield savings accounts and fixed-term deposits can be a safe choice.

Pros and cons:

- **Zero risk of capital loss.**
- **Guaranteed interest**, although typically lower than other investments.
- **High liquidity for savings accounts.**
- **Much lower long-term returns** compared to alternative investment options.

Practical Example: *If I want to set aside money for emergencies, a savings account with a decent interest rate might be the best solution.*

Practical Exercise: Compare the interest rates offered by different savings accounts and choose the most advantageous option.

WHAT IS THE RIGHT BALANCE BETWEEN SAFETY AND RETURN?

Safe investments protect your capital but often yield lower returns than higher-risk ones. Based on your risk profile, the key is to find a balance between security and growth.

Strategies to balance safety and return:

- Keep a portion of your capital in safe assets (gold, silver, bonds, savings accounts).
- Allocate a percentage to more dynamic investments to achieve better returns.
- Invest part of your capital in real estate and adjust your portfolio over time.

Practical Example: *If I want to protect my capital, I might allocate 40%*

to real estate, 30% to physical gold, and the remaining 30% to more dynamic investments for growing my wealth.

Practical Exercise: Develop a portfolio strategy that balances safety and returns in line with your goals.

Safe investments are a crucial component of any solid financial strategy.

Choosing instruments such as gold, bonds, and low-risk funds can protect your capital without completely sacrificing growth.

Remember: A well-balanced portfolio should offer security, stability, and opportunities for long-term growth. The key is to diversify and maintain a clear strategy without being influenced by emotions or fleeting trends.

WHY DIVERSIFICATION MATTERS IN INVESTING

Investing without a diversification strategy is like walking a tightrope without a safety net. One of the most common mistakes, especially for beginners, is to concentrate all their capital on a single investment or sector. If it works, the gain is significant. If it doesn't, you risk losing everything. I've seen this happen many times.

From personal experience, I know that diversification is key to reducing risk and maximizing long-term returns. By allocating capital across various assets, sectors, and markets, we can stabilize our portfolio, reduce volatility, and increase our chances of success.

WHY IS DIVERSIFICATION ESSENTIAL?

Investing is a game of probabilities. While we can't predict market outcomes with certainty, we can minimize risk and prepare.
Main benefits of diversification:

- **Reduces overall risk** – If one investment fails, others may compensate for the loss.

- **Protects against economic surprises** – Financial crises, recessions, or geopolitical events may affect specific sectors but rarely all at once.
- **Increases portfolio stability** – Less volatility means less stress and more security over time.

Practical Example: *If I put all my money into one business and it failed, I would lose my entire capital. However, if I diversify my investments across several sectors, one failure would have a significantly smaller impact.*

Practical Exercise: Review your current portfolio and determine whether it is too heavily concentrated in a single sector or asset.

TYPES OF DIVERSIFICATION

Diversifying doesn't just mean spreading money across random investments. You must select various assets that react differently to market fluctuations.

Main ways to diversify:

- **Asset class diversification** – Combine tangible assets such as real estate, commodities, and digital investments.
- **Geographic diversification**: Invest in various markets (e.g., the U.S., Europe, Asia, and emerging markets).
- **Sector diversification** – Balance investments across technology, healthcare, energy, finance, consumer goods, and more.
- **Time diversification** – Invest gradually over time to mitigate market volatility risk.

Practical Example: *A well-diversified portfolio may consist of 30% in real estate, 20% in commodities like gold, 30% in established businesses, and 20% in emerging sectors, thereby balancing risk and return.*

Practical Exercise: Evaluate your portfolio's composition to ensure a healthy distribution across various asset classes.

HOW TO CREATE A WELL-DIVERSIFIED PORTFOLIO

To develop a successful diversification strategy, you should adopt a systematic approach.

Steps for smart diversification:

- **Analyze your risk profile** – Are you a conservative or aggressive investor?
- **Choose assets with different correlations** – Avoid investing only in instruments that move in the same direction.
- **Use a diversified time horizon** – Plan investments for the short, medium, and long term.
- **Monitor and adjust your portfolio** – Markets change, so regularly rebalancing your assets is essential.

Practical Example: *If my portfolio consists solely of a business venture, I might consider allocating part of my capital to real estate or commodities to reduce risk.*

Practical Exercise: Identify the assets that would best balance your portfolio according to your financial goals.

COMMON MISTAKES IN DIVERSIFICATION

Although diversification is a great strategy, many investors make mistakes that cancel out its benefits.

Most common mistakes to avoid:

- **Over-diversification** – Having too many investments can make management difficult and dilute potential gains.
- **Investing in too similar assets** – If all your investments move in the same direction, diversification becomes pointless.
- **Not rebalancing the portfolio** – If one asset grows significantly, it may unbalance the portfolio and increase risk.

- **Following trends blindly** – Investing only in popular fads without a solid strategy can lead to losses.

Practical Example: *If I have multiple businesses that all function within the same sector, I'm not truly diversifying my portfolio.*

Practical Exercise: Check if you have too many investments in a single sector and find alternatives to improve diversification.

DIVERSIFICATION AS A LONG-TERM STRATEGY

Diversification is not a quick-win tactic; it's a method for protecting capital and building wealth sustainably over time.

How to implement diversification as a long-term strategy:

- **Stay disciplined** – Don't let short-term market fluctuations influence your plan.
- **Monitor and rebalance periodically** – Some assets may grow faster than others, disrupting your initial balance.
- **Keep investing over time** – A consistent investment plan reduces the risk of entering the market at the wrong time.

Practical Example: *If my initial portfolio was well-diversified, but one area has now grown significantly more than the others, it might be time to rebalance.*

Practical Exercise: Set a reminder to review and adjust your portfolio every six months.

Diversification is a crucial strategy to protect your capital and improve financial stability. Distributing investments across various assets, sectors, and markets helps reduce risks and optimize long-term growth opportunities.

Remember: It's not about avoiding risk but rather managing it wisely to build strong, sustainable wealth.

PASSIVE VS. ACTIVE INVESTING

When it comes to investing, one of the first decisions you need to make is how to manage your portfolio. Do you want to be the type of investor who lets your money work automatically, or do you prefer to be active and strategic in seeking the best opportunities? Essentially, it's about choosing between a **passive** and an **active** approach.

Personally, I've always liked having control over my decisions, but I've come to understand that a simpler, automated approach can sometimes help avoid costly mistakes. Let's explore the differences between these two methods, their pros and cons, and how to find the right balance.

PASSIVE INVESTING: STABILITY WITHOUT STRESS

Passive investing is ideal for those who want their money to work without constantly monitoring the markets. The idea is simple: rather than trying to beat the market, you follow it by investing in instruments that offer long-term stability.

Main tools for passive investing:

- **Gold and precious metals** – Protect capital from inflation and economic crises.
- **Income-generating real estate** – Buying property to generate passive income over time.
- **Savings accounts and certificates of deposit (CDs)** – Bank products that offer guaranteed returns.
- **Life insurance and private pension plans** – Long-term strategies for building capital with low risk and tax advantages.

Advantages:

- **Low management costs** – No need to monitor markets daily.
- **Less stress** – Ideal for those seeking security without worries.

- **Protection during economic downturns** – Some assets, such as gold and real estate, are well-suited to market fluctuations.

Disadvantages:

- **Lower returns compared to aggressive strategies** – Security often comes at the expense of potential profits.
- **Less flexibility** – Some assets, like real estate, require a high initial investment and aren't easily liquidated.
- **Dependent on economic context** – The value of assets like property can fluctuate over time.

Practical Example: *If I invest in a rental property, I'll have consistent passive income over time without needing to monitor the market every day.*

Practical Exercise: Find three passive investment options other than ETFs (Exchange-Traded Funds) and compare their historical returns and stability.

ACTIVE INVESTING: MAXIMIZING RETURNS WITH STRATEGY

If passive investing is like putting your money on autopilot, then active investing is like driving manually, trying to optimize every turn to achieve the highest return.

Main tools for active investing:

- **Individual stocks** – Picking specific high-potential securities.
- **Actively managed funds** – Relying on expert managers to choose the best investments.
- **Trading and speculation** – Frequent operations to take advantage of market fluctuations.

Advantages:

- **Potential for higher returns** – If you choose wisely, you can outperform the market.
- **Greater control** – You decide what to invest in and when to enter or exit the market.
- **Crisis protection** – You can adjust your portfolio to avoid heavy losses.

Disadvantages:

- **Time and expertise required** – It's not for everyone; it requires study and analysis.
- **Higher management costs** – Fees, taxes, and research can eat into profits.
- **Higher risk** – A wrong strategy can lead to losses greater than your gains.

Practical Example: *If I invest in shares of an emerging tech startup, I could earn much more than with an ETF, but I also risk losing my capital if the company fails.*

Practical Exercise: Choose three stocks in different sectors and analyze their performance over the past five years.

WHICH STRATEGY SHOULD YOU CHOOSE?

There isn't a one-size-fits-all answer. It depends on your investor profile, the time you can dedicate, and your risk tolerance.

When to choose passive investing:

- If you want a simple, low-effort strategy.
- If your goal is steady long-term growth.
- If you prefer lower costs and less stress.

When to choose active investing:

- If you have financial knowledge and want full control over your portfolio.
- If you can dedicate time to market analysis.
- If you're willing to take more risk for the chance at higher rewards.

Practical Example: *If I'm investing for retirement and don't want to monitor markets daily, a real estate accumulation plan may be safer than active trading.*

Practical Exercise: Assess your level of involvement with your investments and determine which strategy aligns best with your style.

THE BEST APPROACH? A MIX OF BOTH

Many investors adopt a **hybrid strategy**, combining passive and active investing to get the best of both approaches.

How to balance the two approaches:

- Invest the majority of your capital in safe, passive tools (gold, real estate, retirement plans).
- Allocate a portion to more active investments to seize growth opportunities.
- Periodically monitor and rebalance your portfolio as needed.

Practical Example: *If my portfolio consists of 80% in real estate and gold and 20% in higher-yield investments, I get the stability of passive investing along with the upside potential of active management.*

Practical Exercise: Build a portfolio that combines both approaches and analyze the potential benefits.

It's not just about choosing black or white. The real key is finding the right balance between passive and active management based on your needs and abilities. What matters most is having a clear plan and not getting swept away by the latest trends.

Remember: There isn't a perfect strategy; only the strategy fits you best!

USING BANK CREDIT TO CREATE PROFIT

When used wisely, Bank Credit is a powerful financial tool that can accelerate financial growth and generate profit. However, there is a significant difference between using debt as leverage to create value and getting trapped in loans that turn into a burden.

I've seen people ruin themselves financially by taking on the wrong kind of debt, but I've also met entrepreneurs and investors who leveraged credit to amass significant wealth. The key is recognizing the difference between **good debt** and **bad debt** and understanding how to use it to your advantage.

THE DIFFERENCE BETWEEN GOOD DEBT AND BAD DEBT

Not all debt is the same. Some debt can be seen as an investment, while other types are just financial burden that forces you to work just to pay interest without generating any value.

Examples of bad debt:

- **Mortgage on your primary residence** – A home is an asset, but if it doesn't generate income, it's just a fixed expense.
- **Loans for consumer goods** – Financing luxury cars, expensive gadgets or vacations can drain your finances.
- **High-interest credit cards** – Revolving credit becomes a trap if not paid off quickly.

Examples of good debt:

- **Purchasing income-generating property** – A rental property can cover the mortgage and generate cash flow.

- **Starting or expanding a business** – A loan is a smart investment if it helps grow a profitable venture.
- **Investing in education or skills** – Enhancing your professional value can lead to greater earnings in the future.

Practical Example: *If I buy a home with a mortgage to live in, I only incur expenses. However, if I buy one with a mortgage to rent out, the income can cover the loan and generate extra profit.*

Practical Exercise: Analyze a debt you have or are considering and determine whether it qualifies as good debt or bad debt.

INVESTING IN REAL ESTATE WITH BANK CREDIT

One of the smartest ways to use credit is to purchase income-generating real estate. When well-researched, the real estate market allows you to leverage debt strategically.

What types of properties can generate profit?

- **Homes in tourist destinations** – Short-term rentals with high profit margins.
- **Commercial properties** – Longer, more stable lease contracts than residential rentals.
- **Co-living or subdivided rental units** – Maximize return on investment per square meter.

Strategies to maximize profit:

- **Carefully calculate returns** – Rent must cover the mortgage and leave a profit margin.
- **Negotiate favorable financing** – Even a small reduction in interest rate can make a big difference.
- **Avoid saturated markets** – If everyone is investing in the same area, returns may decrease.

Practical Example: *If I purchase an apartment using a fixed-rate mort-*

gage at 3% and rent it out for a 7% yield, I will still make a profit after paying taxes and expenses.

Practical Exercise: Find a property for sale in a high-demand area and calculate its potential return compared to the mortgage costs.

USING CREDIT TO LAUNCH A PROFITABLE BUSINESS

Another way to leverage credit is to secure funding to start or grow a business.

What types of businesses benefit from financing?

- **Businesses with stable demand** – Like e-commerce, digital services, food service, or online education.
- **Franchises** – A well-established brand reduces business risk.
- **Scalable businesses** – Companies that can grow quickly without excessive fixed costs.

How to reduce risk:

- **Create a detailed business plan** – Essential for both getting financing and setting a clear strategy.
- **Calculate the break-even point** – Understand how long it will take to cover your initial investment.
- **Don't borrow more than necessary** – Avoid taking on debt that could jeopardize your business.

Practical Example: *If I open a coffee shop with a €50,000 loan and project a monthly net profit of €5,000, I could recoup the investment in less than a year.*

Practical Exercise: Write out a business idea and determine the capital needed to launch it and the time it may take to become profitable.

RISKS AND STRATEGIES FOR USING CREDIT SAFELY

Credit is useful but must be managed with discipline.
Main risks:

- **High interest rates** – If the cost of borrowing exceeds your returns, the debt becomes unsustainable.
- **Lack of liquidity** – An emergency buffer is essential to avoid financial strain.
- **Misjudging investments** – Overestimating returns can lead to significant losses.

How to reduce risks:

- **Always keep a liquidity reserve** – For each credit–based investment, save at least six months' worth of loan payments.
- **Conduct realistic return analyses** – Consider all costs and potential market fluctuations.
- **Avoid overleveraging** – Regardless of how tempting the opportunity may seem, if the risk of default is too high, it's not worth pursuing.

Practical Example: *If I take out a loan to buy property, I have to consider not just the mortgage but also taxes, maintenance, and possible vacancy periods.*

Practical Exercise: If you're considering a credit-based investment, list all potential risks and how you would mitigate them.

Bank credit, when used wisely, can accelerate your journey toward financial freedom. The key is to use it only to generate income, never to fund unnecessary expenses.

Remember: Debt isn't the problem. The problem is how you manage it. If credit works for you, it's a powerful ally. If you work for it, it's a trap.

IN SUMMARY

Choosing the right investments is a personal decision that requires a good understanding of financial markets, risk levels, and financial goals. Diversifying your portfolio, evaluating risk carefully, and considering both passive and active investing approaches can all contribute to your financial success.

Additionally, evaluate the use of bank credit to generate profits while always weighing the balance between risk and return. Make informed and prudent decisions to build a solid foundation for your financial future.

14 HOW TO OBTAIN ECONOMIC FREEDOM

Many people believe the only way to make money is to start a business and work in it forever. But there's another path: build a business with real value and sell it at the right time. Over the years, I've started several ventures that, once they reached a certain revenue level, I sold to others who wanted to take over and grow them further. This allowed me to reinvest in new projects without being trapped in one single business. That's the entrepreneur's mindset: build assets that generate value and know when it's the right time to monetize them.

In this section, I will focus on the importance of creating assets and passive income streams to achieve financial success. A passive income is a source of income that allows you to earn money without having to actively work for it. Learning to build passive income is a key step toward achieving financial freedom and success in life.

CREATING PASSIVE INCOME: THE KEY TO FINANCIAL FREEDOM

Most people trade their time for money, actively working to earn an income and believing it's the only way to make a living. *"If you stop working, you stop earning!"* I used to hear this. However, I wanted to achieve financial freedom, and I needed a system that would allow me to generate income even when I wasn't physically working. That's where **passive or automated income** comes into play.

Passive income streams are revenue sources that keep generating funds over time without requiring constant active work. This doesn't imply making money by doing nothing (that's a myth); rather, it involves creating assets that work for you while you sleep, travel, or concentrate on other activities.

WHAT IS PASSIVE INCOME AND WHY IS IT IMPORTANT?

Passive income works like this: You invest time, money, or skills upfront and then reap the rewards over time.

Main advantages:

- **No ongoing work required** – After setup, it generates income with minimal effort.
- **Scalable** – A good system can grow without requiring more work from you.
- **Income diversification** – Multiple revenue sources reduce financial risk.
- **Financial freedom** – Frees you from depending on a fixed paycheck.

Practical Example: *A young woman wrote a book and published it on Amazon and other platforms. She wrote it once, yet she continues to earn royalties from sales every month. That's the power of passive income.*

Practical Exercise: Think of an activity that could become a passive income stream. Do you possess any skills or resources that you could utilize?

TOP PASSIVE INCOME SOURCES

There are many ways to create passive income, some require money, while others need time and skills. After years of experience and testing, I've identified a few areas that offer great passive income potential:

1. Real Estate Investments

- Renting apartments or vacation homes.
- Medium- or long-term rentals for students or remote workers.
- Leasing commercial properties to established businesses.

2. Financial Investments

- **Dividend-paying stocks** – Invest in companies that regularly distribute dividends.
- **Bonds and savings accounts** – Low-risk tools that generate periodic interest.
- **ETFs and mutual funds** – Financial instruments that offer returns without active management.

3. Creating and Selling Digital Products

- **E-books and online courses** – Create and sell content through dedicated platforms.
- **Apps and software** – Develop digital tools that generate income with little upkeep.
- **Stock photography and royalty-free music** – Sell media on digital marketplaces without active involvement.

4. Affiliate Marketing

- Promote others' products through affiliate links and earn a commission from sales.

- Works well with blogs, YouTube, or social media platforms.

5. *Automated Businesses*

- **Dropshipping e-commerce** – Sell products without managing inventory.
- **Niche blogs or websites** – Monetize through ads and affiliate links.

Practical Example: *A blogger who creates valuable articles with affiliate links can earn passive commissions without making direct sales.*

Practical Exercise: Which of these strategies aligns best with your skills?

PASSIVE INCOME: THE MYTH OF 'TOTAL AUTOMATION'

Many people believe that passive income means earning money without any effort. However, the reality is that, in most cases, passive income requires initial work and ongoing maintenance.

Here are some hard truths:

- **It requires an initial investment** – time, money, or skills. Passive income doesn't appear from nowhere.
- **Some models require upkeep** – rental properties need maintenance and tenant management, while websites require updates.
- **Diversification is key** – relying on a single income stream is risky if the market changes.

Practical Example: *Creating an online course takes time, but once published, it can produce consistent sales for years with minimal updates.*

Practical Exercise: Determine if you would rather invest time or money to develop your passive income stream.

MISTAKES TO AVOID WHEN CREATING PASSIVE INCOME

Many people fail before they even begin. Here are the most common mistakes:

1. **Expecting immediate returns** – Creating passive income takes time. There are no miracles or shortcuts.
2. **Ignoring taxes and fiscal responsibility** – Every passive income stream is subject to taxation. You need to plan ahead to optimize profits.
3. **Lack of diversification** – Relying on a single income stream is risky; diversification helps protect against market fluctuations.
4. **Not monitoring results** – Even a "passive" income source requires oversight to ensure optimal performance.

Practical Example: *An investor buys an apartment to rent out but fails to consider taxes, maintenance, and vacancy periods. The result? Profits do not meet expectations.*

Practical Exercise: Identify potential obstacles to creating your passive income and develop a strategy to overcome them.

Generating passive income is essential for achieving financial freedom, but it demands dedication and planning.

Let's recap:

- Passive income requires an initial investment (time, money, or skills).
- There are many options, including real estate, finance, digital products, and automated businesses.
- Avoid common mistakes such as insufficient diversification and poor tax planning.

Remember: Don't work for money. Let money work for you.

AUTOMATED INCOME FROM REAL ESTATE: THE RIGHT STRATEGY TO MAXIMIZE PROFITS

Generating automated income through smart investments is one of the most effective ways to build long-term financial stability. Real estate, when managed correctly, can become a solid and lasting source of passive income.

However, not all real estate investments are equal, and some strategies are far more profitable than others. Let's look at the different ways to create passive income through real estate, the best opportunities, and the key strategies for generating returns while avoiding common pitfalls.

WHY INVEST IN REAL ESTATE FOR PASSIVE INCOME?

Real estate offers several advantages as a long-term investment:

- **Consistent cash flow** – Rentals provide recurring income that can cover costs and generate profit.
- **Inflation protection** – Property values typically increase over time, protecting your capital.
- **Leverage** – Banks allow you to buy properties with relatively low upfront capital, increasing your investment power.
- **Diversification** – Including real estate in your financial portfolio helps reduce risk.

However, not all real estate investments yield the same level of profitability. Here's how to select the most effective strategy for you.

WHICH PROPERTIES OFFER THE BEST RETURNS?

Not all properties are the same, and the way you manage them can determine the difference between a successful investment and a financial disaster. Here are the pros and cons of the main options:

Short-Term Rentals for Tourists and Business Travelers

- **PROS:** You can earn significantly more than with a traditional rental, especially using platforms like Airbnb.
- **CONS:** It requires more hands-on management (check-ins, cleaning, customer service), but these tasks can be outsourced to a property manager.

Practical Example: *A friend purchased a small apartment in a tourist city and rents it to travelers at daily rates. In a year, he makes more than twice what he would earn from a long-term rental.*

Renting to Students and Remote Workers

- **PROS:** Stable demand and the option to divide the apartment into multiple rental rooms.
- **CONS:** Students often move frequently, requiring active management and tenant replacement each year.

Practical Example: *A three-bedroom apartment rented to university students in a large city can generate more income than a single long-term tenant, thanks to room-by-room rentals.*

Long-Term Rentals: Why I Don't Recommend Them

From my experience, long-term residential rentals aren't the most profitable strategy. Here's why:

- **Lower income** – After taxes and expenses, net profits are often less than with other options.
- **Tenant issues and eviction delays** – In many countries, laws tend to favor tenants over landlords. If a tenant stops paying rent, the eviction process can take months or even years.
- **Property depreciation** – Long-term tenants may lead to wear and tear, making renovations challenging without extended vacancy periods.

Practical Example: *Many investors believe that long-term rentals offer* *stability. However, when confronted with non-paying tenants and lengthy legal eviction processes, they realize it's not worth the hassle.*

Better Alternative: Renting to students or professionals offers more flexibility and better returns.

STRATEGIES TO MAXIMIZE PROFIT

To achieve the best returns, a focused strategy is essential:

1. Choose the Right Location

- Invest in areas with high tourist, university, or business demand.
- Avoid regions with high delinquency rates or properties that are hard to resell.

2. Optimize Property Layout

- Divide large apartments into multiple units to increase profitability.
- Renovate and furnish in an appealing way to attract tenants willing to pay higher rents.

3. Take Advantage of Tax Benefits

- Some short-term rental models offer tax advantages over long-term leases.
- Consult a tax expert to optimize your net returns.

4. Automate Management

- Use property management software to track payments, expenses, and deadlines.
- Hire a property manager to reduce your workload.

Mistakes to Avoid

- **Buying without market analysis** – Many buy properties without studying demand or potential returns.
- **Underestimating costs** – Taxes, maintenance, and management can eat into profits.
- **Lack of diversification** – Investing in a single property is risky.
- **Overlooking tax effects** – Failing to understand the tax rules for rentals can be significantly expensive.

Practical Example: *I've seen people buy houses in the suburbs, believing they could rent them out easily, only to end up facing months of vacancy due to insufficient demand.*

If you know what you're doing, real estate investing can be an excellent way to generate passive income.

- **Short-term rentals** and **student/professional rentals** are the best options for maximizing returns.
- Long-term leases may seem safer but often come with lower margins and more problems.
- Planning and diversification are essential to avoid unpleasant surprises.

Remember: It's not just about owning property; it's about understanding how to make it profitable.

CHOOSING THE RIGHT SECTOR TO CREATE PASSIVE INCOME

When I first started looking for ways to generate passive income, I made one of the most common mistakes: I jumped into a sector simply because it seemed trendy, without conducting any research or understanding whether it was a good fit for me. The result? I wasted time and money. Then, I realized that choosing the right sector is not about trends or luck; it's about strategy.

Let's explore how to identify the right sector for generating passive income, avoid pitfalls, and capitalize on real opportunities.

THE THREE KEY FACTORS TO CHOOSE THE RIGHT SECTOR

To choose a sector for building passive income, I realized you must evaluate three fundamental elements:

1. Passion and Personal Interest

- Working in a field you're passionate about keeps you motivated over the long term.
- A sector that sparks your curiosity will drive you to dive deeper and innovate.
- Passion helps you overcome early obstacles and stay consistent in your efforts.

Practical Example: *A travel enthusiast could start a travel blog monetized through affiliate marketing and ads, while a tech-savvy individual might launch a YouTube channel reviewing electronic products.*

In the past, I invested in a sector simply because it looked profitable, with no real interest in it. Within a few months, I lost enthusiasm and money, and abandoned the project. That's when I realized that if you want to build something lasting, you need to find a field you're genuinely passionate about.

2. Existing Skills and Knowledge

- Leveraging skills you already possess shortens the learning curve and helps you avoid beginner mistakes.
- Experience in a field makes it easier to spot profitable opportunities.

- If you don't have the skills for a field that interests you yet, think about learning first before investing.

Practical Example: *If you have experience in digital marketing, you might consider starting a consulting business or developing an online course to share your expertise.*

3. *Market Analysis and Profitability*

- A profitable sector should have stable or growing demand. Avoid saturated or declining markets.
- Assess competition: too many players make entry tougher, and too few might signal low demand.
- Estimate earning potential and how long it might take to generate passive income. Some sectors take longer to become profitable than others.

Practical Example: *A growing market like renewable energy might offer better opportunities than declining sectors like traditional printing.*

Practical Exercise: Perform market research on the sector you're interested in, examining demand, competition, and potential growth over the next 5 to 10 years.

MISTAKES TO AVOID WHEN CHOOSING A SECTOR

- **Chasing trends** – A trending industry can quickly become oversaturated.
- **Skipping market analysis** – Investing without knowing the competition is risky.
- **Entering a sector without skills or passion** – Without interest or experience, your chance of failure is high.
- **Ignoring risks and entry barriers** – Some sectors require large investments or involve complex regulations.

Practical Example: *Many inexperienced investors bought stocks without researching the market, only to lose most of their capital when prices crashed.*

Practical Exercise: List potential risks in the sector you're interested in and develop strategies to mitigate them.

HOW TO GET STARTED IN THE RIGHT SECTOR

Once you've chosen the right sector, follow these steps to launch your venture:

1. **Training and Research**
   - Acquire skills through books, courses, and mentorship.
   - Study success stories and effective business models.
2. **Planning and Testing**
   - Draft a detailed business plan with goals and strategies.
   - Run market tests to gauge public response.
3. **Networking and Partnerships**
   - Connect with experts and professionals to learn winning strategies.
   - Consider collaborating with people who can accelerate your success.
4. **Adaptability and Growth**
   - Monitor your investment's performance and make constant improvements.
   - Be ready to pivot if the market demands it.

Choosing the right sector is a fundamental step to building a successful passive income.

- **Passion, skills, and market analysis** are the keys to making an informed decision.
- **Profitable sectors** include real estate, financial investments, online businesses, and renewable energy.
- **Avoid common mistakes** like chasing trends or investing without knowledge to set yourself up for success.

Remember: The secret to success isn't about doing everything; it's about selecting the right sector and mastering the market.

CREATING PASSIVE INCOME WITHOUT INVESTING MONEY

The notion of earning without spending a dime might sound impossible, right? Yet, with the right strategy and a bit of creativity, it's possible to generate passive income from scratch.

I've been there. When I faced financial difficulties, I learned that a lack of money isn't an insurmountable obstacle; it's an opportunity to think smarter and make the most of what you already have. I started several projects with no initial capital, relying solely on my skills, creativity, and a bit of entrepreneurial spirit. Some of them succeeded, others didn't, but every experience taught me something. And you know what the most important lesson was? Money isn't your only resource. Your time, skills, and relationships can be worth far more.

Let's explore ways to generate passive income without spending money, using the resources you already have at your disposal.

LEVERAGE WHAT YOU ALREADY HAVE

If you don't have money to invest, you can still leverage your time, your skills, and the relationships you've built over time. Here are some practical strategies:

Use Your Skills to Create Value

- If you have expertise in marketing, writing, programming, or graphic design, you can start an online business without needing upfront capital.
- **Example:** You can launch a blog, a YouTube channel, or a social media profile focused on a specific topic and monetize it through affiliate links and ads. A close friend of mine started a simple travel blog, writing articles and monetizing

through affiliate marketing. Today, that's his full-time income.

Capitalize on Your Network

- Do you know people who might need a service or support? You can offer consulting or collaborate with others to generate income without investing money.
- **Example:** A social media expert could manage the profiles of small businesses in exchange for a commission on the sales generated.

Work for a Share of the Profits

- Instead of working for a fixed salary, consider taking on projects that use a profit-sharing model. This will allow you to earn equity in the business.
- **Example:** Offer your services to a startup in exchange for a percentage of future profits. I know people who have gained equity in companies this way, companies that are now worth millions.

Practical Exercise: Make a list of your skills and the people who might need your help. How could you monetize these without investing money?

SCALABLE AND LOW-COST BUSINESS MODELS

A scalable business is one that can grow over time without increasing your workload or expenses proportionally. Here are some ideas:

Sell Digital Products

- Creating an eBook, an online course or a guide is a way to earn money without recurring production costs.

- **Example:** A friend wrote a short manual on using LinkedIn to find a job and published it on Amazon Kindle. He invested only his time, but he now earns passive income every month.

Do Affiliate Marketing

- You can promote products from other companies and earn a commission on every sale.
- **Example:** Some people review tech gadgets on YouTube and earn through Amazon affiliate links. Every time someone buys through their link, they get a percentage.

Start an Online Business without inventory

- Dropshipping allows you to sell products online without managing inventory or logistics.
- **Example:** You can create an online store that sells products from third-party suppliers, profiting from each sale.

Practical Exercise: Which business model might suit you best?

AUTOMATE YOUR INCOME WITH TECHNOLOGY

Technology is your greatest ally for earning without having to work manually every day.

Automate Lead Generation

- Create an email marketing system that automatically sends offers to potential customers.
- **Example:** A newsletter that promotes affiliate products or services automatically can earn you money, even while you sleep.

Monetize Social Media

- Creating content for your social platforms can generate passive income through ads or affiliate links.
- **Example:** A niche influencer earns money from ads and sponsorships without having to handle physical products.

Practical Exercise: What tool can you use to automate a source of income?

EARNING FROM REAL ESTATE WITHOUT MONEY

You don't need a large capital investment to enter the real estate market. Here are two strategies that I've seen work effectively:

Manage Properties for Others

- You can offer your services as a property manager for owners who want to rent out on Airbnb but don't have time to handle bookings and guests.
- **Example:** A friend of mine manages ten apartments for different owners and keeps 20% of the revenue. He built a business without owning a single property.

Subletting and Rent-to-Rent

- You rent a property long-term and sublet it for a higher return. *(Be sure to inform the property owner before doing this.)*
- **Example:** An investor rents a house and divides it into individual rooms to rent to students or professionals, increasing the overall yield.

Practical Exercise: Are there real estate opportunities you could take advantage of without investing any capital?

LEVERAGE PARTNERSHIPS TO MULTIPLY OPPORTUNITIES

Strategic partnerships allow you to compensate for a lack of capital with shared skills and resources.

In addition to offering your services in exchange for equity, you can build profitable collaborations with other professionals:

- Team up with experts in complementary fields to launch businesses with no startup costs.
- **Example:** A graphic designer can collaborate with a copywriter to create a social media marketing agency. One handles the content, the other the visuals. No initial investment; just shared skills.

Practical Exercise: Who do you know that could be a good business partner?

Generating passive income without any money isn't a fantasy; it demands a specific mindset shift.

You don't need capital to get started. You can begin with what you already have: your time, your skills, your network, and your creativity.

- Leverage your time and abilities to generate value.
- Choose scalable, automatable business models.
- Use technology to generate income without active labor.
- Build strategic partnerships to access resources without upfront investment.

Remember: The most valuable capital isn't money; it's knowledge and the ability to take action.

IN SUMMARY

Generating passive income is a realistic objective for anyone pursuing financial success. You can establish a revenue stream that provides you with increased financial freedom through passive income sources, choosing the right sector, and implementing cost-effective strategies.

Keep in mind that building a system that runs independently over time requires an investment of time, energy, and initial resources. However, with the right mindset and determination, you can succeed in creating sustainable passive income.

15 HOW TO DEAL WITH FAILURE

Life can be a winding path filled with challenges and obstacles that test our mental strength and motivation. At times, we may feel trapped in a spiral of negativity, overwhelmed by our daily routines. However, overcoming these tough moments and rediscovering the joy of living is possible. In this chapter, we will explore various strategies to be reborn, regain motivation, and renew your enthusiasm for life.

STARTING OVER AFTER FAILURE: REGAINING MOTIVATION AND ENTHUSIASM

Every entrepreneur, professional, or ambitious person will eventually face setbacks. A business that doesn't take off, an investment that falls short, a failed project, or a relationship that ends. I've been through all of these, and I understand how difficult it can be to get back on your feet.

Failure can significantly affect your motivation and lead to frustration, discouragement, and, in the worst cases, a sense of helplessness that turns into inaction. However, failure is not the end of the road; it's a lesson, an opportunity for growth.

The difference between those who rise again and those who give up is their ability to rediscover the motivation and enthusiasm to start anew.

ACCEPTING FAILURE WITHOUT BEING CRUSHED BY IT

Our first reaction to failure is often feelings of guilt or disappointment. This is normal. However, remaining in that phase for too long can lead to paralysis.
How can you deal with failure constructively?

- **Accept it as part of the journey** – Every successful entrepreneur has failed multiple times before succeeding.
- **Avoid excessive self-blame** – Analyze the mistake with clarity without beating yourself up.
- **Separate failure from your identity** – Failing doesn't mean *you* are a failure.

Practical Example: *If my business project doesn't work out, I'll focus on what I learned instead of calling myself incapable. I can refine my strategy and try again with a new approach.*

Practical Exercise: Write a letter to yourself reflecting on what you learned from your failure and how you will use that experience to grow.

FINDING NEW MOTIVATION: LOOKING AHEAD

Once you've accepted the situation, the next step is to redirect your energy toward new goals.
Dwelling on the past won't change anything; taking action will.
Strategies to regain motivation:

- **Refocus your vision** – Why did you start? Is your goal still relevant?

- **Create new stimuli** – Sometimes, changing your context, habits, or approach reignites enthusiasm.
- **Surround yourself with inspiring people** – Talking to those who've overcome tough times can offer a new perspective.

Practical Example: *Did I miss a job opportunity? Rather than staying stuck, I can spend an hour each day learning and discovering new ways to showcase my skills.*

Practical Exercise: Set a specific, tangible goal for the next three months and outline the first three steps to achieve it.

SHIFTING PERSPECTIVE: EVERY FAILURE IS A LESSON

Successful people don't see failure as defeat but as an opportunity to grow. Every mistake contains valuable information if we learn to read it correctly.

How to turn failure into an opportunity:

- **Analyze what worked and what didn't** – No judgment, just objective data.
- **Identify what you can improve** – Are there skills to develop? Strategies to refine?
- **Apply the principle of continuous improvement** – Failing today means doing better tomorrow.

Practical Example: *If my business doesn't succeed, I can ask myself: Was it the product? The market? The business model? What can I improve and try again?*

Practical Exercise: After experiencing a failure, write down three things you've learned and how you'll apply them in the future.

RECHARGING YOUR ENERGY: REDISCOVERING ENTHUSIASM

Failure can drain your motivation. Before restarting, it's essential to recharge both mentally and physically.

How to restore your energy and determination:

- **Do something you're passionate about** – Sometimes, all it takes is a break to reignite creativity.
- **Engage in positive-thinking activities** – Sports, reading, meditation, and travel.
- **Set small daily victories** – Achieving incremental goals helps you regain momentum.

Practical Example: *If I feel stuck, I can spend a week focusing on a side project or a creative activity. Often, taking a mental break brings fresh ideas.*

Practical Exercise: Every day, spend at least 30 minutes doing something that emotionally recharges you.

TAKE ACTION: THE ONLY ESCAPE FROM THE LIMBO

After reflecting, recharging, and redefining your goals, the most important step comes next: taking action.

The biggest risk following a failure is remaining still, waiting for the perfect moment.

How to move forward effectively:

- **Take a first step, even a small one** – Even making a phone call or sending an email can be the beginning.
- **Avoid the procrastination trap** – The perfect moment doesn't exist; act with what you have now.
- **Track your progress without obsession** – Improvement is a gradual process.

Practical Example: *If I lost an important client, I could immediately shift focus to finding new opportunities instead of dwelling on regret.*

Practical Exercise: Choose one concrete action you can take today to move closer to your goal.

A failure doesn't define who you are. What truly matters is how you react, what you learn, and what you do next. Finding motivation and enthusiasm after a setback doesn't come immediately, but it is absolutely possible.

Remember: Those who know how to recover from failure aren't just stronger; they're better equipped for future success.

WHY STAYING POSITIVE MATTERS

Positivity isn't just about attitude; it's a practical tool for facing challenges and building success. Being positive doesn't mean ignoring problems; it means developing the ability to find solutions, stay clear-headed, and face challenges with determination.

In the entrepreneurial and professional world, a positive mindset helps overcome obstacles, attract opportunities, boost productivity, and strengthen relationships. Those who maintain an optimistic attitude are more likely to persevere through tough times, inspire others, and achieve real results.

POSITIVITY AS A COMPETITIVE ADVANTAGE

Setbacks are inevitable in business and life. The difference between those who give up and those who succeed lies in how they react to adversity.

Why does a positive mindset help you stand out?

- **Enhances problem-solving ability** – A confident and open mindset encourages creativity and strategic thinking.

- **Increases stress resilience** – Positive people handle pressure better and avoid being overwhelmed by anxiety.
- **Leads to better decisions** – Negativity focuses only on risks, while positivity also helps identify opportunities.

Practical Example: *An entrepreneur faces an economic crisis. Instead of complaining and freezing in uncertainty, they analyze new strategies, diversify income sources, and turn the challenge into a growth opportunity.*

Practical Exercise: Each time you face a challenge, ask yourself: *"What opportunity could arise from this situation?"*

TRAINING THE MIND FOR POSITIVE RESILIENCE

Positivity isn't a gift you're born with; it's a skill you can develop and strengthen.

Being positive doesn't mean avoiding problems but building mental strength to face them productively.

Strategies to reinforce a positive mindset:

- **Reframe negative thoughts** – Instead of saying, "I can't do this," ask, "How can I make this work?"
- **Use positive language** – Words shape our minds: avoid defeatist expressions and focus on constructive affirmations.
- **Celebrate yourself** – Every small success validates your abilities and boosts your self-confidence.

Practical Example: *If a project fails, analyze what you learned and how to do better next time instead of focusing on what went wrong.*

Practical Exercise: At the end of each day, write down three things you did well and feel proud of.

THE POWER OF GRATITUDE: CHANGING PERSPECTIVE

One of the most effective ways to stay positive is by practicing gratitude.

Shifting your focus from what's missing to what you already have helps build a balanced and resilient mindset.

Benefits of gratitude:

- **Reduces stress and anxiety** – Gratitude helps shift your focus from worries to strengths.
- **Increases fulfillment** – Recognizing the value of what you have makes challenges feel lighter.
- **Boosts motivation** – Focusing on what's good gives you the energy to keep working toward your goals.

Practical Example: *Instead of focusing on a client who rejected your offer, think of those who believed in you and keep improving to attract new ones.*

Practical Exercise: Every morning, write down three things you're grateful for, even simple ones, like an inspiring conversation or small progress in a project.

THE INFLUENCE OF ENVIRONMENT AND PEOPLE

The people we spend time with have a direct impact on our mindset.

Being around negative and pessimistic individuals can drain our motivation while surrounding ourselves with positive people supports a proactive attitude.

How to choose the right environment:

- **Be around inspiring people** – Seek mentors, colleagues, and friends who radiate positive energy.
- **Limit time with toxic individuals** – If someone constantly belittles you or spreads negativity, reduce contact.

- **Consume uplifting content** – Books, podcasts, and motivational videos can shift your mindset in a positive direction.

Practical Example: If you notice that someone's presence makes you anxious or pessimistic, ask yourself, "Is this relationship helping me grow or holding me back?

Practical Exercise: Review the people you interact with most often and assess which ones positively impact your life.

TURNING POSITIVITY INTO ACTION

Positivity without action is merely theory. For a positive mindset to be effective, it must translate into concrete actions.
Strategies to turn positivity into results:

- **Take action instead of waiting** – Being optimistic doesn't mean sitting still; it means using that energy to move forward.
- **Focus on solutions, not problems** – Every challenge holds an opportunity for improvement.
- **Build success habits** – Positivity becomes a lifestyle when you create productive routines.

Practical Example: If your business is in a rut, plan a strategy to expand your market or improve your product instead of complaining.

Practical Exercise: Every week, choose one challenge you're facing and write down three actions you can take to improve it.

Staying positive doesn't mean ignoring problems; it means facing them with a mindset that allows you to find solutions, generate opportunities, and keep your motivation high.

Positivity is a conscious choice, a habit to cultivate, and a competitive advantage in both work and life.

Remember: While you can't control everything that happens, you can control your attitude and how you respond to challenges.

REDISCOVERING ENTHUSIASM: HOW TO REKINDLE PASSION FOR WHAT YOU DO

Enthusiasm is the engine that drives ideas into action, the fuel that makes work exciting and life-fulfilling. However, sooner or later, everyone faces moments of apathy and demotivation. This is a natural phase, but it becomes problematic when these feelings linger, extinguishing passion and turning every task into a burden.

I've experienced this several times. There were mornings when I woke up, and everything ahead seemed dull, repetitive, and meaningless. It wasn't laziness; it felt as if my energy had been drained. I was certain I was on the right path, but deep down, something had faded. I needed to learn to identify the causes and, most importantly, find strategies to reignite that spark.

IDENTIFYING THE CAUSES OF LOST ENTHUSIASM

The first step in regaining enthusiasm is to understand why you've lost it. There can be many reasons, but they often come down to a few common factors:

- **Monotonous routine** – Doing the same things every day without new stimuli can make everything feel predictable and boring.
- **Lack of visible progress** – If it feels like you're working hard without any visible results, motivation drops dramatically.
- **Mental and physical exhaustion** – Burnout is one of the leading causes of apathy and disinterest.
- **Lack of a clear goal** – Without a defined direction, everything can seem meaningless.

Practical Example: *I realized that whenever I lost my enthusiasm, one of* these reasons was at play. Perhaps I was too focused on the problems rather than the solutions, or I was pushing myself beyond my limits without allowing time to recharge.

Practical Exercise: Take 10 minutes to reflect and write down what might be causing your loss of enthusiasm.

REIGNITING PASSION THROUGH SMALL THINGS

We often look for drastic solutions to regain motivation, but in reality, it's best to start with the little things. Sometimes, a small change can make a big difference.
Strategies to reignite passion:

- **Try something new** – Even a small variation in your daily routine can offer a fresh perspective.
- **Make time for what brings you joy** – Rediscovering hobbies and passions helps recharge mental energy.
- **Make your work more engaging** – Introducing new challenges or changing your approach can restore excitement to daily tasks.

Practical Example: *I recall a time when everything felt stagnant. The solution? I decided to spend at least one hour a day doing something I genuinely enjoyed without worrying about the outcome. Gradually, the enthusiasm came back.*

Practical Exercise: Make a list of five activities that make you feel excited and integrate at least one into your weekly routine.

SETTING ENGAGING AND ATTAINABLE GOALS

Enthusiasm flourishes when we have a clear goal that motivates us to take action. However, if a goal is too vague or too far off, it can lead to frustration instead of satisfaction.
How to set goals that spark enthusiasm:

- **Choose goals that excite you** – They shouldn't just be necessary but inspire you.
- **Break them into concrete steps** – Every small milestone achieved brings renewed motivation.
- **Track your progress** – Seeing even small results helps maintain momentum.

Practical Example: *When I start a new project, instead of saying 'I want it to take off,' I break it down: first research the market, then test an idea, and finally, I validate it. This way, each small win fuels my motivation to keep going.*

Practical Exercise: Write down an important goal and break it into three clear, achievable steps.

FINDING ENTHUSIASM THROUGH INSPIRATION

Sometimes, enthusiasm doesn't arise from within; it must be sparked by external stimuli.

Finding sources of inspiration is crucial for maintaining high motivation.

Where to find inspiration:

- **Read success stories** – Learning how others overcame tough times can offer a new perspective.
- **Surround yourself with passionate people** – Other people's energy is contagious.
- **Listen to podcasts or motivational content** – Sometimes the right phrase at the right time makes all the difference.

Practical Example: *Whenever I feel stuck, I spend 15 minutes each day reading a personal growth book or watching a motivational video. It always works for me.*

Practical Exercise: Find a source of inspiration that motivates you and spend at least 10 minutes a day engaging with it.

CREATING AN ENVIRONMENT THAT FOSTERS ENTHUSIASM

The environment in which we live and work greatly impacts our mood. Rediscovering enthusiasm becomes much harder if it's chaotic, oppressive, or lacks stimulation.

How to optimize your environment:

- **Create an inspiring workspace** – A pleasant space influences your mood positively.
- **Avoid negative people** – Negativity is contagious; better to be around those who uplift you.
- **Organize your time strategically** – Don't overload yourself, make room for activities that recharge you.

Practical Exercise: Identify three changes you can implement in your environment to make it more inspiring.

TAKING IMMEDIATE ACTION TO BREAK THE STALEMATE

The true secret to reigniting enthusiasm is taking the first step.

Action, even the smallest, creates momentum and rekindles motivation.

Strategies to act without procrastinating:

- **Start with something simple** – One small step is better than staying stuck.
- **Create a short-term plan** – Knowing what to do helps you stay focused.
- **Reward your progress** – Even small wins deserve recognition.

Practical Example: *Whenever I feel stuck, I ask myself: what is the simplest thing I can do today to get moving again? It always works.*

Practical Exercise: Write down one small step you can take today to start your journey toward greater enthusiasm.

Enthusiasm isn't something that's lost forever. It's a flame that can be reignited with small steps, new habits, and fresh inspiration.

Remember: Don't wait to feel enthusiastic before acting. Act, and the enthusiasm will follow.

SEEKING NEW INSPIRATION

Loss of motivation often arises from monotony, lack of stimulation, or the sensation of being trapped in repetitive daily habits. To reignite creativity and the desire to act, opening yourself to new sources of inspiration is essential. Inspiration doesn't come naturally; it must be actively sought, feeding the mind with new ideas, experiences, and exploration.

Finding new inspiration means expanding your horizon, challenging yourself, and seeking stimulation in unexpected places, people, and knowledge.

EXPANDING HORIZONS THROUGH NEW EXPERIENCES

You need to disrupt your routine and try new activities to break mental stagnation.

Inspiration often comes from exposure to different situations that force us to see things from a new perspective.

Ways to explore new experiences:

- **Travel, even to nearby places** – A change of scenery stimulates creativity and sparks new ideas.
- **Attend events and conferences** – Listening to experts and innovators opens your mind to new possibilities.
- **Explore unfamiliar environments** – Discovering new

communities, industries, or disciplines enriches your thinking.

Practical Example: *When I feel stuck in my work, I may go to an event in an entirely different field to uncover new ideas and connections.*

Practical Exercise: Find an event or activity outside your comfort zone and participate actively within the next 30 days.

FINDING INSPIRATION IN THE STORIES OF OTHERS

Hearing the stories of people who have faced and overcome challenges is one of the most powerful sources of inspiration.

Success and resilience stories remind us that difficulties are part of the journey and that change is possible.

Where to find inspirational stories:

- **Read biographies of successful people** – Learning about their paths can give you fresh ideas for overcoming your own challenges.
- **Watch documentaries and interviews** – Hearing directly from those who've pushed through hard times can be incredibly motivating.
- **Talk to mentors or people you admire** – One-on-one conversations with experienced individuals help clarify your own direction.

Practical Example: *If I'm facing a tough period in my business, I can read the biography of an entrepreneur who overcame similar obstacles.*

Practical Exercise: Find a biography, documentary, or interview of someone who inspires you and write down at least three lessons you can apply to your life.

CONTINUOUS LEARNING AS A SOURCE OF INSPIRATION

Personal and professional growth is tightly linked to learning.

Our minds expand when we learn something new and become more receptive to opportunities.

Ways to incorporate learning into your life:

- **Take online or in-person courses** – Even one hour a week on a new topic can make a big difference.
- **Read books on topics that spark your curiosity** – Not just for work but for the sheer joy of discovery.
- **Participate in hands-on workshops** – Active learning stimulates the brain more than passive consumption.

Practical Example: *If I feel that I've lost my passion for my field, I can take a refresher course to gain new skills and rekindle that interest.*

Practical Exercise: Choose a new topic that piques your curiosity and dedicate 30 minutes each week to it, whether through books, courses, or educational videos.

THE POWER OF NEW CONNECTIONS

Sometimes, new inspiration comes from the people we meet.

Expanding your network and engaging with individuals who think differently can open your mind and offer fresh perspectives.

How to create inspiring connections:

- **Join networking events or professional communities** – Meeting people with similar interests stimulates creativity.
- **Find a mentor, or become one** – Teaching and learning from others spark new ideas.
- **Join discussion groups or mastermind circles** – Regularly exchanging ideas with others helps maintain motivation.

Practical Example: *If I feel unmotivated in my work, I can look for a group of professionals to share ideas with and find new stimulation.*

Practical Exercise: Identify one person you'd like to connect with and send them a message to start a conversation.

STIMULATING CREATIVITY THROUGH NEW SENSORY EXPERIENCES

Inspiration comes not only from knowledge but also from sensory experience and creative expression.
How to stimulate creativity and find inspiration:

- **Listen to music that inspires you** – Sound can influence mood and productivity.
- **Explore different forms of art** – Photography, painting, theater, or any creative activity can help you see things from a new perspective.
- **Change your workspace or living environment**. Even rearranging your furniture or moving to a new location can bring fresh energy.

Practical Example: *If I feel mentally blocked, I take a walk in a museum or a natural setting to shift my perspective.*

Practical Exercise: Choose a creative activity that you've never tried before and dedicate at least an hour to it this week.

Inspiration doesn't come by chance; it must be actively pursued. Opening your mind to new experiences, learning continuously, connecting with inspiring people, and nurturing creativity are vital strategies for revitalizing energy, enthusiasm, and fresh ideas.

Remember: The more you explore the world around you, the more likely you are to find the inspiration you need to achieve your goals.

REBOOTING: REGAINING DRIVE AND CONFIDENCE

There are times in life when we feel stuck and drained of energy and stimulation. Rebooting doesn't mean changing everything overnight but making small, intentional changes that reignite our confidence and desire to move forward.

A personal reboot isn't just about appearance or fleeting motivation; it's an internal and external renewal process that helps us recover momentum, self-belief, and determination.

THE IMPACT OF AESTHETIC CHANGE ON SELF-CONFIDENCE

How we look directly affects how we perceive ourselves and face the world. Feeling good about our appearance can immediately affect our confidence and how we handle each day.

How a small change can make a difference:

- **Update your style** – Even a new accessory or haircut can bring a fresh perspective.
- **Improve posture and body language** – Standing tall and walking confidently influences how others see you and how you feel about yourself.
- **Declutter your wardrobe** – Let go of what no longer represents you and invest in items that make you feel comfortable and confident.

Practical Example: *If I want to shift my attitude, I can start by dressing in a way that makes me feel empowered and ready to face new challenges.*

Practical Exercise: Identify one small aesthetic change you can make today to feel better about yourself and do it.

TAKING INITIATIVE ON WHAT YOU'VE ALWAYS POSTPONED

Often, we feel stuck because we've left too many projects or dreams on hold. Constant procrastination creates frustration and dissatisfaction. Starting something you've always wanted to do can reignite energy and motivation.

How to reboot through action:

- **Identify a project you've always postponed** – Even a small one, as long as it's meaningful to you.
- **Take the first step, no matter how small** – You don't have to plan everything, just start.
- **Enjoy the process** – Don't focus only on the end result but on the satisfaction of making progress.

Practical Example: *If I've always wanted to learn a new language, instead of saying 'someday,' I can start today with a simple online lesson.*

Practical Exercise: Write down a goal you've been postponing and outline one small action you can take today to get started.

REDEFINING YOUR IDENTITY AND PURPOSE

Sometimes, rebooting means rediscovering who we are and what we truly want. This requires stepping back and reflecting on our values, passions, and what makes us feel fulfilled.

How to redefine your identity:

- **Reflect on what truly excites you** – What makes you feel alive and motivated?
- **Review past experiences** – Which activities have given you real satisfaction?
- **Write a statement of intent** – Define who you want to become and the steps you'll take to grow into that version of yourself.

Practical Example: *If I feel lost, I can write a personal mission statement that outlines what I want to achieve in the next six months and use it as a guide.*

Practical Exercise: Write a sentence describing who you want to become in the coming months and how you can move closer to that version of yourself.

RENEWING RELATIONSHIPS TO FIND NEW ENERGY

The people around us have a huge impact on our energy and motivation. Sometimes, rebooting also means refreshing your social connections and distancing yourself from those who hold you back.
How to improve relationships to reboot:

- **Seek new connections with inspiring people** – Attend events, join groups, or expand your network.
- **Limit time with negative people** – If someone drains your energy, consider reducing their influence.
- **Reconnect with old contacts** – Sometimes, a conversation with someone who once inspired you can reignite a spark.

Practical Example: *Whenever I need a boost of energy, I can look for opportunities to connect with people who share my interests and exchange fresh ideas.*

Practical Exercise: Contact someone who once inspired you and schedule a meeting or conversation to share ideas and gain motivation.

Rebooting doesn't mean overhauling your entire life overnight. It means making small changes that help you feel stronger, more motivated, and more confident.

Remember: Every significant transformation begins with a first step. The perfect time to reboot your life is now.

TURNING OBSTACLES INTO OPPORTUNITIES

There are moments in life when obstacles feel overwhelming, and it seems like everything is working against us.

I've faced situations where I thought I had lost everything and moments when failure appeared inevitable. Yet, each time, I discovered that behind every challenge was an opportunity I hadn't noticed yet.

ADOPTING A RESILIENT MINDSET

Resilience isn't just a buzzword; it's a true survival tool in business and life. Being resilient means accepting that obstacles are part of the journey and understanding that we can choose how to confront them.

How to strengthen resilience:

- **Accept that difficulties are part of the path** – If you expect everything to go smoothly, every problem feels like a disaster. But if you know obstacles are normal, you'll see them as growth opportunities.
- **Focus on solutions** – Whenever I've faced a tough moment, I've asked myself: "What are my options? How can I overcome this?" Looking for solutions instead of complaining changes everything.
- **Be flexible** – Sometimes, the road to success isn't what you planned. I've had to change course many times and each time, I discovered new opportunities I wouldn't have considered before.

Practical Exercise: Think about a recent challenge you faced. Write down three ways you could have turned it into an opportunity.

SHIFTING PERSPECTIVE: FROM OBSTACLE TO OPPORTUNITY

Often, a problem is simply a matter of perspective. What feels like a defeat today could turn out to be the turning point of your life.

How to shift your perspective:

- **Look for the hidden lesson** – Every obstacle has something to teach you. I've learned more from my failures than from my successes.
- **Find the opportunity behind the difficulty** – I once lost an important client and initially felt discouraged. Then, I realized I could use that free time to focus on an even bigger project.
- **Replace negative thoughts with strategic thinking** – Instead of asking, "Why did this happen to me?" try asking, "How can I use this experience to grow?"

Practical Exercise: Take an obstacle you're currently facing and write down at least one positive opportunity that could arise from it.

USING FAILURE AS A GROWTH LEVER

Failure isn't the end of the road; it's a necessary step toward success. If you've never experienced failure, it means you've never dared enough.

How to use failure to your advantage:

- **Analyze what went wrong** – Not to feel sorry for yourself, but to learn with a critical eye.
- **Adopt an experimental mindset** – Every experience is a test; every mistake is feedback.
- **Restart with greater awareness** – Use what you've learned to refine your strategy.

Practical Exercise: Write down three lessons you've learned from a recent failure and explain how you can apply them in the future.

TURNING CHALLENGES INTO ENGINES OF INNOVATION

The greatest innovations are born from problems that need solving.

If we learn to see obstacles as opportunities for improvement, we can turn difficulties into competitive advantages.

How to use challenges to innovate:

- **Think outside the box** – If one method doesn't work, try another.
- **Observe what others do and find your unique edge**
- **Experiment** – Don't wait for the perfect solution; test and improve as you go.

Practical Exercise: Identify a challenge you are currently facing and write down one innovative idea you could develop to overcome it.

STRENGTHENING DETERMINATION THROUGH DIFFICULTIES

Obstacles test our determination. But those who persist eventually turn even the toughest challenges into stepping stones toward success.

How to build stronger determination:

- **Stay true to your goals but flexible in your approach**
- **Build a support network** – Having people who believe in you gives you the strength to keep going.
- **Remember your "why"** – When everything feels hard, reconnect with the deeper reasons that made you start.

Practical Exercise: Write down your "why," the deeper reason for your journey, and read it whenever you encounter an obstacle.

Obstacles aren't barriers; they're opportunities in disguise. We can turn any challenge into an advantage if we learn to shift our perspective, see difficulties as growth opportunities, and persist in tough times.

Remember: Don't wonder whether you'll overcome the obstacle; consider how you'll turn it into your greatest opportunity.

THE IMPORTANCE OF CONSCIOUS CHANGE

Routine brings security, but it can also become an invisible cage. When our days become repetitive and unstimulating, we risk losing enthusiasm, curiosity, and the desire to improve. We must introduce new stimuli, break out of habitual patterns, and rediscover the joy of exploration.

You don't need to overhaul your life; just opening up to small, new experiences can refresh your mental energy and allow you to see the world through new eyes. Routine often creeps in gradually and unconsciously.

We tend to engage in the same activities daily because it feels easier and safer, but this repetition can lead to stagnation. To create genuine change, we need to understand how our habits might limit our growth.

Recognizing the signs that it's time for change:

- You feel bored or unmotivated, even without a clear reason.
- Your days pass by without excitement or stimulation.
- You notice you're avoiding new experiences out of fear or laziness.

Practical Example: *If I notice that each day feels the same, I can begin making small changes, such as picking up a new hobby or trying a different morning routine.*

Practical Exercise: Identify three areas of your life that feel repetitive and brainstorm ways to make them more stimulating.

TRYING SMALL CHANGES TO BREAK THE MONOTONY

You don't need to transform your life overnight. Change can start with small, daily actions that interrupt the autopilot of routine.
Simple ways to add variety to your day:

- **Take a different route to work** – You'll notice new details and break the monotony of your commute.
- **Modify your morning habits** – Try waking up earlier, starting a new activity, or rearranging the order of your routine.
- **Choose one new activity each week** – From cooking to reading a different genre, novelty stimulates the mind.

Practical Example: *If I always start my mornings the same way, I might consider adding a new habit, like writing down a positive thought or taking a short walk.*

Practical Exercise: Choose one habit you can change in your daily routine and try it out for a week.

STEPPING OUTSIDE YOUR COMFORT ZONE AND EMBRACING UNCERTAINTY

Real change happens when we move beyond what's familiar. Leaving your comfort zone means facing new experiences without fear of failure and embracing uncertainty as part of personal growth.
How to step out of your comfort zone:

- **Embrace new challenges without fear of mistakes** – Every error is a chance to learn.
- **Say "yes" to unexpected experiences** – Accept invitations and try things you'd usually avoid.
- **Do something that scares you but also intrigues you** – Overcoming small fears boosts confidence.

Practical Example: *If I've always avoided public speaking out of fear, I can start by giving a short talk in front of a small group.*

Practical Exercise: Identify one experience you've avoided due to fear or insecurity and plan how you'll face it in the next few days.

EXPANDING YOUR PERSPECTIVE THROUGH NEW EXPERIENCES

Different experiences expand our worldview and help us uncover talents and passions we weren't aware we possessed. Exploring new environments, cultures, and disciplines stimulates the mind and enriches our understanding of the world.

Ways to expand your horizons:

- **Travel, even nearby** – Visiting new places, even in your own city, helps you see things differently.
- **Meet people with different interests** – Hearing new perspectives offers fresh insights.
- **Explore unfamiliar subjects** – Read, take courses, or talk with experts outside your usual field.

Practical Example: *If I've only ever read one type of book, I can try diving into a completely different topic to spark new ideas.*

Practical Exercise: Pick an activity, book, or experience outside your usual interests and dedicate time to exploring it this week.

CARVING OUT TIME FOR REFLECTION AND RENEWAL

To stay motivated and energized, it's essential to take time for yourself to recharge and reflect on your progress.

Activities to recharge your mind and body:

- **Meditation or mindfulness** – Even a few minutes daily helps reduce stress and boost focus.
- **Walks in nature** – Being in a new, natural setting helps clear the mind.
- **Disconnecting from social media and technology** – Turning off your phone for a while allows you to reconnect with yourself.

Practical Example: *If I feel overwhelmed by routine and busyness, I can set aside 15 minutes each day just for myself, without any distractions.*

Practical Exercise: Schedule a time in your day for relaxation and reflection away from external distractions.

Every small step outside your comfort zone is a step toward a richer, more fulfilling life.

Remember: Breaking free from routine doesn't require upending your life; it entails making gradual changes that infuse new energy and positive momentum.

IN SUMMARY

Rebirth, rediscovering motivation, and reigniting enthusiasm for life require commitment and consistency. It's not a straightforward journey, but with determination and these strategies, you can overcome negativity, find inspiration, and relaunch yourself with purpose.

Remember: You are the director of your life, and you have the power to create your own success. Approach each day with positivity, gratitude, and an open mind. Let enthusiasm guide you toward personal fulfillment and lasting success.

CONCLUSION

Everything I've shared on these pages—every lesson, mistake, and win—comes from my real-life experience, and I hope it can help you on your journey. Every obstacle overcome is a step forward, an opportunity to grow, learn, and improve.

If there's one thing I want you to remember after reading this book, it's this: success isn't just about money or brilliant ideas; it's about mindset, action, and perseverance.

Open your mind, challenge the rules you've been taught, and start building your business and your future on your own terms. And above all, don't wait for the perfect moment… because the perfect moment is *now*.

If you think you're too young to start a project, let me tell you something: there is no such thing as the "right age" to begin. And if you think it's too late, know this: many entrepreneurs find their path well after 40, 50, or even 60.

Ray Kroc was 52 when he turned McDonald's into a global giant. Colonel Sanders founded KFC at 65. Sam Walton launched Walmart at 44. Vera Wang began her fashion career at 40, and Arianna Huffington started the Huffington Post at 55.

On the other hand, there are teenagers who made their fortune before turning 20 simply because they never believed the excuse, "I'm not ready." Time passes anyway, whether you take action or not. And here's the truth: If you don't start today, you probably never will.

It doesn't matter where you start, what matters is that you *start*.

The world is full of opportunities, but none will come knocking at your door.

If you have an idea that has been lingering in your mind, stop thinking about it and take the first step.

Success belongs to those who act, not to those who wait.
It's not an impossible dream; it's yours to turn into reality!

www.ingramcontent.com/pod-product-compliance
Lightning Source LLC
Chambersburg PA
CBHW051605010526
44119CB00056B/785